WHAT OTHERS ARE SAYING

"Those of us who pray for America know that when the sins of our forefathers are confessed and remitted, the doors of heaven over our land open even wider. *Healing America's Soul* provides an amazingly vivid and insightful guidebook for this event and more. It is new information that every serious intercessor needs."
Dr. C. Peter Wagner, Founder
Wagner University, Author of over 70 books

"*Healing America's Soul* is one of the most important books of the decade for those of us who are interested in praying for God's blessings and revival to be poured out from heaven.

"It is an entirely biblical approach to identificational repentance, a well-attested biblical prayer pattern that asks the Lord to forgive historic sins that otherwise give Satan ongoing authority to keep sowing increasingly darker forms of the same sin patterns in our country and culture. This book has been raised up by God for such a time as this!"
Dr. Gary S. Greig, PhD
Vice President for Bible and Theology
Gospel Light Publications

"Every intercessor could benefit from *Healing America's Soul*. I highly recommend it."
Bob E. Lichty, Director
YWAM Blessing Center, Charles City, VA.

"Pastor Bob Fox has done an excellent job of preparing a road map of historical facts dating back to Jamestown's founding when our Judeo-Christian Nation was established. In your hand is a book that will help reveal the mysteries of Jamestown and what can be done to heal those who were unjustly treated."
H. Wade Trump, III
Pastor, Jamestown Christian Fellowship Church
Williamsburg, Virginia

This book is about the power of repentance to heal our nation through repentance for the sins of our forefathers. This is sometimes called Identificational Repentance.

Well-known author and pastor **Dutch Sheets** says, "There is no more important issue facing the Church than...identificational confession and intercession. No issue will have greater impact on the coming harvest than this one."[1]

1. Jim Goll, Father Forgive Us! Intercessory focus on Yesterday's Sins, (Destiny Image, 1999), xiv.

HEALING AMERICA'S SOUL

Lessons from Jamestown. Promises from God

STUDY EDITION

BOB FOX

HIS HEROS
PRESS

CONTENTS

Cover design by Orlen Stauffer
Editor: Kelly Bixler
Originally Published in 2004 as
Healing America's DNA
Published by His Heros Press in 2021
Copyright © 2021 by Bob Fox
Study Edition in 2023
ISBN: 978-1-7366916-0-1
All rights reserved.

Contact the author at:

https://healing-americas-soul.com

Email: bob@healing-americas-soul.com **for a free digital gift**

https://www.facebook.com/bobfoxauthor/

I dedicate this book to the dozens of pastors and ministry leaders I have worked with for over thirty years here in the Tidewater/Hampton Roads region of Virginia. These godly men and women come from Black, White, Asian, Native American and Island ethnic groups who worship as Catholics, Orthodox, Messianic Jews, Protestants and mainline and evangelical Christian communities. They are committed to seeing the Kingdom of God expressed in holiness, humility, prayer and power—here in the very location that birthed America.

Pastor Ken Gerry was one of those fiery, dedicated leaders and a dear friend who just went home to glory after surgery complications. Ken truly was closer than a brother to me and to so many others.

A special thanks to the late **Dr. Charles Wolfe**, former President of The Plymouth Rock Foundation in Plymouth, Massachusetts for encouraging me to write this book.

I also dedicate this book to **Ken Custalow,** a Virginia Native American and one of the godliest men I have ever met. Ken lived on the Mattaponi Tribe Reservation not far from me. He helped me understand how to write Chapter Thirteen called *Abuse of Native Americans*.

Lastly, I dedicate this book to my wonderful wife, *Beth*—a gifted artist, loving mom, Bible and math teacher, cherished grandma, pastor's wife and wise Christian counselor. This book would not have been written without her kind and encouraging support.

You're the best, Honey! Thank you!

ANGEL 24

A NOVEL BASED ON THIS BOOK

A historical, supernatural thriller about the intense spiritual warfare between angels, demons and rebel angels that almost destroyed the Jamestown Colony.

Angel 24 tells the dramatic story of an emotionally damaged angel named Scion who survived the Great Rebellion in heaven and now is assigned to protect the 1607 Jamestown Colony from the wicked schemes of his former best friend.

It's the story of John Smith, Pocahontas and her Powhatan tribes as few have ever imagined. Sample chapters at the back of this book!

Book details at https://angel24book.com or use this QR code:

SPIRITUAL WARFARE AUTHOR
BOB FOX

ANGEL 24

FIGHTS TO DEFEND THE 1607 JAMESTOWN COLONY FROM
THE WICKED SCHEMES OF HIS FORMER BEST FRIEND!

CHAPTER 1

WHY I WROTE THIS BOOK

STARTING IN 1992, I BEGAN TO WORK WITH MANY PASTORS AND Christian leaders in Hampton Roads, Virginia to reach our region with the Gospel by working together across racial and denominational lines.

In 1995, I resigned from a thriving church we had started to pursue a regional ministry among pastors that I called "city-church" work. This abrupt shift in ministry focus came as a result of a powerful encounter with God in 1994 in Toronto, Canada. After 17 years as a pastor, I sensed God calling me to build relationships of trust and affection among Christian leaders in Hampton Roads so we could release God's Kingdom here **together!**

So, from 1995 to 2000, I worked with many Christian leaders from many denominations in Hampton Roads and across America (through a national ministry called Mission America) to bring the Gospel to more people in our communities. But despite many meetings, much prayer, several written group covenants, and lots of sincere efforts, we made little lasting progress.

After five years of hard work, I was greatly disappointed, to say the least. It took many months for me to recover from the death of that dream.

Along the way, I took a course at Regent University by George Otis of the Sentinel Group about how "spiritual mapping" a region could reveal the source of demonic strongholds in a city or region that can hinder the Gospel in that region. I began to see that our failures as Christian leaders to build the Kingdom here were *being blocked by historic spiritual issues that we needed to address.*

As I read books by Cindy Jacobs, Dr. Peter Wagner, John Dawson and others, God gave me more insights. I learned that confession and repentance for the sins of *previous generations* are powerful biblical practices for two purposes: **to reconcile** groups of people and, secondly, **to release** groups from the spiritual iniquities of those past corporate sins. This is now called Identificational repentance. Chapters 8 & 23 describe this in detail. This book is mainly about identificational repentance for the sins of our Christian forefathers who began what became America in Jamestown, Virginia, just 45 minutes from my home.

I highly recommend John Dawson's excellent book, *Healing America's Wounds,* and his powerful video series of the same name. *They both* focus primarily on *reconciling* relationships through identificational repentance, while this book is more about the power of identificational repentance to *release* our land spiritually from the evil power of past sins. In practice, both reconciling people groups and breaking the power of evil from past sins often happen simultaneously if repentance is done properly.

At church one day, I met Dr. Charles Wolfe, a former economist at Columbia University and past President of the Plymouth Rock Foundation, who suggested that I study the 1607 Jamestown Colony to better understand America today. I also became friends with Dr. Gary Greig, an Old Testament Professor at Regent University, who taught about identificational repentance extensively. See Chapter 23 for his scholarly notes. Most importantly, and to my surprise, I sensed the Lord telling me to write this book to help heal Hampton Roads and America.

So, in 2001, I began to do the spiritual mapping research which produced the first edition of this book called *Healing America's DNA in 2002.* This 2023 edition is a major update with study questions. After retiring from being a pastor after 35 years, I plan to speak and teach on this as much as I can.

I am fully convinced that God is calling His American Church to repent for many current and past sins so He can heal America through another Great Awakening like the first two that swept millions of Americans into the Kingdom in the 18th and 19th centuries.

BLESSINGS TO ALL,
    Bob Fox
    New Year's Day, 2023

CHAPTER 2

A QUICK SUMMARY

WITH A LIST OF SINS & SAMPLE PRAYERS

"But if they will confess their sins **and the sins of their ancestors**...I will remember the land" (Leviticus 26:40-42).

AMERICA AND THE AMERICAN CHURCH ARE IN TROUBLE WITH GOD due to their sins, including the corporate sins of our forefathers. See Chapter Six

The Bible teaches us that we have "corporate identities" before God that bring us blessings and curses and help create our 'spiritual DNA." See Chapter Eight.

The special focus of this book is that God wants His people to confess and repent for the corporate sins of our forefathers so that He can "remember" and heal our land. By confessing our current personal and corporate sins and the sins of our forefathers, God promises to heal our land.

Confessing and repenting for the corporate sins of others is sometimes called "**identificational repentance.**" Watch Dr. Peter
Wagner's 40-second explanation here[1] or in
the following QR code.

Although not well-known, this pattern of

Dr. C. Peter Wagner
Fuller Theological Seminary

 confession and repentance is firmly rooted in the Bible as a means for God's people to heal their nation. Eight books of the Old Testament mention this critical prayer principle. See Chapter Eight. Jesus Himself demonstrated identifica- tional repentance on a whole new level on the cross! See Chapter Three.

Why Jamestown?

The earliest sins of America's Earliest Christian Forefathers were committed in the 1607 Jamestown Colony in Virginia. The 1620 Plymouth Colony also brought more of America's forefathers here but this book focuses on the Jamestown Colony whose sin patterns are still making the soul of America sick with sin in 2023. In a word, "Jamestown is a model of the righteous and unrighteous roots of America."[2]

THE MAIN SINS OF OUR FIRST CHRISTIAN FOREFATHERS

- The main sins are against Native Americans, blacks and women.
- Choosing to love money more than God's priorities in almost every sector of the colony.
- Failure to love God with all their hearts, soul and strength
- Severe abuse of white and black servants/slaves, adults and children, for financial gain and pleasure
- Fornication and rape with white, Powhatan and black women
- Murder of a wife by her husband for personal gain in 1610
- Pervasive dishonesty and lies to whites, Powhatans and women for personal gain
- Violently and deceitfully stealing the land and food of the Powhatans.
- Not loving Powhatans, whites and blacks as our neighbors

- Discrimination, bigotry and violence against non-Anglican Christians
- A very carnal Christian colony full of hatred, discord, jealousy, fits of rage, selfish ambition, dissensions, factions and envy, drunkenness and orgies.
- Selling a harmful drug (tobacco) for personal gain
- Idol worship and human sacrifices of the Powhatans
- Divination practices of the English
- Colonial and government laws were passed to support human rights abuses against Powhatans, blacks and women.
- Prideful domination over others

SAMPLE PRAYERS OF CONFESSION

Money Over God

Lord, forgive our Christian forefathers for choosing to make money their master more than God. Jesus, you said we had to choose between money and God as a master. We confess that our forefathers usually chose to seek money in many ways that dishonored You. Please forgive this great sin against You.

Breaking the Great Commandment

God of glory, we confess that our Jamestown Christian forefathers did not love you with all their hearts, soul and strength. Please forgive this great sin against You.

Cruel Abuse

Father God, forgive our Jamestown ancestors for creating and supporting systems of cruel, unchristian abuse against the Powhatan natives, British white servants, African black slaves and women for personal gain. Please forgive this great sin against You.

Breaking the Second Great Commandment

Father of mercy, we confess that most of our forefathers in Jamestown did not obey your command to love each other, white servants, black slaves and Powhatans as neighbors to be loved. Please forgive this great sin against You.

Sexual Sins

Jesus, please forgive our Jamestown forefathers for many sins of fornication and rape against white, black and Powhatan women. Please forgive this great sin against You.

Murder of a Wife

Father, please forgive the treachery and wicked slaying of a wife by her husband for personal gain in the "Starving Time" of 1610. Please forgive this great sin against You.

Dishonesty

Spirit of Truth, we confess the many lies and dishonesty of our Jamestown forefathers to the Powhatans, to each other and to women for personal financial gain. Please forgive this great sin against You.

Stealing

God of Justice, we confess that our forefathers stole the land of the Powhatans with deceit and violence. Please forgive this great sin against You.

Breaking The New Commandment of Jesus

Jesus, we confess that our forefathers broke the new commandment you gave us "to love one another as I have loved you". Instead, we discriminated against non-Anglican Christians, often harshly and violently. Please forgive this great sin against You.

The Sins of the Flesh

Spirit of God, we confess that our forefathers chose many times not to be led by You in their behavior. Instead, they acted with hatred, discord, jealousy, fits of rage, selfish ambition, dissensions, factions and envy, drunkenness and orgies. Please forgive this great sin against You.

Drug Abuse Economy

Lord Jesus, we confess that our forefathers at Jamestown severely damaged many thousands of human bodies by growing and selling tobacco as the main export from the colony for decades for personal financial gain. Please forgive this great sin against You.

Idol Worship

God Almighty, we confess the sins of idolatry and human sacrifice committed by our Powhatan forefathers. As original owners of the Jamestown lands that began America, their actions carry a great impact on that land. Father of mercy, they did not know You and they acted in ignorance. Please forgive this great sin against You.

Divination

Spirit of Truth, we confess that our Christian forefathers sought guidance from created objects rather than from you, the Living God. Please forgive this great sin against You.

Abusive Laws

Father and Great Judge of the Universe, we confess the evil of laws our Christian forefathers created to create and maintain abuse against white servants, black slaves, women and Powhatans—all for personal gain and pleasure. Please forgive this great sin against You.

Pride

Humble Jesus, we confess the deeply-seated pride of our Christian forefathers that resulted in their harsh domination over others.

WHATEVER WE DO, we must seek to receive the blessing of our Native Americans, blacks and women. These three groups were signed against and wonder the most in the Jamestown Colony and probably in America as a whole.[3]

A sample service of confession and repentance for Hampton Roads, Virginia is found in Chapter 24.

Discussion Questions

1. What sins listed above surprised you?

2. Which ones did you expect to see? Why?

3. Do you see these sin patterns in America today? Explain.

4. Has your church ever spoken about these sins of our forefathers? Should they? Why or why not?

5. Do you think Lev. 26: 40-42 could apply to America today? Why or why not?

---

1. Healing America's Wounds Video Series, Part Three, starting at 4:05 minutes
2. Healing America's Wounds Video Series, Part One, starting at 31:00 minutes
3. Ibid, starting at 17:45 minutes

CHAPTER 3

FROM MOSES TO JESUS
STANDING IN THE GAP FOR OTHERS

"I looked for someone among them who would build up the wall and
stand before me in the gap on behalf of the land so I would not
have to destroy it, but I found no one" (Ezekiel 22:30).

WE CHRISTIANS HAVE UNIQUE ACCESS TO GOD AS "THE PRIESTHOOD
of all believers".[1] We can "stand in the gap" on behalf of our nation
through confession and repentance so that God will nullify His earthly
penalties on the corporate sins of our nation, present and past. The
founders of the Old Covenant and the New Covenant—Moses and
Jesus— did this for others as we will see below.

Confession and repentance are powerful! Such prayers can save
individuals, families, churches, cities and nations from God's penalties
for sin. Public repentance for sin even saved the entire *pagan city* of
Nineveh from imminent destruction by God.[2] Even exceedingly
wicked kings like Ahab[3] and Manasseh[4] were shown mercy by God
when they confessed their sins, repented and humbled themselves
before God.

There are many ways to confess and repent for sin, both personal
and corporate sins. The outward forms are not as important as the
hearts of the people, the thoroughness of their confession and repen-

tance, and their follow-through with changed behavior after the words of repentance have been said to God and to others.

Metanoia is the Greek word for repentance. The first part, *meta*, means change; "noia" comes from the Greek word *nous* for the mind. Repentance means **we change our minds** about something and confess it as a sin and consciously choose not to do it again.

Starting in 1976, millions of Christians began confessing their sins and the sins of America during a national prayer event called Washington for Jesus. America was not doing well spiritually and many leaders called for humble repentance before God.

At the same time, Jimmy & Carol Owens toured the country calling people to "stand in the gap" for America. They encouraged American believers to repent for their sins and the sins of America with their musical called "If My People", based on II Chronicles 7:14.

Use this QR code to listen to their beautiful theme song.

"If My People" Song on Youtube

MOSES STOOD IN THE GAP

As the founder of the Old Covenant, Moses demonstrated identificational repentance for the sins of the new Jewish nation. As Israel traveled to the Promised Land for Egypt, God wanted to wipe out the entire Jewish nation several times due to their sins and rebellion against God.

But Moses "stood in the gap" for Israel several times by *confessing the sins of the nation and pleading with God* to forgive Israel for its sins. And God did. (Ex. 32:10, Deut. 9, Num. 14:19, 16:22)

> "Therefore He said that He would destroy them, had not
> Moses His chosen one **stood in the breach before Him**,
> to turn away His wrath from destroying *them*." Psalm
> 106:23

Abraham also tried to do that for Sodom and Gomorra (Gen 18:23-32). Later, David did the same thing for his generation of Jews (2

Samuel 24:17). Ezekiel also tried this in Ezk. 9:8 but God would not listen then due to the greatness of Jerusalem's sins.

Jesus Stood the Gap

The most profound, beautiful and powerful example of someone "standing in the gap" in identificational repentance before God on behalf of others is Jesus on the cross!

Identificational repentance in the Bible is confessing and repenting for the sins of the nation so that God's just earthly penalty for those sins can be annulled. What biblical leaders did with *words* in identificational repentance, Jesus did primarily by His obedient *actions* on Calvary!

As the founder of the New Covenant, Jesus, as a man, *identified with the sins of all mankind* by **taking those sins in His own body** on the cross, and then He **presented His body full of mankind's sins** to God on the cross to atone for the guilt of all humanity. Because Jesus stood in the gap for us, God forgave the eternal punishment for all those sins. When God saw Jesus dying on the cross, full of mankind's sin, God saw His Son's obedient death as an *act* of confession and repentance for all mankind. Read these scriptures slowly with a grateful heart.

"He **bore our sins in His body** on the cross, so that we might die to sin and live to righteousness; for by His wounds you were healed." (1 Peter 2:24)

"**He made Him** who knew no sin **to be sin on our behalf** so that we might become the righteousness of God in Him." (2 For. 5:21)

"For he bore the sin of many, and **made intercession for the transgressors.**" (Is. 53:12)

This is the greatest act of identificational repentance in the Bible!

In the following pages, I believe Jesus is inviting you to learn how to be part of His "priesthood of all believers" and stand in the gap for the corporate sins of our cities, regions and our nation.

Will You?

Discussion Questions

1. Read some of the scriptures cited above and describe how Moses stood in the gap before God for rebellious Israel.

2. Can you tell the stories of how Abraham and David also stood in the gap for the nation of Israel?

3. How did Jesus identify with humanity? Why?

4. Why is the cross the greatest example of identificational repentance in the Bible?

5. Has God changed His mind about this biblical practice? Why or why not?

6. What could you do to encourage this kind of prayer for the healing of America?

---

1. 1 Peter 2:9
2. Jonah 3:10
3. I Kings 21:29
4. II Chronicles 33:13

CHAPTER 4

SHORT TESTIMONIES

WHEN THESE BIBLICAL PRINCIPLES ARE FOLLOWED

A RELEASE OF POWER

Around 1996, I attended a service at a non-denominational church called New Life Christian Center in the Oceanview section of Norfolk, Virginia. My good friend, **Ken Gerry,** the host pastor, had invited a mutual friend. an Episcopal priest named **Marty O'Rourke**, to preach! Normally, mainline Episcopalians were not invited to preach in non-denominational churches.

Knowing of the severe Anglican persecution of non-Anglicans in colonial Tidewater (Chapter 17), I leaned over to Marty and suggested that he publicly apologize to Ken on behalf of the Anglicans who had persecuted non-Anglican churches like Ken's in our colonial past.

Episcopalians are the direct spiritual descendants of the Anglican Church in America. I felt that God would be honored by such an apology. I was not aware of any Episcopal priest having done anything like this in Virginia up to that point.

Despite some initial reluctance to do something not planned for the service, they agreed to do it.

Standing face to face in front of the congregation, Marty began to say that he wanted to make an apology to Ken's church on behalf of the Anglican Church.

Without any warning or expectation on our part, **the power of God came down upon both of them, knocking them both to the floor!** After a moment of shock, they both sheepishly got off the floor and finished the apology. Ken extended forgiveness to the Anglican Church on behalf of the non-Anglican denominations who had been persecuted by Anglicans.

That response is quite unusual, but then, so was the apology —*which may not have ever happened in Virginia before.*

I think God was trying to say how pleased He was with that apology by bringing both leaders to their faces before Him. It reminds me of how God showed His pleasure when Solomon was dedicating the temple (1 Kings 8:11). The priests in that account also ended up on their faces as God's glory cloud entered the temple!

THE TRANSFORMATIONS VIDEO SERIES

Well-known Argentinean evangelism strategist Ed Silvoso has said that no one knows better than a mayor of a large city that *there are no human solutions to the systemic problems of big cities* around the world. Mayors know better than anyone that no amount of money, programs, or force is going to stop violent crime, drug abuse, sexual misconduct, family violence, homelessness and poverty in their cities. All mayors can hope to do is somehow minimize and manage those evils.

Video Documentaries of revival in our day!

But the incredible true documentaries called the *Transformations Video Series*[1] from the Sentinel Group now show how many of the problems cities face have been changed by the power of the Gospel! These videos show documentary footage about how God changed cities, regions and nations. These videos are so encouraging to city officials worldwide that:

- **A South African mayor personally distributed videos to 100 other mayors;**
  - Some law enforcement officers in America have used the teachings in the videos as a crime reduction strategy.

The Transformation Video Series vividly documents how revival broke out in a place like Cali, Columbia; Hemet, California and cities across Uganda, villages among the Canadian Inuit tribes and in many of the Fiji Islands.

Watch their six-minute overview of the series here [2]for free. These are stories of revival in our time—in the last thirty years!

Why did revival break out in those places?

Because in each video documentary, Christians appropriated the promises of Lev. 26: 39-42 and II Chron. 7:14 in deep, gut-wrenching repentance for personal and the corporate sins of their community, present and past.

Transformation Series
Overview

This remarkable series of documentary videos shows the power of repentance to restore cities, regions and nations. These videos demonstrate the truths of this book better than this book ever could.

If you do nothing else from reading this book, **buy and watch those videos.** They can be purchased for $6 each from here.[3]

BREAKING God's Curses in Fiji

Christians in Fiji have recently seen what happens when a nation deals with the sins of one's ancestors! In George Otis's video documentary called *Let the Sea Resound* [4], you can watch the amazing 2003 story in which Fiji Islanders broke *a God-given curse for their ancestors' sin* of killing and eating a British Methodist missionary 136 years ago![5]

God Healed the Land & Sea

The Bible tells us that God will sometimes curse the land due to

the egregious sins of the people living there. "For the land **has become defiled,** therefore I have brought its punishment upon it, so the land has vomited out its inhabitants" (Lev. 18:25). This happened in some of the Fiji Islands.

But just like II Chronicles 7:14 promised, even the flora and the fauna of the Fiji Islands were restored to health by the obedience and humility of the Church in Fiji! Click this link to see a short video about this incredible story or use this QR code.

After a significant time of **repentance for the sins of their ancestors,** Fijians are seeing fish returning to local waters where fish had not been for years, a poisonous stream is now drinkable and crops are improving greatly—as this report confirms:

Healing of the land in Fiji by deep repentance

All over the Fiji Islands, whenever the spiritual and civil leaders come into one accord to repent of the sins that have defiled the land (the sins of the shedding of innocent blood, sexual sins, idolatry and witchcraft, and the breaking of covenants) both the land and the water are cleansed and become productive and fruitful again.[6]

HEALING CHINESE HEARTS

I was in Buenos Aires, Argentina in November 1997, at a conference led by Ed Silvoso[7] on how to heal our cities by the power of the Gospel. While sitting on a bus with about 50 Chinese young adult attendees from Hong Kong, an older Japanese man entered the bus— but he did not sit down.

He asked permission to speak to the Chinese people on the bus. A sudden hush came over the passengers. No one knew what he was about to say and no one knew him.

He began to apologize for Japan's WWII atrocities in China, including the "rape of Nanking"[8] in 1937. He went into some detail about how terrible the Chinese people suffered at the hands of his nation's brutal soldiers. All the air seemed to leave the bus. It was hard to hear such things. It was also difficult for the man to say them. He barely kept his emotions in check.

As he concluded—and without warning— a cloudburst of tears and moans erupted on the bus from Asians who normally do not show such emotions in public. Even though they had not been alive in WWII, those young Chinese knew the stories their grandparents told them about the war. Now, for probably the first time in their lives, a Japanese man expressed real sorrow for the horrific acts of his forefathers against their forefathers. He confessed the sins of Japan and asked for their forgiveness. The memory of that moment still gives me chills. The air was electric with compassion.

Incredibly, the man just walked off the bus and disappeared into the crowd outside while the Chinese tried to compose themselves. His work was done. Two people groups had been reconciled at least partially by the heartful confession and repentance of one humble, Christian man. It was a beautiful moment that no one there could ever forget.

Let's do more of that!

---

1. https://www.sentinelgroup.org/documentaries (20 Dec 2022). These amazing videos are not only $6 each! I encourage to get them all, especially Transformations: A Documentary, Transformations II: The Glory Spreads, Let the Sea Resound, An Appalachian Dawn and An Unconventional War. I love them!!! You will too.
2. https://www.youtube.com/watch?v=dBvxWl7jXro (20 Dec 2022)
3. https://www.sentinelgroup.org/documentaries
4. https://vimeo.com/ondemand/letthesearesound (17 March 2020)
5. The Virginian-Pilot, November 14, 2003, A13
6. Inger J. Logelin, in an email to supporters from Sentinel Group called *From South to North*, dated Oct 11, 2004. This story is also seen int he video called "Let the Sea

Resound" by George Otis. A similar story in the Canadian north is also told on another of Otis's videos called Transformations II (https://www.youtube.com/watch?v=X420Z1O8hAk) (4 Dec. 20222)

7. http://www.antioch.com.sg/events/hei/hec.htm (28 Dec. 20222)
8. https://www.britannica.com/event/Nanjing-Massacre (28 Dec. 2022)

CHAPTER 5

WHEN NATIONS REPENT

MANY NATIONS KNOW THIS IS IMPORTANT

"On either side of the river was the tree of life...and the leaves of the tree were for the **healing of the nations**. **There will no longer be any curse**" (Rev. 22:2-3).

SINCE THE 20TH CENTURY, GOD HAS BEEN MOVING HIS CHURCH worldwide and even non-believers to publicly confess and repent for the corporate sins of their group—*mostly the sins of their forefathers!* We need to capitalize on this new trend of corporate repentance occurring all over the globe. God is behind this! As Walter Wink, a noted theologian says, "Apologies by nations are a fairly recent phenomenon, and may indicate a small step toward maturity by the human race."[1]

Note that many of these confessions of past wrongs by secular leaders are primarily aimed at **reconciling** their nation with other groups but it is likely that God also uses such apologies to **release** them from the spiritual penalties for the sins of their forefathers.

1. August 18, 1777: Before we were a nation, the **State of Massachusetts-Bay** called a Day of Public Fasting, Humiliation and Prayer to win the war with Great Britain. The declaration specifically says that the "*sins of the People of*

this Land" have led to this war.[2] The delegate from Massachusetts, John Adams had earlier remarked in 1777: "We will surely defeat them if we fear God and repent of our sins."[3] They did repent and the war was won.

2. March 6, 1799: President **John Adams** calls the entire nation a Day of Humiliation, Fasting and Prayer to end the war with Britain.

3. March 30, 1863: **Abraham Lincoln's** Proclamation Appointing a National Fast Day:" *And whereas, it is the duty of nations as well as of men to own their dependence upon the overruling power of God, to* **confess their sins and transgressions** *in humble sorrow yet with assured hope that genuine repentance will lead to mercy and pardon."*[4]

4. March 4, 1865: **Lincoln** confesses that America's sins in slavery have brought on the terrible Civil War as God's judgment on America. [5]

5. **1984: Congress apologized** for protecting Nazi war criminal Klaus Barbie who slaughtered Jews in WWII in Lyon, France.[6] The US Army had used Barbie as a paid informant during the war and helped him escape to Bolivia.

6. August 10, 1988: **President Reagan** signed the Civil Liberties Act of 1988, apologizing and making restitution to the 120,000 American citizens and permanent residents of Japanese ancestry who had been forcibly relocated and virtually imprisoned during World War II by the federal government from 1942-1946. George H W Bush and Bill Clinton, later sent individual apology letters to former internees as their claims were processed. [7]

7. 1993: the 103rd **US Congress** in Joint Resolution 19 formally apologized to Hawaiians for the overthrow of Queen Liliuokalani a century ago.[8]

8. August 1993: **Anglican Church of Canada** through The Primate of the Anglican Church of Canada, Archbishop Michale Peers, apologizes to its native students abused in church schools. [9]

9. July 15, 1995: "**The Southern Baptist Convention** voted on June 20 to adopt a resolution renouncing its racist roots and apologizing for its past defense of slavery. Southern Baptist leaders declared publicly for the first time their repentance for upholding slavery, as they "lament and repudiate historic acts of evil such as slavery from which we continue to reap a bitter harvest."[10]

10. January 27, 1995: On the 50th anniversary of the liberation of Auschwitz, **Germany's Chancellor, Helmut Kohl,** publicly apologized for the Auschwitz death camp as "the darkest and most horrible chapter of German history". [11]

11. October 1, 1997: "**France's Roman Catholic clergy** have apologized for the church's silence during the systematic persecution and deportation of Jews by the pro-Nazi Vichy regime: 'We confess that silence in the face of the Nazi's extermination of the Jews was a failure of the French church...We beg God's forgiveness and ask the Jewish people to hear our words of repentance.'" [12]

12. 1997: **President Clinton** apologized to the elderly victims of the infamous Tuskegee syphilis experiments ago.[13]

13. 1997: **Tony Blair,** Prime Minister of Great Britain, apologized for the treatment of the Irish during the potato famine in the nineteenth century.[14]

14. April 3, 1998: "**Britain** Apologizes to Jews & Others... for being 'sometimes insensitive' in the aftermath of its seizure of the assets of some 25,000 victims of the Nazis during World War II and promised a new compensation plan."[15]

15. 1988: **President Ronald Reagan** signed the Civil Liberties Act, which offered every Japanese-American interned in the camps during the war a formal apology and $20,000 in compensation[16]

16. 1999: The new **Japanese prime minister**, Keizo Obuchi, spoke an expression of contrition "to the visiting president of Korea, Kim Dae Jung, for the Japanese occupation of Korea in the first half of this century."[17]

17. Dec. 1-5, 1999: **Mathieu Kérékou,** the **President of Benin** and Other African Leaders Apologized to African Americans for Selling Africans to White Slave Traders.[18]This footnote has a link to a video about this.[19]

1. Oct 15, 2000: "The **German Catholic Church** has admitted that it employed slave laborers during the Nazi regime...The Protestant Church in Germany decided...to contribute $5 million to...recompense former slave laborers."[20]

A video about this historic apology by the President of Benin.

2. March 12, 2000: Speaking as head of the Roman Catholic Church and leader of the nation of Vatican City, **Pope John Paul II** publicly asked God's forgiveness[21] for the sins of Catholics through the ages, including wrongs inflicted on Jews, women and minorities in the infamous tortures of the Inquisition. To his great credit, Pope John Paul II, during his time as pope, made about **one hundred** separate public apologies for the mistakes, sins and atrocities committed by the Catholic Church over many centuries such as the Sack of Constantinople, the forced conversion of natives in the Americas and in Africa, the global sexual abuse of children under church care, the African slave trade, the burning of "heretics" like Jon Hus, the silence of the bishops and the papacy to the WWII Holocaust, etc.

3. June 11, 2001: **Pope John Paul II** apologized directly to Orthodox Church and Muslim Leaders. He asked God to "forgive Roman Catholics for sins committed against Orthodox Christians..." He also said to Muslim leaders, "For all the times that Muslims and Christians have offended one another, we need to seek forgiveness." [22]

4. Oct 26, 2001: "**Pope John Paul II** apologized specifically to China... for the errors of missionaries in colonial

times."[23]

5. 2001: "The Indianapolis-based **Christian Church** (Disciples of Christ) admitted that its apathy prolonged the suffering of enslaved blacks."[24]

6. May 5, 2003: "**Protestants** in the Swiss canton of Zurich have made a public apology for the persecution during the 16th century Reformation era of a radical Christian movement called Anabaptists, whose present-day successors include many Mennonites and the Amish community in North America..."[25]

7. July 2003: The **Zimbabwe Council of Churches** (ZCC) apologized for "standing by while its country's people have starved to death due to food shortages and while violence, rape, intimidation and torture have 'ravaged the nation'". [26]

8. April 22, 2005: "**Japan's prime minister** apologized Friday for his country's World War II aggression in Asia..."[27] (This was one of about two dozen formal apologies Japan has made since 1972 to China for WWII atrocities!)

9. November 23, 2005: **The Anglican Church** acknowledges Crusades were ungodly. "'The Crusades were a serious betrayal of Christian beliefs,' the Archbishop of Canterbury, Dr. Rowan Williams, said yesterday"[28] in Pakistan to Muslims.

10. May 10, 2006: **France** officially commemorates the victims of the French slave trade for the first time. In what is tantamount to an apology "... President Jacques Chirac said facing up to the colonial past was a 'key to national cohesion'... Hundreds of thousands of slaves were taken by French ships from Africa to plantations in the Caribbean before France banned the practice in 1848. It was, Mr. Chirac said, an 'indelible stain on history... The greatness of a nation resides in its capacity to bear full responsibility for the darkest periods of its history,'" French Envoy Brigitte Girardin declared. [29]

11. 2006: "This year, the **Church of England**...voted to acknowledge its complicity in the slave trade."[30]

12. November 26, 2006: "**Tony Blair** is to make a historic statement condemning Britain's role in the transatlantic slave trade as a 'crime against humanity' and expressing 'deep sorrow' that it ever happened."[31]

13. An apology was made to the **President of Zimbabwe** by representatives of nine nations for the sins of their forefathers in Africa. [32]

14. February 26, 2007: **Spanish Envoy** declares that the 1492 expulsion of Jews from Spain was Spain's greatest mistake. The consul general, Francisco Jose Viqueira "echoed King Juan Carlos' apology to the Jewish people for the suffering they had endured. According to the consul, the expulsion was Spain's greatest political and historical mistake, since the Jews and their culture were an integral part of the country." [33]

15. February 24, 2007: **The Virginia General Assembly** becomes the first state in America to formally apologize for American slavery. "The resolution says government-sanctioned slavery 'ranks as the most horrendous of all depredations of human rights and violations of our founding ideals in our nation's history, and the abolition of slavery was followed by systematic discrimination, enforced segregation, and other insidious institutions and practices toward Americans of African descent that were rooted in racism, racial bias, and racial misunderstanding'." The measure also expressed regret for "the exploitation of Native Americans."[34]

16. March 21, 2007: "**London's mayor** apologized Wednesday for his city's role in the African slave trade, to mark the 200th anniversary of the law that abolished the slave trade in Britain's colonies... [calling it] a "monstrous crime... He acknowledged earlier formal apologies made by the city of Liverpool and the Church of England."[35]

17. March 26, 2007: **Maryland lawmakers** voted on Monday to formally apologize for the state's role in the slave trade, expressing "profound regret" that the state once "trafficked

in human flesh... The Annapolis City Council also is considering a resolution calling for atonement for the city's "participation in the involuntary servitude of African men, women and children and calls for reconciliation among all citizens of Annapolis"[36]

18. February 13, 2008: **Prime Minister Kevin Rudd** presented an apology to Indigenous Australians for the forced removal of aboriginal children from their homes. "We apologise for the laws and policies of successive Parliaments and governments that have inflicted profound grief, suffering and loss on these our fellow Australians. "We apologise especially for the removal of Aboriginal and Torres Strait Islander children from their families, their communities and their country." [37]

19. November 16, 2009: Australian **Prime Minister Kevin Rudd** proclaimed a national apology for the tens of thousands of Migrant Children who were sent to Australia from Britain under false pretenses and never allowed to know their real parents. He said Australia was "sorry for the physical suffering, the emotional starvation and the cold absence of love, of tenderness, of care."[38]

20. February 24, 2010: British Prime Minister **Gordon Brown** offered a "full and unconditional" apology to tens of thousands of British children exiled overseas who suffered physical and sexual abuse in orphanages and labor farms in Commonwealth countries.[39]

21. 2016: **Pope Francis** asked forgiveness from Protestant and other Christian Churches "for the non-evangelical behavior of Catholics toward Christians of other churches" after the Protestant Reformation in 1517. [40] The slaughter of Protestant "heretics" by Catholics was extremely bloody, and massive and went on for decades. Modern scholars estimate 50 million died in the religious violence that followed in persecutions, counter-persecutions and religious wars.[41]

22. March 11, 2022: The Northern Ireland Assembly publicly apologized[42] for the forced migration of children overseas to serve the needs of their colonies where they were often abused in multiple ways. Details here.[43]

23. December 5, 2022: **Pope Francis,** on what he calls a "Pilgrimage of Penance", apologized to the indigenous people of Canada for the Church's role in the atrocities committed in the residential school system.[44]

---

1. tinyurl.com/5a6up9au p. 48 of the PDF (20 Dec 2022)
2. https://wallbuilders.com/proclamation-fasting-humiliation-prayer-1777-massachusetts-bay/ (20 Dec, 2022)
3. Ibid
4. https://www.historyplace.com/lincoln/proc-3.htm (17 Dec 2022)
5. https://www.facinghistory.org/resource-library/speech-president-lincoln-second-inaugural-address-0?hsa_tgt=kwd-300212519657&hsa_grp=63212501410&hsa_src=g&hsa_net=adwords&hsa_mt=b&hsa_ver=3&hsa_ad=444127870032&hsa_acc=4949854077&hsa_kw=lincoln%27s%20second%20inaugural%20address&hsa_cam=1661698525
6. https://www.smithsonianmag.com/smart-news/five-times-united-states-officially-apologized-180959254/ (6 Dec. 2022)
7. http://www.children-of-the-camps.org/history/civilact.html (17 March 2020)
8. https://archive.nytimes.com/learning.blogs.nytimes.com/2012/01/17/jan-17-1893-hawaiian-monarchy-overthrown-by-america-backed-businessmen/?_r=0 (6 Dec. 2022)
9. http://www.religioustolerance.org/sch_resid4.htm (17 March 2020)
10. https://www.theatlantic.com/politics/archive/2015/04/southern-baptists-wrestle-with-the-sin-of-racism/389808/ (17 March 2020)
11. https://aeon.co/essays/a-national-apology-has-the-power-to-change-the-future
12. http://www.cnn.com/WORLD/9710/01/france.catholics/ (17 March 2020)
13. https://www.smithsonianmag.com/smart-news/five-times-united-states-officially-apologized-180959254/ (6 Dec. 20222)
14. https://www.independent.co.uk/news/blair-issues-apology-for-irish-potato-famine-1253790.html (17 March 2020)
15. https://www.independent.co.uk/news/holocaust-debt-families-get-british-apology-1154040.html (17 March 2020)
16. https://www.smithsonianmag.com/smart-news/five-times-united-states-officially-apologized-180959254/ (6 Dec. 2022)
17. https://www.nytimes.com/1998/10/09/world/japan-apologizes-forcefully-for-its-occupation-of-korea.html (17 March 2020)
18. https://bobfox.org/the-apology-that-shook-a-continent/ (5 Dec. 2022)
19. This video is a 30-minute documentary of that historic event: https://youtu.be/UdAqaUyItuE (3-29-2023)

20. https://cathnews.com/cathnews/11326-german-catholic-church-used-nazi-forced-labour (17 March 2020)
21. https://www.latimes.com/archives/la-xpm-2000-mar-13-mn-8338-story.html (3 Jan. 2023)
22. https://www.latimes.com/archives/la-xpm-2001-may-05-mn-59656-story.html and http://www.cnn.com/2001/WORLD/meast/05/06/pope.syria.03/ (17 March 2020)
23. https://www.nytimes.com/2001/10/25/world/the-pope-apologizes-for-the-catholic-church-s-errors-in-china.html (17 March 2020)
24. http://www.washingtonpost.com/wp-dyn/content/article/2006/06/02/AR2006060201531_2.html?nav=hcmodule (3 June 2006)
25. https://episcopalchurch.org/library/article/zurich-protestants-beg-forgiveness-persecuting-mennonites-and-amish (17 March 2020)
26. https://reliefweb.int/report/zimbabwe/zimbabwe-churches-say-sorry-inaction (17 March 2020)
27. https://www.nytimes.com/2005/04/23/world/asia/japan-apologizes-for-wartime-aggression.html (17 March 2020)
28. https://www.telegraph.co.uk/news/uknews/1503762/Crusades-betrayed-Christian-beliefs-Williams-tells-Muslims.html (17 March 2020)
29. http://news.bbc.co.uk/2/hi/europe/4756635.stm (17 March 2020)
30. https://www.theguardian.com/uk/2006/feb/09/religion.world (17 March 2020)
31. http://observer.guardian.co.uk/politics/story/0,,1957278,00.html (17 March 2020)
32. https://bobfox.org/statements-of-confession-at-harare-zimbabwe-2006-and-berlin-2005-2/ (5 Dec 2022)
33. http://www.ynetnews.com/articles/0,7340,L-3369892,00.html (17 March 2020)
34. https://www.theguardian.com/world/2007/feb/26/usa.topstories3 (17 March 2020)
35. https://www.inquirer.com/philly/news/nation_world/20070824_Londons_mayor_apologizes_for_slave_trade.html (17 March 2020)
36. https://www.eastbaytimes.com/2007/03/27/maryland-legislature-apologizes-for-slavery/ (17 March 2020)
37. https://en.wikipedia.org/wiki/Stolen_Generations#Australian_federal_parliament_apology (17 March 2020)
38. https://www.nytimes.com/2009/11/17/world/asia/17migrants.html This is part of the British system of forcibly exporting children to their colonies from England without their parent's consent and then telling the children their parents were dead. **The first shipment of 300 of such children was to the Jamestown Colony in 1619.**
39. https://www.theguardian.com/society/2010/feb/24/british-children-sent-overseas-policy
40. https://www.thetrumpet.com/13544-pope-apologizes-for-killing-protestants (10 Dec. 2022)
41. Ibid
42. https://www.youtube.com/watch?v=NeEjuCx21MY&t=3300s (23 Dec.2022)
43. https://www.childmigrantstrust.com/news (23 Dec. 2022)
44. https://www.npr.org/2022/07/29/1114468497/in-canada-the-pope-delivers-an-apology-to-indigenous-peoples (5 Dec. 2022)

CHAPTER 6

AMERICA IS IN TROUBLE
WITH GOD

"Righteousness exalts a nation, but sin is a reproach to any people"
(Proverbs 14:34).

THE SOUL OF AMERICA IS SICK WITH SIN. AS YWAM LEADER JOHN
Dawson says, "This is a nation that has a covenant with God and a
pact with the devil."[1]

A large measure of the American Church is also greatly weakened
by sin. But God has made promises in Leviticus 26: 39-42 and II
Chronicles 7:14 to heal a nation when His people in that nation
sincerely confess and repent for their current sins and the sins of their
forefathers.

Twenty-five hundred years ago, Ezra and Nehemiah activated these
promises to restore sin-sick Israel from God's judgment by leading
Israel in confession and repentance for their current sins and the sins
of their forefathers.

In the last thirty years, these biblical promises have been activated
multiple times all over the world in cities and regions with incredible
results! [2]

The deepest roots of sin in the American Church began in the 1607

Jamestown Colony in Virginia. Confessing these sins before God can help activate God's promises to remember and heal our land.

God is patiently waiting for the American Church to activate these powerful promises now. God wants to heal America's soul!

The choice is ours.

SIN SICKENS

As many of us know, serious, unrepentant, persistent sin will cause a person or a nation to become spiritually broken. As nations sin persistently, they eventually experience God's righteous reproach for sin which leads to increasing chaos, moral darkness, and a toxic culture. That nation is spiritually sick.

Moral darkness, mental confusion, and economic losses often follow. *This is where America is in 2023.*

Our decadence as a nation and the sin and passivity of the American Church has brought God's reproach on us as a nation. Sadly, much of America's sin-sickness may be partly the result of lukewarm American churches that have not prayed, preached, repented, or acted in ways to prevent such widespread sin in our nation.

Sexual Sin

Sexual sins of all kinds have infected and afflicted many congregations and Christian leaders in America. Sexual sin is often the "elephant in the room" in American churches. Pornography is a bigger epidemic than COVID-19 among Christians, even among pastors. "Most pastors (57%) and youth pastors (64%) admit they have struggled with porn, either currently or in the past, " according to a 2016 Barna survey. [3]

Fornication by Bible-believing Christians may be at an all-time high. 49% of "born-again" Christians believe that cohabitation by a man and woman is not wrong. 35% of the same group thinks fornication is morally acceptable. [4]

Few pulpits seem to address it. Worse yet, pedophilia has been rampant among the spiritual leaders of one major denomination for at least fifty years all over the world, damaging tens of thousands of children—*with the criminal complicity of its denominational leaders.* Beyond that, in 2022, at least six major American denominations with over ten million members now consider the 3000- year- old biblical teachings on homosexuality to be *completely incorrect.*

Division, strife, anger, bitterness, gossip, hatred, unforgiveness, and racism by people of all colors combined with a massive vacuum of repentance and corporate prayer in churches has spawned *the perfect demonic storm* to weaken the American Church with devastating success. In 2020-2021 alone, COVID-19, vaccine debates, racial anger, violent protests, empty Sunday services, political divisions, and economic losses have greatly weakened the Church and nation even more drastically.

The Loss of Truth and Freedom

Into this spiritual sickness of the American Church and America's culture, a denial of reality and a totalitarian mindset have begun to take root in the culture and even in some Christian organizations in America.

When a person chooses to deny their birth gender, that is their subjective preference. When a society decides that something as theologically and scientifically proven as the definition of gender is up for debate, the "nose of the camel is under the tent". *All truth, all reality is now at risk.* When that same society *forbids and punishes* any dissent against this new identity ideology, *all freedoms are also at risk.* Free speech no longer is free—and the loss of other freedoms will surely follow. "Big Brother" has arrived—with the blessing of foolish government and media leaders. Foolish leaders are one of the judgments God levies against sinful nations.[5]

GOD'S LOVING JUDGMENT ON AMERICA

"The wages of sin is death," God says in Romans 6:23. The loss of reality and freedom are part of America's Kafkaesque wages of sin. America is staggering morally, emotionally, relationally, economically, spiritually, and *mentally* due to sin. 2020-21 was only the latest version of our nation living without God's full protection. *The worst is yet to come*—including the persecution of Christians who are becoming enemies of our culture due to our biblical beliefs. We are living in a Romans 1:18-32 moment:

> The wrath of God is being revealed from heaven against all the godlessness and wickedness of people...Therefore **God gave them over** in the sinful desires of their hearts to sexual impurity...so God gave them over to **a depraved mind** so that they do what ought not to be done...they not only continue to do these very things but also approve of those who practice them.

But God promises to make ALL things work together for good to His children (Romans 8:28). When Christians experience more of the painful wages of sin in our nation, **that pain will awaken the sleeping giant of the American Church to prayer, repentance, and biblically-based action.** That will prepare America for another **Great Awakening**—a massive revival that alone can save America from its downward spiral into greater sin and chaos.

The simple truth is that God disciplines those He loves.

> "For those whom the Lord loves, He disciplines and scourges every son whom He receives" (Heb. 12:6).

God always prefers not to punish sin. But as a loving Father, He has allowed our nation's troubles *to show us our desperate need for His help.* He is like the father in the story of the Prodigal Son in Luke 15. He gave his rebellious son enough time and resources to learn that he needed to return to his father in repentance.

Read the Book of Judges in the Bible.

The same pattern is there: increasing sin leads to national chaos allowed by God which eventually produces desperate repentance by God's people, which leads to God's deliverance of the nation from evil. *There are seven cycles of that in Judges!*

Christians Leaders Agree

Around 1997, I met Dr. Bill Bright, the legendary founder of

Campus Crusade for Christ (now called Cru), at a meeting in St. Louis with 120 other evangelical leaders in America for three days of prayer for America. This meeting took place right after one of Dr. Bright's annual 40-day fasts for America. In private, I asked him, "Dr. Bright, what is God saying to you about America?"

Sin cycle sin Book of Judges

Instantly, he replied, *"Judgment!"* Dr. Bright said the same thing in 1980 at Washington For Jesus, "Unless we repent and turn from our sin, we can expect to be destroyed."[6]

Many Christian leaders agree that America and the American Church are both now under the increasing judgment of God. Bill Bright, Jack Hayford, Alice Smith, Henry Blackaby, Pat Robertson, Mike Bickle, and David Wilkerson have said as much many times. [7]

Years ago, Billy and Ruth Graham said that unless God judges America for its sins, He will have to apologize to Sodom and Gomorrah on Judgment Day!

A Matter of National Security

God rules the destinies of nations. "Unless the Lord guards the city, the watchman stays awake in vain" (Ps 127:1). America has many enemies who want to inflict terrible damage on us. Only God can protect America from its enemies and disaster. This urgent call to repent is a national security issue of the highest importance!

God's Promised Solution

The only way back to "health" for the soul of America is through deep, heartfelt **repentance for personal and corporate sins** by Christians— **including the sins of our American forefathers**— based on the powerful promises in Leviticus 26: 39-42 and II Chronicles 7: 1-14. Read them slowly and remember that God *never* breaks His promises.

"So those of you who may be left will rot away because of their iniquity in the lands of your enemies; and also *because of the iniquities of their forefathers*, they will rot away with them.

But if they will confess their sins **and the sins of their ancestors**—

their unfaithfulness and their hostility toward me, which made me hostile toward them so that I sent them into the land of their enemies... I will remember my covenant with Jacob and my covenant with Isaac and my covenant with Abraham, and **I will remember the land."** (Lev. 26:39-42)

If I shut up the heavens so that there is no rain, or if I command the locust to devour the land, or if I send pestilence among My people, and My people who are called by My name humble themselves and pray and seek My face and turn from their wicked ways, then I will hear from heaven, will forgive their sin and **will heal their land**. (II Chron. 7:13-14)

Remember the story in II Chronicles 7?

As the first Jewish temple in Jerusalem was being dedicated, *heaven came to earth!* God's fire fell to consume the burnt offerings. The glorious presence of God was so strong that the priests could not enter the temple. Then, like a loving father, God appeared to Solomon one night to give the young king a special set of promises he could use *to nullify God's judgment on Israel* if God's people in Israel were to sin greatly.

The American Church needs to appropriate these promises today!

As John Dawson says in his excellent book called Healing America's Wounds

God's Main Purpose for This Book

This book calls the American Church to **confess and repent** for its current personal and corporate sins, *including the sins of our forefathers at Jamestown* **to prepare us for a national revival that alone can restore our land.** As John Dawson puts it so well, "A repentant church, confessing the sins of the nation before God, is America's only hope."[8]

God does not want to judge America. He looking for Christians to "stand in the gap before Me for the land so that I would not destroy it"

(Ezekiel 22:30). 2600 years ago, God found no one to repent for Israel and so *God destroyed Israel*, "the apple of His eye".

God is again looking to His Church in America—His royal priesthood— to stand in the gap for America. *Will we?*

Repenting with you for America,

Bob Fox
January 1, 2023

❧

Discussion Questions

1. What signs of moral decay do you see in the American Church and American culture?

2. According to the Bible, why is repentance important to God? Give examples.

2. Where in the Bible does someone confess the present and past sins of the Jewish community?

3. How can you be part of the solution to the problems you see in the American Church and our culture?

---

1. Healing America's Wounds Video Series, Part One, starting at 22:45 minutes

2. See https://www.sentinelgroup.org/documentaries for a partial list of documentaries about these amazing stories. Here is a video from that series: tinyurl.com/y3nb7dnt

3. https://www.barna.com/the-porn-phenomenon/

4. https://www.barna.com/research/morality-continues-to-decay/

5. Isaiah 19:13

6. https://www.christianitytoday.com/ct/1980/may-23/washington-for-jesus-revival-fervor-and-political.html (19 Dec 2022)

7. Here is an old blog I started on this subject: https://severe-mercy.blogspot.com/2007/

8. Dawson, John. *Healing America's Wounds* (Regal Books, CA, 1994), p. 89

CHAPTER 7

PREGNANT WITH AMERICA!

THE JAMESTOWN COLONY BIRTHED AMERICA

[*THE FOLLOWING ACCOUNT IS A HISTORICAL RECONSTRUCTION FROM THE sparse details known about the Jamestown colonists' first landing on the shores of Virginia. Since many of the details of the First Landing were not recorded in any document we now have, some of the details in this reconstruction are suggested by the facts that are known from other historical documents of that era.]*

After four months thrashing through the thick waves of the stormy Atlantic, three small, battered English ships gratefully dropped anchor on Sunday[1], April 26, 1607, a few hundred yards off a glistening white beach in a new, mysterious world at the mouth of what the local Indians called "great shellfish bay" — "Chesepioc" in their language. [2]

The Susan Constant, Godspeed and Discovery sailed to Virginia

Rising sharply above the foamy, surf-soaked sand, 50-foot dunes, topped with short scrub pines and heavy brush, gleamed in the morning sun. To the 145 weary, home-sick British men aboard the Godspeed, the Susan Constant and the Discovery, the creamy-white dunes may have looked like dwarf versions of England's white cliffs of Dover. "Land—at last!" they whispered to each other.

Eagerly, like birds about to be released from a cage, Christopher Newport, Admiral of the fleet, Edward Maria Wingfield, future president of the colony's council, Bartholomew Gosnold, a member of the council, and about 30 others, ventured ashore. Most of the men flung themselves overboard into the small boats, excited to see what lay beyond the tall dunes. "Today, we'll celebrate! We made it!" they shouted.

For most, dreams of gold, glory and adventure filled their weary minds. Their varied hopes reflected the collage of motives in the 1606 Charter that King James had given them just a year before. They came for God and gold, ministry and money, evangelism and economics. King James had the spiritual authority to initiate all those goals. At that time, he was King of England, Ireland, Scotland and Wales and the Head of the Church of England. But this blend of often-opposing motives would prove hard to balance in the days and centuries ahead. The 1606 charter to the Virginia Company, which sent the three ships, dictated *a spiritual* as well as an economic and governmental mission.

However, that mission was not to start on April 26th. Trouble was already brewing. This day would not end well.

During the scouting trip ashore with about 30 sailors, a few Chesapeake Indians attacked with bows and arrows, leaving two colonists wounded. Just when the exhausted seafarers thought that they had finally reached safety and refreshment, an unprovoked attack speckled the soft white sands of Virginia with drops of English blood. The violence, discouragement and anger of that first day in America would be a foretaste of what the colony would consistently endure in the years to follow.

After this unprovoked attack, tempers flared even more among the exhausted travelers. The colonists' nerves were already raw from months of living in cramped, dark cargo spaces beneath the incessant pounding of cold, heavy waves. Reverend Robert Hunt, the sole clergyman aboard the three ships, and Capt. Newport agreed that the men were not ready to worship God and dedicate the land to the Lord Jesus Christ as they had planned. As the fleet's chaplain, Pastor Hunt called for three days of prayer and fasting to help the men calm down and cleanse their hearts. Rev. Hunt encouraged everyone to repent from any anger and dissension in their hearts and to be reconciled with one another.[3] He knew from the scriptures that God specifically commands that His followers must get right with one another before coming to worship and prayer (Matt.5:23-24).

THIS LAND DEDICATED TO THE GOSPEL

Finally, on Wednesday[4] morning of April 29, purified by prayer, several small boats splashed ashore again through the cold surf for the second landing on what they now called Cape Henry, named after the king's son, the Prince of Wales. With them was a large wooden cross, constructed from a spare mast. Wearing the robe of an Anglican bishop in a representative fashion, Parson Hunt led the men in the planting of the cross and in dedicating the new land they now stood on as seen in this famous painting.[5]

Rev. Hunt dedicating the cross in 1607

Under the glare of a cloudless azure sky, with seagulls skirling overhead, and with a dozen heads bowed around him, Pastor Hunt began to pray. He offered prayers of thanksgiving for the safe voyage and prayers of blessing for the new colony that they were about to establish for God and the king. Taking out his well-worn Anglican Prayer Book of 1559, Rev. Hunt began to read the scriptures for Morning Prayer for April 29: [6]Psalm 29, II Kings 11 and Acts 26; these were the same scriptures that Anglicans all over England had prayed that day. He could almost hear the voice of his dear friend, Rev. Richard Hakluyt, the great visionary for this colony, who had read and prayed these same bible verses only hours before in London.

As he read Acts 26: 17-18, he suddenly felt the overwhelming Presence of the One Whose book he was now reading. The words seemed to leap off the page where Paul described how God directed him to "the Gentiles, to whom I am sending you, to open their eyes so that they may turn from darkness to light and from the dominion of Satan to God, that they may receive forgiveness of sins and an inheritance among those who have been sanctified by faith in Me."

Finally, choking with emotion, he raised his eyes and his trembling hands to heaven and prayed, "from these shores the Gospel shall go forth to not only this New World but also to the entire world."[7] In doing so, Rev. Hunt prayed the only prayer that Jesus ever asked his followers to pray for others: that God would send Christians into His harvest all over the world. "The harvest is plentiful, but the workers are few. Ask the Lord of the harvest, therefore, to send out workers into His harvest field."

The air was suddenly unusually still. The gulls now glided silently in a tight arc above the motionless clump of men around the tall, weather-beaten cross. The surf behind them pounded out the same rhythmic beat on the soggy sand. It seemed that nothing discernible changed.

But high above the earth, where men cannot see or hear, all heaven broke out in thunderous applause as the Son of God stood up and shouted a victory shout that reverberated throughout the heavens and shook the gates of hell.

"*Victory for Jesus!*" the heavenly hosts sang at the top of their lungs.

"*Victory for the Lamb!*" the 24 elders shouted as they fell before Him.

"*Victory for His Kingdom!*" the cloud of witnesses repeated.

Never before in the history of the world had a nation been born like this! Never before had God been glorified in this way by the first settlers of a land as they entered it. For a moment in time, Christian men stood before God with pure hearts to glorify Him in the founding of a new nation that would take the Gospel to this land and every land for which Jesus died. This First Landing was a first on earth...and in heaven.

The dream of the Rev. Richard Hakluyt was coming true. Like Christopher Columbus before him,[8] Rev. Hakluyt felt that the Lord had given him the vision to help found a colony in the New World to complete the Christian evangelization of the entire world that Jesus commanded in Matthew 28:18-20. Today, Christians call this the "Great Commission". Hakluyt foresaw a Christian community here in America that would raise its children to become missionaries for the Gospel to the Native Americans here and the peoples of every nation.

Among the founders of the Virginia Company that sent these three ships, Hakluyt is one of only eight men named in the king's charter to oversee the establishment of the first Virginia colony in the area of the Chesapeake Bay. Part of his evangelical goals was included in the king's charter dated April 10, 1606. According to the charter, one of the purposes of the colony was to further

...so noble a Work, which may, by the Providence of Almighty God, hereafter tend to the Glory of his Divine Majesty, in propagating of Christian Religion to such People, as yet live in Darkness and miserable Ignorance of the true Knowledge and Worship of God...[9]

Hakluyt made sure that the charter explicitly stated the evangelistic goals of the colony—to win the lost in the New World. Being a close friend of Hakluyt, Rev. Hunt's prayer must have echoed Hakluyt's passion for national and international evangelism to flow from this new land just as Puritan leader John Winthrop would later preach in the northern half of the Virginia colony in Plymouth, Massachusetts.[10]

A PREGNANT LAND

April 29th was a day of conception. The seeds of God's word, purposes and presence were planted at the entrance to the womb: the Chesapeake Bay area, later called Tidewater. In the next few days, that seed would tack its way up the James River—a tributary of the bay—to lodge itself in the flat, marshy lowlands of what is now Jamestown, Virginia: the first permanent Protestant Christian settlement in America.

The land was now pregnant with the Kingdom of God! The "spiritual DNA" of America was born. America began to take form in Southeastern Virginia. The union of God's Kingdom and this land was finally accomplished after other earlier attempts—both British and Spanish—had failed.

Jamestown gave birth to the first Protestant American Church and much of the American government. The 2006 Virginia General Assembly even calls the 1606 Charter that founded Jamestown and Plymouth, the "birth certificate of American Civilization."[11] Ultimately, this Tidewater "pregnancy" gave birth to one of the most unique creations of God on earth, the United States of America.

In the chapters to follow, we shall examine some of the "birth defects" in our spiritual DNA that we have inherited from this first permanent English colony. These "spiritual DNA defects" need to be identified and dealt with so that God's full purpose in giving birth to The United States of America and its Church can come to pass.

What exactly is "spiritual DNA" and how does it affect a region or nation? And why is "spiritual DNA" important to understand identificational repentance? The next chapter addresses these important questions.

Click here[12] to watch a 24-minute podcast video I made about this event near the actual site where the colonists first landed. Or use the QR code below.

Discussion Questions

1. Why is it very likely that America was dedicated to the spread of the Gospel worldwide?

2. Who had a vision for the colony to be a global missions base?

3. What could the churches of America do better to fulfill that vision?

---

1. http://www.timeanddate.com/calendar/index.html?year=1607&country=1 (17 Match 2020)

2. https://joannedi.wordpress.com/2014/08/18/the-chesapeake-bay-and-our-native-american-heritage/ (19 March 2021)

3. M.J. Raeburn, *America's Dedication to God Series, Booklet One: Richard Hakluyt's Contribution,* (His Story Seminars INC, Virginia Beach, 1994), 3-4 *As mentioned earlier, the actual role of Chaplain Hunt here is conjecture based on his known character, Anglican spiritual practices and Hunt's ministry to the colonists in Jamestown.*
4. http://www.timeanddate.com/calendar/index.html?year=1607&country=1
   (17 May 2006)
5. Picture Credit: Stephen Reid Scottish, 1873 - 1948 The Landing at Cape Henry, April 1607, 1928 Overall: 50 x 62 in. (127 x 157.5 cm) Overall, Frame: 54 ½ x 66 ¼ in. (138.4 x 168.3 cm) Chrysler Museum of Art, Norfolk, VA Gift of the Organizations and Citizens of Norfolk and vicinity in memory of Alethea Serpell, past President, Council of Assembly Tidewater Virginia Women. 35.14.1
6. The 1559 Anglican Book of Prayer was used by the settlers for many decades in Virginia.
7. Ibid.,
8. Christopher Columbus, a devout Christian, wrote of this great quest in his journal in 1492 just before he sailed West. He sadly reminded King Ferdinand and Queen Isabella in his journal of what Marco Polo had told the Pope in the late 1200s after his historic travels to Asia: the **Great Khan of China requested 100 priests** to teach his people about the religion of Marco Polo who had visited him in China. Think of it—all of China turning to Jesus in 1300 AD! **It is one of the most tragic tales of Church history that no priest ever made it to China in response to the Great Khan's plea for Christian workers. Columbus actually responds to this great tragedy in his journal.** He sailed west to find a route to China to fulfill the request of the Great Khan. Columbus writes:
   ...and in the present month, in consequence of the information which I had given your Highnesses respecting the countries of India and of a Prince, called Great Can, which in our language signifies King of Kings, how, at many times he, and his predecessors had sent to Rome soliciting instructors who might teach him our holy faith, and the holy Father had never granted his request, whereby great numbers of people were lost, believing in idolatry and doctrines of perdition. Your Highnesses, as Catholic Christians, and princes who love and promote the holy Christian faith, and are enemies of the doctrine of Mahomet [Islam], and of all idolatry and heresy, determined to send me, Christopher Columbus, to the above-mentioned countries of India, to see the said princes, people, and territories, and to learn their disposition and the proper method of converting them to our holy faith; and furthermore directed that I should not proceed by land to the East, as is customary, but by a Westerly route, in which direction we have hitherto no certain evidence that any one has gone (In http://www.fordham.edu/halsall/source/colum bus1.html).
   Sir Francis Drake's circumnavigation of the globe in 1577-80 proved to him that there were many people on earth still waiting to hear the Gospel. Drake and godly leaders longed to send missionaries to tell them (M.J. Raeburn. *America's Dedication to God Series: Booklet One: Richard Hakluyt's Contribution* (His Story Seminars, Virginia Beach, VA.), 2.
9. The Virginia Charter of 1606, in W. W. Hening, "The Statutes of Virginia," 1619-1792 (Richmond, VA, 1809-1823), vol. 1, pp. 57-66; https://web.archive.org/web/20050301092128/http://www.yale.edu/lawweb/aval-

on/states/va01.htm Yale Law School Avalon Project. *This charter is still part of the legal statutes of Virginia!*

10. John Winthrop, Puritan leader in the Massachusetts Colony echoed Hakluyt's vision of America with his image of America as a city on a hill, taken from Matthew   5:14.https://www.americanyawp.com/reader/colliding-cultures/john-winthrop-dreams-of-a-city-on-a-hill-1630/ (March 2021)

11. On March 2, 2006, the entire Virginia General Assembly declared that they "hereby commend the 400th Anniversary celebration of the 1606 First Virginia Charter, which may be thought of as *the birth certificate* of American Civilization..." as seen in http://www.firstcolledge.us/ (17 March 2020).

12. https://vimeo.com/manage/videos/767056941 (21 Dec 2022)

CHAPTER 8

SPIRITUAL DNA

AMERICA IS SPIRITUALLY CONNECTED TO THE JAMESTOWN COLONY

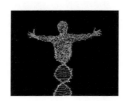

"Look at me, listen to me. Pay attention to this prayer of your servant that I'm praying day and night in intercession for your servants, the People of Israel, **confessing the sins** of the People of Israel. And I'm including myself, **I and my ancestors**, among those who have sinned against you" (Nehemiah 1:6 MSG Version).

IN THE LAST DECADE OF THE TWENTIETH CENTURY, SCIENTISTS finally mapped the billions of DNA codes in humans that God uses to make every person on earth. Without a doubt, this is one of the most stunning scientific feats in all of human history!

Millions of people are now having their DNA "mapped" to find who their ancestors were and to find missing family members. It seems true that knowing the ethnic and cultural groups of our ancestors can tell more about why we look, think, and act the way we do.

WHAT IS SPIRITUAL DNA?

"Spiritual DNA" is a term we will use to describe how our present and past family and non-family connections can shape our character, thinking and actions. Spiritual DNA can also influence our spiritual condition.

Although calling it spiritual DNA is a modern expression, *this concept is firmly rooted in the Bible.* The Bible clearly describes powerful spiritual connections between us and our forefathers—*both family and non-family ancestors, present and past.* These connections can result in God's **blessings or** God-given **earthly penalties** being passed down from one generation to another **due to the sin of their forefathers**. The Bible is full of examples of this concept of people suffering *earthly* penalties for the sins of their ancestors. **No one can lose their salvation due to the sins of their forefathers.**

The entire Bible declares that people "die"—i.e, lose the right to eternal life— only because of their **own sins**. This is what Ezekiel and Jeremiah meant in Jeremiah 31:29-30[1] and Ezekiel 18:1-4 [2]when they spoke of the children's teeth not being set on edge when the fathers eat sour grapes.

In these two passages, both prophets are speaking of *eternal death for sin*, not earthly penalties for sin. As we shall discuss later, since their Exodus from Egypt, the **Jews always knew that earthly penalties could come from the sins of their ancestors**.

But besides biblical revelation, most people would agree that every person receives "spiritual DNA" from their family. "Like father, like son"; "He's a chip off the old block"; and "The apple doesn't fall far from the tree" are just three common ways we express the truth that parents pass some of their character, personality, and physical makeup to their children.

The older I get, the more I see how similar I am to my father emotionally, spiritually and morally—*even though I was not raised by him or even around him for most of my growing years.* Unfortunately, his military career and my parents' divorce kept us apart after I turned eight. I saw him only a couple of times a year for 10 years— yet I share many of dad's strengths and weaknesses of character. To my amazement, I turned out a lot like my dad—*for which I am very grateful:* he is a great man in my eyes and, I believe, in God's eyes. [3]

VIRGINIA SETTLERS INTERGENERATIONAL CONNECTIONS

In colonial times, Individuals in Virginia were stereotyped by traits that were thought to be hereditary in their extended families. Anglican Clergyman Jonathon Boucher (1738-1804) believed that "family character, both of body and mind, may be traced thro' many generations; as for instance, every Fitzhugh has bad eyes; every Thorton hears badly; Winslow's and Lees talk well; Carters are proud and imperious; and Taliaferro's mean and avaricious; and Fowlkes cruel."[4] Virginians often pronounced these judgments on one another. The result was a set of family reputations that then acquired the social status of self-fulfilling prophecies. [5]

Note that *character traits* were passed down as well as physical traits. Don't we see this all the time? Goodness runs in some families and sinfulness runs in others from generation to generation. Alcoholism runs in my family. Persistent anger runs in other families. Fear often haunts generations of children in other families. These spiritual DNA patterns are also seen in biblical families.

SPIRITUAL DNA & CORPORATE IDENTITIES

To understand these spiritual DNA connections, it is important to understand that each person on earth has identities before God that are rooted in the groups they belong to.

In the Bible, God sees people primarily as individuals, then as families, churches, cities and nations. Amazingly, we see in the Bible that families, churches, cities and nations each have specific sin patterns, spiritual bondages, corporate guilt and God-given callings! These groups can be called *corporate identities* that we each have because we are affiliated with that group. This is who we are *corporately* —as God sees us. Because our corporate identities can carry *blessings and penalties* from God, these corporate identities also form part of our spiritual DNA that we inherit from previous generations.

BIBLICAL EXAMPLES

The Seven Cities

The seven churches in the Book of Revelation were not just individual church congregations like we have today. They were regional, city-wide churches. The Church of Ephesus probably had hundreds of house churches in it because Paul spent three years there serving that city-wide church.

Note this: All the people in the seven "city-churches" in the Book of Revelation (Rev. 1-3) were **commended or corrected** by Jesus according to their corporate identity as city-wide churches, even though each person in each city may not have individually deserved that specific commendation or correction. But because they belonged to that corporate identity of a city-wide church, they shared in the **praise or warnings of judgment** that Jesus gave to each of the seven churches.

Similar judgments were promised by Jesus on entire Jewish cities who had seen his miracles but still not believed (Matthew 11:20-24). "And you, Capernaum, will not be exalted to heaven, will you? **You will descend to Hades**; for if the miracles had occurred in Sodom which occurred in you, it would have remained to this day" (Matthew 11:23). So, if you were a citizen of that city, you might face this terrible judgment because Jesus decided that the city of Capernaum was more accountable because of the miracles done there.

CORPORATE IDENTITY BLESSINGS

The Jews

Most Christians and Jews would agree that Jews often enjoy a higher level of personal and corporate blessings mainly because of their national corporate spiritual identity as the nation of Israel, God's original chosen people.

This national corporate identity is rooted in the covenant God made with the founding fathers of Israel at least 4000 years ago: Abraham, Isaac, Jacob and Moses: "He will not forsake thee, neither destroy thee nor forget the covenant of thy fathers which he swore unto them"

(Deut. 4:31). The Old Testament describes this covenant. That covenant gave them great favor with God even when many generations violated God's laws, simply because they had that corporate identity as Jews!

Likewise, God's blessings persisted on **King David's descendants** in many ways, even mitigating God's condemnation of David's son Solomon for his repeated idolatry with many false gods. God was kinder to Solomon because he had a *corporate identity* as a physical son of David!

> So the Lord said to Solomon, "Since this is your attitude and you have not kept my covenant and my decrees, which I commanded you, I will most certainly *tear the kingdom away from you* and give it to one of your subordinates. [12] Nevertheless, **for the sake of David your father, I will not do it during your lifetime.** I will tear it out of the hand of your son. [13] Yet I will not tear the whole kingdom from him but will give him one tribe **for the sake of David** my servant and for the sake of Jerusalem, which I have chosen.[6]

Look also at how God spared Judah under a wicked king named Jehoram because of King David! In 2 Kings 8: 18-19, Jehoram

> ...did evil in the sight of the LORD. However, the LORD was not willing to destroy Judah, **for the sake of David** His servant, since He had promised to give a lamp to him through his sons always.

God withheld His judgment on each person in the nation of Judah due to **each person's corporate identity** connection to one of its past government leaders, King David!

In this example, note how God sees the iniquities of many people in an entire nation as being **counted in heaven as a corporate entity**, even though it must be true that not every person—especially their children— committed those sins.

> But in the fourth generation, they shall come hither again: for the iniquity of the Amorites *is* not yet full. (Gen 15:16)

These are just a few examples of blessings or curses that can come upon individuals just by being associated with certain groups or regions!

Not convinced? Read on.

ORIGINAL SIN

The most profound example of a negative spiritual inheritance from a corporate identity is what some theologians call Original Sin.

Original sin comes from Adam. As the ancestor of every person on earth, Adam's sin has influenced all humanity to sin. Romans 5:12-21 spells this out:

> Therefore, just as sin entered the world through one man, and death through sin, and in this way death came to all men because all sinned...*For just as through the disobedience of the one man, the many were made sinners* (vs. 12,19).

This is where all humans acquired a *corporate identity* as humans because we are descendants of Adam—the first human! This is also part of the most basic *corporate spiritual DNA* we inherit from the sin of our first forefather!

Penalties We Inherit

The sins of our corporate identity forefathers can involve us in God-given penalties for their sins.

Because of our spiritual and physical corporate connection with Adam, all humans share Adam's earthly penalties for his sin. Understanding these temporal, God-given penalties is crucial to grasp the *significance of our spiritual DNA that comes from our corporate identities.* We are never punished in eternity for someone else's sin but our spiritual connections to them via corporate identities can make us liable to earthly penalties.

1. Curses

Adam's sin resulted in curses from God that all humanity has inherited from their corporate identity with Adam:

Men would have to earn a living "by the sweat of [their] brow" instead of living in a fertile garden with abundant, readily available food resources (Gen.3:19).

"Cursed is the ground because of you." The ground itself would be difficult to cultivate at times (Gen. 3:17-18).

Adam would physically die (Gen 3:19b).

Eve's part in Original Sin also caused all women to birth children with great pain (Gen.3:16).

2. Propensity to Sin

Generational sins are sins that seem to be repeated from one generation to the next within an individual, family, group, region or nation. The *propensity to sin* in a particular way seems to run in families and affiliated groups. *"We have sinned even as our fathers did" (Psalm 106:6).*

For example, the sin of alcohol abuse runs strongly on one side of my family tree. This is a part of my family's spiritual DNA.

Violent feuds among Scottish-born settlers in colonial Appalachian America were probably more common than in other places in America. Just think of the vicious **Hatfield and McCoy's** thirty-year feud. Why? Such families had roots in the clans of Scotland where feuding was legendary...and very sad.

Sexual promiscuity is very common among certain populations in America who are descendants of promiscuous cultures in other nations.

For generations, the Church in India has had a problem misappropriating money. It is a moral weakness in the Indian Church and nation.[7]

These are examples of sins that have rolled down from one generation to another affecting the spiritual makeup of many individuals and some sub-groups within the larger group. We inherit both good and bad spiritual traits from our ancestors: propensities to sin as they did, as well as propensities to do good.

This is what the New Testament means when it refers to the influence of our ancestors on the present generation: "...knowing that you were not redeemed with perishable things like silver or gold from your *futile way of life inherited from your forefathers...*" (1 Peter 1:18). This echoes passages such as II Kings 17:14, 22-23: "However, they did not listen, but stiffened their neck like their fathers, who did not believe in the LORD their God."

GENERATIONAL SIN IN ABRAHAM'S FAMILY: LYING

Abraham lied about his wife twice. He feared that men would kill him to steal his beautiful wife, Sarai, so he denied that she was his wife and said that she was his sister (Gen 12:13, 20:2). It was a half-truth. Sarai was his sister by another mother, but with the same father.

Issac told the same lie about his wife, Rebecca years later. Ironically, *he told the same King Abimelech the same lie that his father Abraham had told Abimelech* (Gen.26:7-8).

This sin of lying shows up in a more magnified way in his grandson, Jacob. Jacob connived with his mother to deceive his father, Isaac, to steal his older brother's birthright blessing as firstborn (Gen 27:6-30). Jacob later deceived his crafty uncle Laban (Gen 31:30) by secretly fleeing from Laban, who previously deceived Jacob several times (Gen 29:21-27). While fleeing, Rebecca, lied to her uncle Laban about the theft of his household idols (Gen 31:34).

Simeon and Levi, two sons of Jacob, deceived and later murdered an entire village to take revenge on a man who raped their sister (Gen 34:13-31).

Another of Jacob's sons, Judah, lies to his daughter-in-law, Tamar, saying that he will give his last son to her in marriage (Gen 38:11, 14, 26). Tamar later deceives Judah, disguised as a prostitute.

Ten of Jacob's sons cruelly lied to him about Joseph's disappearance. They led their father to believe that a wild animal had killed Joseph, his favorite son (Gen 37:31-35).

Joseph also later deceived his brothers when they came to Egypt for food, but for good reason: to reconcile with his brothers. Joseph seemed to break the family's generational sin of deception through his extremely honest and unselfish behavior. Joseph's example probably influenced his brothers to also be more honest. (See Gen 45:5-10).

This is one of the key principles, as we will see later, in changing the spiritual DNA of a region: to break the power of that generational sin, the descendants **have to walk in the opposite spirit** of the generational sin. That is what repentance is. Joseph did that for his family. Any Christian can help break family strongholds if they are willing to break that generational sin pattern in their own life.

GENERATIONAL SIN IN KING DAVID'S FAMILY: LUST

David is of the tribe of Judah, Jacob's son. Judah was a fornicator (Gen 38:18) yet God brought forth His Messiah, Jesus, from the Tribe of Judah (Gen 49:8-10). What a merciful God we serve!

David's great-great-grandmother, Rahab, was a prostitute (Joshua 2:1, Matt 1:5). David and Bathsheba committed adultery with each other (2 Sam. 11). Later, David's son Amnon, raped his half-sister, Tamar (2 Sam. 13). Then, Absalom had sex with David's concubines on the roof of a house (2 Sam. 16:22).

Solomon had a profound lust for women.

He had 1000 wives and concubines. Solomon's lust was so strong that he even married foreign women who worshipped other gods—this despite *two powerful visions* Solomon had from God (1 Kings 11:9). He "loved many foreign women" (1 Kings 11:1) who eventually turned his heart from the Lord (1 Kings 11:4).

This brought God's wrath on the nation and eventually split the nation into two parts (1 Kings 11:1-14, 12:24).

INHERITING EARTHLY PENALTIES DUE TO GENERATIONAL SIN

Consider Ps. 79:8: "Do not remember the iniquities of our forefathers against us"? The Psalmist prayed that so God would not punish the current generation for the sins of past generations.

Even more dramatic is Leviticus 26:39:

So those of you who may be left will rot away because of their iniquity in the lands of your enemies; and **also because of the iniquities of their forefathers,** they will rot away with them.

THE EARLIEST AND Clearest Example

The clearest example of this biblical truth is seen in the first of the Ten Commandments:

> You shall not make for yourself an idol... You shall not worship them or serve them; for I, the Lord your God, am a jealous God, **visiting the iniquity of the fathers on the children,** on the third and the fourth generations of those who hate Me... (Ex.20:2-6 and repeated in Ex. 34:7)

In the experience of many Christian ministers, sins of idolatry always carry a generational penalty from God on the family's descendants.

Idolatry can be participation in false religions, (including Freemasonry), spiritism and all forms of the occult. Seeking supernatural information from sources other than God (horoscopes, Ouija boards, seances, etc.) can also be considered idolatrous to God.

Heinous sins committed by our ancestors (perhaps also up to the third generation) like premeditated murder, incest and rape can also impose earthly penalties on their descendants.

Note that God does not say he sends the **sin** of the parents to their descendants. OT Professor, Dr. Gary Greig comments:

> In the Old Testament, the Hebrew language distinguishes between "sin" and iniquity." In Hebrew, the term "sin" (*khet', khat'at*) refers to the act of sin, and the word "iniquity" (*'awon*) refers to the act of sin as well as the associated guilt and consequences of sin.[8]

Simply put, God will not send anyone to hell for the sins of their ancestors, but He does attach guilt (iniquities) and earthly penalties to their descendants primarily for **serious ancestral sins** like idolatry, murder, sexual sins of all kids, etc. At a minimum, iniquity (awon) from the sins of ancestors seems to corrupt the character of the descendants, **making them more prone to sin in the same way** as their ancestors which leads to demonic bondage in that sin similar to the bondage their ancestors experienced.

OT EXAMPLES OF PENALTIES FROM CORPORATE IDENTITIES

In II Samuel 21:1-14, King Saul's past sin brings famine to all of Israel under a new king. This vivid example of generational sin also shows how a righteous king broke God's curse on the nation for the past sin of King Saul.

> There was a famine in the days of David for three years. David inquired of the Lord and the LORD answered, 'It is for Saul, and for his bloody house, because he slew the Gibeonites.

Saul and his followers had broken a godly covenant that Joshua had made with the tricky pagan Gibeonites hundreds of years earlier (Joshua 9:16). When the deception was discovered, the Jews wanted to kill the Gibeonites, but Joshua wisely replied, "This we will do to them, even let them live, so that wrath will not be upon us for the oath which we swore to them" (Joshua 9:20).

When King David understood that God had brought the curse of a famine on the entire nation because of what King Saul had done, he went to the pagan Gibeonites and asked them what he needed to do to make things right between them and Israel. Seven of Saul's grandchildren had to die to appease the Gibeonites. After that, the Bible says, "...after that God was moved by prayer for the land" (2 Samuel 21:14).

God's wrath came upon the entire nation because a former king broke a treaty with a pagan people! The famine affected everyone in David's kingdom even though some of those people may not have even been alive when Saul's sin was committed. *Just being Jewish made them liable* to that guilt penalty from an earlier generation.

This is why God commands Israel in Leviticus 26:39-42 to confess the sins of their forefathers **to break the penalties from those sins off the current generation!**

ACHAN

Joshua reminded the Israelites of their bloody defeat in the battle for the city of Ai due to one man's sin (Joshua 7:1) at Jericho "Did not Achan the son of Zerah act unfaithfully in the things under the ban and wrath fall on all the congregation of Israel? And that man did not perish alone in his iniquity."[9] Note that Achan's entire family was executed by Israel's leaders because of the father's sin even though it is unlikely that all the children were even aware of the father's sin.

RUEBEN

As the first-born son of Jacob, Rueben should have received double honor above his brothers. Instead, Jacob prophesied that Rueben was penalized because of his sexual sin. "Uncontrolled as water, you shall not have preeminence, because you went up to your father's bed. Then you defiled it—he went up to my couch" (Gen 49:4). *Those God-given penalties on Rueben affected every generation of that tribe!*

While Rueben was still included among the twelve tribes of Israel, eminent Bible commentator Albert Barnes notes: "...this blessing is abated and modified by his past conduct. His tribe has its seat on the east of the Jordan, and never comes to any eminence in the common-wealth of Israel."[10]

AHAB

God cursed every male descendant of King Ahab, King of Israel, for the sins of his wife Jezebel,[11] who was a witch.[12] As a result, God assigned an assassin named Jehu to kill all the males in that family. Jehu killed King Joram, son of Ahab and Jezebel, on the very ground where Jezebel had Naboth murdered to satisfy Ahab's greed.[13]

Similarly, all the male descendants of wicked King Jeroboam (even the slaves) were *cursed by God* and assigned to be killed by God's command.[14] Wicked King Baasha's household was also condemned to die by God due to the sins of the king.[15] The sins of those two fathers brought physical destruction from God to their households.

THE EXODUS OF THE JEWS

The entire younger generation of Israel was cursed to spend 40 years in the desert due to *the sins of their parents.* "Your sons...will suffer for your unfaithfulness until your corpses lie in the wilderness."[16]

Caleb's obedience, however, during that same time resulted in his children receiving a great inheritance from God.[17] This is an example of a **generational blessing.**

MANASSEH

King Manasseh's gross sins brought God's judgment on Israel generations later (II Kings 24: 1-4): God sent the enemies of Israel against Israel under King Jehoiakim partly for the sins of Manasseh—**four kings earlier!**

Dr. Gary Greig, an Old Testament professor and an expert on this topic, writes:

> Spiritual oppression [that I call curses] may result from generational sin, as is taught explicitly in such passages as Hosea 4:12-13 and implicitly in the context of Exodus 20:5 and Deuteronomy 5:9. Both the latter passages comprise the second of the Ten Commandments and set the generational sin cycling principle of God's character in the framework of the sin of idolatry. [18]

GENERATIONAL SIN PENALTIES IN THE NT

In the New Testament, even the Apostles believed in the Old Testament concept of children being punished for the sins of their parents:

'Rabbi, who sinned, this man or his parents, that he would be born blind?' Jesus responded, 'Neither this man nor his parents sinned,' said Jesus, 'but this happened so that the works of God might be displayed in him.' (John 9:1-3)

In his response, **Jesus did not deny the principle** of ancestral sin penalties passing down the generations that started with *the 10*

Commandments! Jesus just said that the principle did not apply in this situation.

In Matthew 23:32-45, Jesus alludes to the earthly **generational penalties** that will fall on the Jews of his generation due to the sins of their forefathers for hundreds of years:

> **Fill up, then, the measure of your fathers [guilt]**... so that on you may come all the righteous blood shed on earth, from the blood of righteous Abel to the blood of Zechariah the son of Barachiah,-whom you murdered between the sanctuary and the altar.

BREAKING SIN PENALTIES BY IDENTIFICATIONAL REPENTANCE

According to Old Testament scholar, Dr. Gary Greig, "Identificational repentance is a person or group identifying with the sins of others, past or present, and repenting to God for those sins so that the God-given penalties (which the devil will exploit) are broken off of those repenting and off of those connected to the people repenting." See Chapter 23 for Dr. Greig's scholarly notes on this.

Eight books of the Old Testament talk about the God-given penalties affecting the current generation because of Israel's forefathers.

Moses

Moses "stood in the gap" before God to plead for the lives of Israel when they made the golden calf (Numbers 14:19, Psalm 106:23), but he also wrote about the *God-given earthly penalties of ancestral sin on the current generation* later in his book of Leviticus:

> So those of you who may be left will rot away because of their iniquity in the lands of your enemies; and **also because of the iniquities of their forefathers,** they will rot away with them. (Leviticus 26:39).

Then, Moses shows them the solution to their sins and the sins of their ancestors in the next three verses (40-42):

But if they will confess their sins and the sins of their ances-tors—their unfaithfulness and their hostility toward me...I will remember my covenant with Jacob and my covenant with Isaac and my covenant with Abraham, and I will remember the land.

Daniel made a long, detailed confession[19] of Israel's current and the sins of Israel's forefathers to appease God's earthly wrath on Israel:

"O Lord, in accordance with all Your righteous acts, let now Your anger and Your wrath turn away from Your city Jerusalem, Your holy mountain; for *because of our sins and the iniquities of our fathers*, Jerusalem and Your people have become a reproach to all those around us...While I was speaking and praying, confessing my sin and **the sin of my people Israel**..." (Daniel 9:16, 20)

Nehemiah and Ezra

Both men were used by God to restore and rebuild the nation of Israel after the Jews were released from 70 years of captivity by the Babylonians— a terrible penalty God imposed on them for centuries of their unrepentant sins.

The priest **Ezra** prays to God in Ezra 9:7, confessing the sins of Israel—**present and past**— and recognizes that the sins of their ancestors are part of their present guilt before God:

From the days of our ancestors until now, our guilt has been great. Because of our sins, we and our kings and our priests have been subjected to the sword and captivity, to pillage and humiliation at the hand of foreign kings, as it is today.

Nehemiah called on God, "confessing the sins of the sons of Israel which we have sinned against You; *I and my father's house have sinned*" (Nehemiah 1:6). Nehemiah also confessed before God, "Our kings, our leaders, our priests and **our ancestors** did not follow your law" (Neh. 9:34).

The Jews at that moment were quite aware that God destroyed Jerusalem because of the sins of their ancestors! That is why they deeply repented of both their sins and the sins of their ancestors as they were rededicating the rebuilt city in Nehemiah 9 & 10.

As an interesting side note, Daniel, Ezra and Nehemiah all confess the sins of Israel's forefathers **in chapter nine of each book!** There may not be another trifold example of a specific prayer focus like that in the entire Bible

Jeremiah wrote, **"Our fathers sinned, and are no more. It is we who have borne their iniquities"** (Lamentations 5:7,16).

In Jeremiah 14:20, he also writes, " We acknowledge, O LORD, our wickedness And the iniquity of our fathers, For we have sinned against You." See also Jer. 3:25.

And in 32:18, Jeremiah writes: "You show love to thousands but bring the punishment for the parents' sins into the laps of their children after them."

Note that this last verse is one chapter after the verse in Jer. 31 about the children's teeth not being set on edge due to the parents eating sour grapes— which is often used as proof against this principle of earthly penalties from the sins of our forefathers.

King Josiah admitted that "great is the wrath of the LORD that burns against us *because our fathers have not listened to the words of this book,* to do according to all that is written concerning us."[20] 2 Kings 23 details the special temple service of repentance and the practical deeds of repentance that King Josiah did to cement his commitment to leading Judah in obedience to God's word.

Asaph

"Do not remember the iniquities of *our* forefathers against us." (Ps. 79:9)

Isaiah

"See, it stands written before me: I will not keep silent but will pay back in full: I will pay it back into their laps—*both your sins and the sins of your ancestors,*" says the Lord. (Is. 65:6-7)

What Moses, King Josiah, Jeremiah, Daniel, Ezra, Nehemiah and Asaph have spoken of in the above passages is now called *identificational repentance* by many Christian leaders like George Otis, Peter

Wagner, Cindy Jacobs, Ed Silvoso, John Dawson, Jim Goll, Dutch Sheets and others.

Each of these leaders would say that *repenting for the current and past sins of groups is crucial for the glory of God to break out over regions and nations.* Such prayer breaks the God-given penalties incurred by the sins of our forefathers.

A Good Question

But you may ask," Why have we not heard about identificational repentance in our church pulpits in the past?

That's a good question! The answer is that this type of repentance was used in the Bible *mainly for healing the Jewish nation*—not for personal matters.

CONCLUSION

This chapter attempted to show how "spiritual DNA" is a good metaphor for understanding how the soul of America is impacted by blessings and penalties that come from America's corporate identities' history—just as a person's physical and spiritual DNA is influenced for better or for worse by that person's ancestors.

According to Leviticus 26:39-42 and II Chronicles 7:14, **only God's covenant people**—Christians for sure and probably faithful Jews living under the Old Covenant—have the authority to heal America's soul by correcting the "defective genes" in the spiritual DNA of America through confession and repentance for current and ancestral sins.

Thank God that through Jesus, the eternal curses against us for our sins are negated: "Christ redeemed us from the curse of the Law, having become a curse for us—for it is written: "CURSED IS EVERYONE WHO HANGS ON A TREE" (Gal.3:13)

Now, as God's "royal priesthood" (1 Peter 2:9), Christians have the authority of Jesus to "stand in the gap on behalf of the land" and call upon God to annul *the earthly penalties for the iniquities of our forefathers.* God is waiting for His people to do this for America.

And I sought for a man among them, that should build up the wall, and **stand in the gap before me for the land,** that I should not destroy it; but I found none. Ezk.22:30

Will you and your church stand in the gap for America? Please pray about this.

☙❧

Discussion Questions

1. What character traits have you inherited from your parents and grandparents?

2. Define "corporate identities." Why are they important to us spiritually?

3. Where in the NT do you see the corporate identities of people?

4. Name the sin that ran through Abraham's bloodline. And King David's?

5. Give an example of a God-given multi-generational penalty for someone's sin in the Bible.

6. Defines what the Hebrew word *awon* means?

7. Which seven books in the Bible describe the principle of identificational repentance for the sins of previous generations?

8. Briefly define identificational repentance.

------

1. "In those days people will no longer say, 'The parents have eaten sour grapes,   and the children's teeth are set on edge.' Instead, **everyone will die for their own sin**; whoever eats sour grapes—their own teeth will be set on edge.
2. Then the word of the Lord came to me, saying, ² "What do you *people* mean by using this proverb about the land of Israel, saying,
    'The fathers eat sour grapes, but *it is* the children's teeth *that* have become blunt'? As I live," declares the Lord God, "you certainly are not going to use this proverb in Israel anymore...The soul who sins will die."
3. By the way, if you want to know what kind of wife or husband someone will make? *Get to know their parents! My years of counseling couples has proven that true many times.*
4. David Hackett Fisher, Albion's Seed, (Oxford University Press, 1989) 275 quoting Jonathon Boucher, ed., Reminiscences of an America Loyalist (Boston, 1925), 61.
5. Ibid, 61
6. I Kings 11:11-13
7. Told to the author by two prominent Christian leaders in India.

8. University Prayer Network newsletter of May 30, 2003 written by Dr. Greig

9. Joshua 22:20

10. Albert Barnes, *Albert Barnes Notes on the Bible*, citation on this verse from the electronic version found at https://www.studylight.org/commentaries/eng/bnb/genesis-49.html (19-March 2021)

11. II Kings 9:7-8

12. II Kings 9:22

13. II Kings 9:24-26

14. I Kings 14:10

15. I Kings 16:3

16. Numbers 14:33

17. Numbers 14:24

18. Gary Greig, "Class Notes on Identificational Repentance" (Regent University, Virginia Beach, VA.: 1996).

19. Daniel 9:4-19

20. 2 Kings 22:13

CHAPTER 9

SPIRITUAL MAPPING

HISTORICAL RESEARCH REVEALS
SPIRITUAL CONNECTIONS

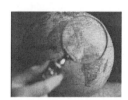

THIS IS A SPIRITUAL MAPPING BOOK. SPIRITUAL MAPPING IS SIMPLY creating a spiritual profile of a community based on careful historical research of that community. It enables us to see the spiritual realities in a region behind what we know about the current physical world. Let me illustrate.

In the early '70s, I flew F-4 Phantom jets for the Marines as a reconnaissance pilot.[1]

Capt. Bob Fox, USMC

The long nose of my Mach-2 jet had cameras designed to see and record what the enemy was doing--- *or what they had been doing.* I was trained to make pictorial maps of enemy actions even when human eyes could not see the ground from the air. I could take pictures with my SLR (Side-Looking Radar) camera right through dense fog or in the dark of night.

I could even take a picture of the ground on a clear day with infrared film and tell you what the enemy was doing there in the recent past!

This is because infrared film shows how warm or cool things are in relationship to one another. You can buy a roll of 35mm infrared film in a camera store and take pictures of your home's exterior to see where heat is leaking out of your home on a cold day! On that developed film, warm areas will look different from colder areas.

Using 100-foot rolls of 16x4 inch infrared film negatives, my F-4B could photograph the ground where a truck or plane *had been parked* in the sun in the last hour or two. The film would pick up the *heat differential* between the warm ground and the cooler spot where the shadow of the truck or plane had been.

The film was so good that you could actually tell what kind of plane had been parked there by the shape of the cooler shadow area. Using those infrared images, our military could know something about *enemy activity in the past* which gave them clues about our adversary's *plans in the present.*

Spiritual mapping is just that: a way to research and unravel the clues left in history that show what might be happening in the present spiritual world *in a city, region, or nation.*

When we look at spiritual mapping research through the lenses of the scriptures, we can better see what God was doing and what Satan was doing to counter the Kingdom of God. This "spiritual intelligence" helps us identify the schemes of the enemy in that place so we can more effectively destroy the works of the devil in that region today.

GEORGE OTIS

George Otis, Jr. leads The Sentinel Group[2], one of the most authoritative spiritual mapping ministries in the world. The Sentinel Group documents the growing use of spiritual mapping among pastors, evangelists and intercessors around the world for promoting spiritual revival and community transformation.

Sometime in the '80s, **George Otis, Jr**. coined the term spiritual mapping. He defines it as "the discipline of diagnosing the obstacles to revival in a given community through fervent prayer and diligent research."

Well-known prophetess Cindy Jacobs says that spiritual mapping is the researching of a city to discern any inroads Satan has made that prevent the spread of the gospel. Guatemalan Christian leader Harold Caballeros says that *"what an X-ray is to a physician, spiritual mapping is to intercessors."*[3]

If you want to know more about spiritual mapping, read his two classic books, *Informed Intercession* and the *Twilight Labyrinth*. John Dawson also has a good chapter on this topic in *Taking Our Cities for God.*[4]

Research on the roots of evil in cultures and cities

To write the second book, *Twilight Labyrinth*, George traveled to fifty countries and interviewed thousands of people. *In Twilight Labyrinth*, he shares many dramatic examples of how the spiritual history of a region can dramatically affect the present condition of that region. *Some of his stories will astound you.*

After taking a weeklong intensive class at Regent University from George years ago, I became convinced that spiritual mapping is a powerful way to *undo the schemes of the devil* in our region and nation. This is why I wrote this book, as I mentioned in Chapter One.

Although the term "spiritual mapping" is relatively new, numerous passages of Scripture address the reality of invisible cosmic forces and the importance of spiritual warfare, both of which are foundational to this new discipline. (See, for example, I Chronicles 21:1, Job 1, Daniel 10, Acts 13:4-12, Ephesians 6:10-20, I Peter 5:8, Rev 12:12.)

There is even precedent in the Bible for the practice of spiritual mapping, or something very like it (cf. Numbers 13, Joshua 18 and Acts 17).

"SPIRITUAL MAPPING" FOR AN INDIVIDUAL

For those of you who are new to this concept of spiritual mapping, here's an example of the value of a "spiritual map" of a person. This will help you get a better feel for spiritual mapping on a regional scale.

I have counseled people as a pastor for over 35 years. I "majored" in counseling as a pastor. Out of my own need to find healing from a very difficult childhood and out of a desire to see my parishioners set free from some of the same damaged emotions and demonic interference I had experienced because of my own damaged emotions, I became a serious student of spiritual healing.

I once headed a large counseling department in a 1200-member evangelical church in Tidewater. I saw had the opportunity to see the principles of spiritual mapping work with all kinds of people. I counseled elders, deacons, pastors, seminary professors, teenagers, children and couples. I quickly learned that to help them, *I had to know about their personal history.* What they had done and what was done to them had huge implications for understanding the emotional and spiritual issues they struggled with.

In a real sense, I had to create a "spiritual map" of their life history to better target my prayers and their prayers in the counseling session.

If I knew how someone was treated as a child by their parents; what sins the person normally struggled with; what major traumas they had experienced; what major sins were committed against them and what serious sins their parents and grandparents committed— then I could usually discern how to dismantle some of the lies, spiritual brokenness and bondages in that person's spiritual makeup.

Armed with that "spiritual map", I could lead them in prayers of confession, forgiveness, repentance, and break demonic bondages that usually gave them some relief from persistent problems they experienced. Sometimes, the results were immediately dramatic and life-changing.

The same spiritual principles that damage and heal individuals also damage and heal groups, cities, regions and nations.

Later, as I worked with many other pastors and Christian leaders to bring spiritual healing to Tidewater, I began to see that *the Body of Christ in Hampton Roads had to deal with the sins of our past* for our region — and this nation that God birthed here—to move forward in the Lord's purposes.

As the motto over the doorway to the National Archives building in Washington DC reads, **"The past is prologue."** In other words, what happened in the past affects the future.

This is why this book studies the history of Jamestown so closely. The original "spiritual DNA" of America and the oldest sins of America's forefathers all began in the 1607 Jamestown Colony. This book's spiritual map of Jamestown can give us invaluable clues on how to heal America's soul!

Now that you know more about the theology and practical use of spiritual DNA and Spiritual Mapping, you will better understand the conclusions I have reached in the remaining chapters as we look at the roots of America's sin-sick soul.

⚜

Discussion Questions

1. What about spiritual mapping makes sense to you? What doesn't?

2. Have you ever shared a "spiritual map" of your life with someone to help you experience greater healing in your emotions? How did that help or not help?

3. View one of the Transformation video clips here [5] What did you learn?

1. I find it ironic that I am doing *spiritual data reconnaissance* now in writing this book. I think it is part of *my* spiritual DNA.
2. https://www.sentinelgroup.org/
3. https://strategicprayercommandmin.com/
4. Dawson, John. Taking Our Cities for God (Creation House, Lake Mary, FL, 1989), p.79
5. https://www.youtube.com/playlist?list=PLdS21FNaABqcYe2s8KBsuB2WZyzcqemiM

CHAPTER 10

FIFETEEN GUIDING PRINCIPLES

BASIC RESEARCH ASSUMPTIONS

"Finally, brethren, whatever is true, whatever is honorable, whatever is right, whatever is pure, whatever is lovely, whatever is of good repute, if there is any excellence and if anything worthy of praise, dwell on these things" (Phil. 4:8).

IN THIS BIBLICAL ANALYSIS OF THE JAMESTOWN COLONY, WE WILL use these fifteen principles to guide us.

THE BIBLE & GOD

1. The Bible is our ultimate standard for evaluating human behavior because the Bible is true in all that it claims to teach: "All Scripture is inspired by God and profitable for teaching, for reproof, for correction, for training in righteousness" (2 Tim. 3:16; 2Pet.1:20-21).

2. Faith in Jesus is the only way to salvation, and Jesus is God (John 14:6; John 1:1, 14).

3. God is totally sovereign in the affairs of mankind (Isaiah 45:14, 23-24; Rom. 14:11; Phil. 2:10-11; Heb. 6:13).

4. God planned the time and place of America's founding: "From one man, He made every nation of men, that they should inhabit the whole earth; and he determined the times set for them and the exact places where they should live" (Acts 17:26, NIV).

5. Sin affects every dimension of life: People and nations pay penalties physically, emotionally, spiritually, relationally, politically, economically and environmentally due to sin (Genesis, chapters 3, 4, 6; Proverbs 14:34).

6. The guilt and consequences of past and present sin can affect an individual, a group, a region or a nation. The national security, economy and well-being of any nation are greatly determined by its current sins and the sins of its former generations.

THE SPIRITUAL WORLD

7. Angels, demons, the Devil and God are real spiritual beings. The influence and existence of demons are easily demonstrated in biblical literature and the history of Christianity. If demons are not real, Jesus is a fraud for dealing with them so often and so openly (Ephesians 6:11-12; Matthew 10:8; Mark 16:17).

8. The spiritual world of God, the devil, angels and demons influence and control the physical world more than the physical world controls the spiritual world. The Bible claims that the devil controls much of the known world. "We know that we are of God and that the whole world lies in the power of evil one (I John 5:19). However, God is in ultimate control of everything—the devil is only "God's devil", a mere creature. The devil can do only what God allows him to do. In the final analysis, God uses everything for His purposes, for His glory and His children.

9. There is a constant invisible war going on between the forces of God and the powers of evil for the souls of humanity, as exemplified in these verses with strong battle imagery:

> Finally, be strong in the Lord and in the strength of His might. Put on the full armor of God, so that you will be able to stand firm against the schemes of the devil. For our struggle is not against flesh and blood, but against the rulers, against the powers, against the world forces of

this darkness, against the spiritual forces of wickedness in the heavenly places (Eph. 6:10-12).

America's founding at Jamestown has been deeply marked by intense spiritual war.

TIDEWATER VIRGINIA BIRTHED AMERICA

10. This book contends that the healing of America is partially dependent upon a thorough confession and repentance for the sins *our earliest Christian forefathers* committed in the Jamestown Colony. That colony was located in what is now called the Tidewater or Hampton Roads region of Virginia where I live. It seems reasonable to conclude that the spiritual DNA of our region birthed the original spiritual DNA of the United States of America for three reasons: the primacy of origin, the scope of geography and the breadth of influence.

Primacy of Origin

This Tidewater region hosted the first permanent British colony in North America at Jamestown.

That colony would later morph into the 13 Colonies and, later, the United States of America. God also used other places in America, with different spiritual DNA to birth America—such as the northern Virginia colony in Plymouth, established by the Puritans and Pilgrims 13 years later in 1620. Nevertheless, the first strands of the "spiritual genetic code" that became America's spiritual DNA first grew in Tidewater, Virginia. Thus, Tidewater/Hampton Roads Virginia may be called the *Womb of America*.

Jamestown map given to the Spanish by a spy

Scope of Geography

The Jamestown Colony eventually grew into British Virginia—which claimed the entire United States in geography by the time of its Second Charter in 1609 from King James I in which the king claimed all land "from sea to sea, west and northwest" for Great Britain.[1]

The British planned to settle in just two areas initially—the Chesapeake Bay and the Plymouth, Massachusetts area. The famous Mayflower Compact of 1620 says that they came "to plant the first Colony in the *northern* Parts of Virginia."[2] From the beginning of the Virginia Colony, both the Virginia and the Massachusetts regions were called Virginia under the Virginia Company's charters from the King.

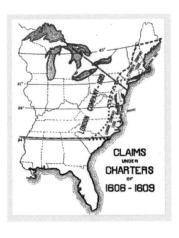

To be precise, the first Virginia Charter of 1606 claimed all land from north latitudes 34 to 45 degrees, essentially from Cape Fear, NC to Halifax, Nova Scotia! The Chesapeake Colony was assigned the land and near islands between 34 and 40 degrees and the Massachusetts Colony of Virginia got latitudes 38 to 45. This created an overlap by three degrees of latitude that either colony could claim.

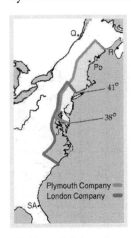

The Plymouth Colony of Massachusetts was called the Northern Virginia Colony

By the time of the third Virginia Charter in 1612, the British claimed from 30 to 41 degrees north latitude[3] (North Florida to Maine and Bermuda) and the Bermuda Islands 600 miles offshore, while still claiming all the land across the continent to the mysterious western sea we now call the Pacific Ocean.[4]

Almost all of what is now the contiguous United States was claimed for Britain by this third Virginia Charter in 1612.[5] From sea to shining sea, the Virginia Colony was, in theory, legally, the "Continent of Virginia".

BREADTH OF INFLUENCE

Finally, in influence, Virginia's actual political rule operated as far as the Mississippi River and the Great Lakes until 1774! Virginia gave up most of those lands to help form other states after the defeat of the British in 1776. By the time of the Revolution, Virginia was still the largest and most populated of all the 13 colonies.

Therefore, for all three reasons stated above, the Virginia Colony holds much of the key spiritual DNA that influences America today—for better and for worse.

THE BRITISH "DNA" OF AMERICA

11. It is difficult to overstate the high degree of influence the British had on the Virginia Colony, Jamestown and the 13 colonies that grew into the United States. While the Algonquian tribes had been the dominant native groups in the Tidewater region for thousands of years, their culture and influence were mostly suppressed by the British conquerors who took over their lands in s short period.

> The east coast of North America was English for 175 years before it became American. The English first explored it in 1497 under Cabot and claimed it in 1584 under Raleigh, who proudly named it Virginia for their virgin queen, Elizabeth. It was the beginning of their vast empire overseas.[6]

England, in its quest for the development of an empire that could compete with Spain and France, carved out its colony between the claims of Spain to the south in Florida and France to the north in Nova Scotia.

Although the French had two small, temporary colonies in South Carolina (1562) and Florida (1563),[7] and although the Spanish founded the first permanent settlement in the eastern United States at St. Augustine, Florida in 1565[8], neither nation was able to maintain its claims in North America against the growing colonies of Great Britain.

So, after several unsuccessful efforts to colonize North America, the first English permanent settlement appeared at Jamestown, Virginia in 1607. The British claims to its colony at Jamestown lasted—*miraculously!* Therefore, for all these reasons, it seems obvious that the deepest and strongest roots of who we are as Americans come from our British lineage!

Businessmen

If England was "the ship" that founded America, the sails and rudder of that ship were English businessmen. **The Virginia Company,** which founded the Virginia Colony, was composed of London business stockholders bent on enriching themselves and the British Crown with North American wealth—just as Spain had done in Latin America.

Despite the intense missionary vision of some clergy in England for the colony, **business values** drove most of the decisions in the colony, including the forced importation of white and black indentured adults and children, black slaves, the massive growing of addictive tobacco crops and the cruel abuse of the Powhatan natives—all covered up by many lies by the businessmen as the colony continued to fail for years. As we shall later, their strong focus on making money *at any cost* led to many sin patterns in the colony that persist in America today.

THE CHURCH OF TIDEWATER, VIRGINIA

12. Some of the healing of America needs to start in the Tidewater/Hampton Roads region since this region is the "womb of America" where most of America's major sin patterns began. The correction of Tidewater's " defective spiritual DNA genes" by the Church of this region may affect the nation that was birthed from here! **"Fruit follows root"** in agriculture and the scriptures. This region is the original "root" of America's soul.

> "If the first piece of dough is holy, the lump is also; and if the **root** is holy, **the branches are too**" (Rom 11:16).

13. The Church is the key. Throughout the Bible, God commissions His people to "stand in the gap" for the land.

"I searched for a man among them who would build up the wall and stand in the gap before Me for the land so that I would not destroy it, but I found no one" (Ezekiel 22:30).

As **God's priesthood of believers** on earth,[9] Christians have been given authority from Jesus to stand in the gap for others as Jesus did for all of us on Calvary. The Church can nullify the God-given sin penalties of others by confession and repentance on behalf of individuals, regions and for nations

If you forgive the sins of any, they are forgiven them; if you withhold forgiveness from any, it is withheld. (John 20:23).

BIBLICAL HONESTY

14. Some people will see the book as being too negative about the Jamestown Colony. Few Americans want to focus on the sins and weaknesses of our founding fathers. We owe so much to them. But *deep regional or national restoration requires acute honesty.*

   The Bible is notoriously frank about people—even its heroes: Adam, Moses, David, Solomon, Paul, and Peter—all were great believers whose sins were exposed by God for the entire world to see.

   Look at the founding fathers of Israel, the 12 sons of Jacob. Ten of them conspired to kill their brother Joseph and then broke their father's heart with lies about Joseph's disappearance. Judah later had sex with his angry daughter-in-law, Tamar, who disguised herself as a prostitute to trick Judah into sex (Gen. 38). Two other sons of Jacob wiped out an entire village because one man raped their sister (Gen. 34). Abraham lied about his marriage to Sarah twice (Gen. 12:13; 20:2-3) and Jacob and his mother, Rebecca, deceived his father, Isaac, to steal the blessing of the first-born from Esau (Gen. 27:19). Clearly, Israel's founders sinned, yet God still used them to found the one, chosen nation that brought forth the Savior of the World, Jesus!

   God Only Uses Imperfect People

   15. Finally, to keep a biblical perspective on this critique of America's founding, let us remember that our founding fathers were no worse than the people God used to start the *nation of Israel*. Except for Jesus, God never had perfect people to start anything. See Chapter 22 for more comments on this.

America was solidly built on Christian foundations—**but by very flawed people**—just as the biblical nation of Israel—the "apple of God's eye"—was founded by the often sinful, twelve sons of Jacob. The founders of the Jamestown Colony claimed to be Christians—and perhaps many were—but their behavior fell far short of biblical standards.

If we were to evaluate our founding fathers according to the standards of their day, we might reach many different conclusions than mine in this book. The behavior of our founding fathers was probably quite acceptable in many ways according to 17th-century British culture! They courageously attempted something few people would dare to try.

Yes, they abused many people along the way. Yes, the love of money drove them to many sins, yet few of their peers would have found fault with them for that. But *God's values are different,* as revealed in the Bible. When anyone's life is measured against biblical standards, it will always come up short. *Our founding fathers were no different— and neither are we.* We all need the forgiveness of God that comes through confession and repentance.

IN 2023, God wants to use some imperfect Christians to heal the soul of America. *Will you be one of them?*

Discussion Questions

   1. Which of these fourteen principles challenged you the most?

   2. Which ones did you agree with easily?

   3. Name three reasons why the Tidewater region of Virginia could be considered the "womb that birthed America"?

   4. Give examples of persons in the Bible with flawed characters.

---

1. https://www.gutenberg.org/files/36181/36181-h/36181-h.htm#pg_4
2. https://en.wikipedia.org/wiki/Mayflower_Compact (19 March 2021)
3. **St. Augustine was at 29 degrees latitude!** The English tried to avoid conflict with the Spanish claims there so the English started their southern border one degree north of the Spanish claims!
4. Edward Wright Haile, *Jamestown Narratives: Eyewitness Accounts of the Virginia Colony*, Roundhouse, Champlain, Virginia, 14-16.
5. https://www.encyclopediavirginia.org/Third_Charter_of_Virginia_1612 (17 March 2020)
6. Parke Rouse, Jr., Virginia, The English Heritage in America (New York: Hastings House, 1966), 13.
7. https://www.carolana.com/Carolina/External_Influences/french_in_carolana.html (1 December 2022)
8. https://en.wikipedia.org/wiki/St._Augustine,_Florida (1 December 2022)
9. 1 Peter 2:9: "But you are A CHOSEN RACE, A royal PRIESTHOOD..."

CHAPTER 11

TIDEWATER'S PROTOTYPES
A GIFT TO SHARE WITH THE WORLD

"Do not call to mind the former things···Behold, I am going to do something new...I will even make a roadway in the wilderness" (Is. 43:18-19).

PROTOTYPE BLESSINGS IN TIDEWATER

As the first location to birth America, Tidewater is "a prototype location with prototype blessings." Webster's Dictionary says, "A prototype is someone or something that serves as a model or inspiration for those that come later."[1]

Although this book focuses mainly on the "defective genes" that need to be fixed in the spiritual DNA of Tidewater, we also want to mention one of Tidewater's "good genes" that has become part of America's spiritual makeup: The Tidewater gift to create prototypes in culture, government, technology, medicine, art, media and religion is a wonderful part of the spiritual DNA of America. *These are things to give thanks to God for!* Here are a few examples.

A PLACE OF REFUGE

French Huguenots tried to find refuge in what is now Florida and Carolina in the 1500s, but the Jamestown Colony became the first permanent place of refuge for Europeans in what has become America. The Plymouth Colony would be next in 1620.

First Provided By Native Americans

Famine-plagued Jamestown settlers were kept alive much of the time by the hospitality and kindness of Tidewater's Native Americans. More than any other Native American, God used a 10-year-old Indian princess called Matoaka and nick-named Pocahontas (Playful One) by her father, to bring peace, communication, support and food to the starving, inept, British colonists during the first few years along the shores of the James River.

She was the daughter of Powhatan, the powerful chief of the Algonquian Indian confederacy in Tidewater. She dramatically helped the colony survive. "Every once in four or five days, Pocahontas with her attendants brought him [Smith] so much provision that saved many of their lives that else for all this had starved with hunger."[2] She befriended Capt. John Smith—whether or not she saved his life from execution[3]— became a Christian named Rebecca, married John Rolfe, and represented her people at the court of King James I in London. After her marriage to Rolfe in April 1614, Powhatan and his tribes treated the colonists with unusual hospitality and kindness that lasted until 1622.[4] Unfortunately, an untimely death at age 22— probably from a sickness contracted in England— ended the life of this great lady. Her only son, Thomas Rolfe later came to Virginia to inherit his father's estate.[5]

In 1616 John Smith wrote that Pocahontas was "the instrument to pursurve this colonie from death, famine, and utter confusion."[6] America owes a great debt of gratitude to this impetuous little Indian princess. She was God's "woman of peace"[7] to our needy and sinful founders. She was America's first Christian heroine and Christian stateswoman.

A Refuge from the Sea

Tidewater has one of the largest and best-protected harbors in the world. Ships seeking refuge from storms or pirates have found safe harbor here ever since it was founded. Yet, many ships were wrecked off the shores before they could reach safe harbors.

Between 1874 and 1915, more than 185 shipwrecks occurred just off the beaches of present-day Virginia Beach. To save the passengers and crews of those sinking ships near the beaches, five lifesaving stations were constructed. These lifesaving stations became the primary source of assistance for ships in distress in Tidewater until 1915 when the U.S. Coast Guard was formed.[8]

A Refuge for "Distressed Cavaliers"

"Virginia [was] the only city of refuge in His Majesties dominion, in those times, for distressed cavaliers."[9] These younger sons of nobility (Cavaliers) were able to flee the conflicts of England to build the "Virginia gentleman" culture that brought much good to America in terms of competent businessmen, law and order, good education for some, and much leadership for the government of Virginia—and later for the United States.

A Refuge for British Families Wanting a Fresh Start

By coming to the Virginia Colony, poor British families would be free from many of the class structures that kept people from becoming prosperous and independent. The Virginia Colony gave them all that and more. The "American Dream" of starting with nothing and making something worthy of greatness began in the Virginia colonies.

CHRISTIAN PROTOTYPES

First Permanent Protestant Colony

America was initially founded by Protestant Christians. Jamestown began that process. The official city Seal of Virginia Beach confirms the centrality of Christianity to the founding of America!

The city seal has a cross on it to depict the First Landing Cross erected to dedicate this land to Jesus Christ on April 29, 1607.

Hunt and his fellow voyagers planted the cross on a bluff above the beach. The original wooden cross stayed there for about 150 years and was used as a navigational aid for ships.

Today, a concrete cross stands near the spot at Cape Henry where the settlers may have come ashore that day. [10]

America's First Protestant Church

America is the first nation founded in the New World by Protestants (Anglicans, to be exact), starting in

The Cross at Cape Henry

Jamestown. The **first Protestant Church** built in the Western Hemisphere was at Jamestown. The Protestant Reformation that began in 1517 in Europe under Luther, Calvin and Zwingli first took root in North America in the Jamestown Colony. From there, the Protestant Gospel was spread across North America by British and American missionaries. This new Protestant theology, the use of the King James Bible and at least two national Great Awakenings became the real basis for the greatness of our nation for centuries.

First Native Marriage to a Protestant

The first native in Virginia (and probably in North America) to convert to Protestant Christianity was **Pocahontas.** She was baptized with the name of Rebecca, then married to tobacco pioneer John Rolfe and later presented to the court of England looking like this picture here.[11]

The **marriage of John Rolfe and Pocahontas** on April 5, 1614, was the first ever for any Native American in North America to a European. Their Christian marriage led to a period of peace between the English and Powhatans called "The Peace of Pocahontas."

Protestant Evangelism

While most came to the colony for mercantile motives, God's passion for the lost still burned in some fervent Christian settlers and London partners of the Virginia Company. Some in the colony were the **first in North America** to persistently reach out to the native tribes with the Protestant Gospel birthed in the recent Protestant Reformation. The 1620 Plymouth Colony continued this practice. William Bradford, of the key leaders in that colony, stated in his diary

that the Pilgrims came here to evangelize the natives and then take the
Gospel to the world from there.[12]

The **Rev. Alexander Whitaker**,
known to historians as the "Apostle of
Virginia," a ministry he started in 1611.
He was responsible for the baptism
and conversion of Pocahontas, as seen
below. [13]

Lady Rebecca Rolfe

Rev. Robert Hunt

Embodying the best of the spiritual DNA in Tidewater, Reverend
Robert Hunt's Christian character and fervent faith were unsurpassed
in the new colony. He was the **first Anglican priest and Protestant
pastor** to serve in the New World. Author Peter Marshall says of Rev.
Hunt:

> When not involved in priestly functions, he did more than his share of
> the physical work, hoping in vain to influence the other Gentlemen by
> his example. He personally took charge of the building of Jamestown's
> first grist mill for the grinding of corn. And since no one else was

willing to assume the responsibility for the sick, he did so, and this soon became a full-time occupation. He would clean them when they were too sick to clean themselves, make sure that they got their fair share of whatever meager rations were their lot, bring them water when they thirsted, and in general, fulfilled the Lord's exhortation, 'Inasmuch as ye have done it unto one of the least of these My brethren, ye have done it unto Me' (Matthew 25:40, KJV). Most of all, he would hear confessions and pray with them as the end drew near, as it almost inevitably did when someone came down with "the fever" or "the bloody flux" (which may have been typhoid, from shallow wells too close to their waste area).[14]

Rev. Hunt serving communion at Jamestown

Many in the colony found their way to heaven through the loving ministry and prayers of Rev. Hunt. Finally, in 1609, two years after arriving, "good Mr. Hunt" died along with many others in a season of famine and disease that characterized Jamestown for years. Rev. Hunt was a revered man, sorely missed, as the words of his memorial demonstrate:

He was an honest, religious man and courageous Divine [a name for a minister]; he preferred the service of God to every thought of ease at home. He endured every privation, yet none ever heard him repine. During his life, our factions were oft healed and our greatest extremities so comforted that they seemed easy in comparison with what we endured after his memorable death. We all received from him the Holy Communion together as a pledge of reconciliation, for we all loved him for his exceeding goodness. He planted the first Protestant church in America and laid down his life in the foundation of America.[15]

Rev. Hakylut

The main Christian visionary behind Virginia's First Charter was an Anglican clergyman named Richard Hakluyt. He was one of the eight signers of the First Charter and the main proponent to evangelize the Virginia natives as seen in Article III:

> We greatly commending... by the providence of Almighty God...in propagating of Christian religion to such people...and may in time bring the infidels and savages, living in those parts, to human civility, and to a settled and quiet government. [16]

Despite everything the colonists would do wrong, centuries later, God fulfilled Pastor Hakluyt's dream to make America *the most productive missionary nation on earth for many decades.*

The first Christian Thanksgiving may have occurred here on December 4, 1619, (a year before the better-known one in Massachusetts) according to a book published by the Norfolk County Historical Society of Chesapeake. The Colonists reportedly celebrated the blessings of that year on the banks of the Elizabeth River in the Southside area of Tidewater where the Berkeley[17] section of Norfolk is now. They feasted and offered prayers of thanksgiving.[18] Given the starvation diet the early colonists usually lived on, it is easy to imagine that prayers of Thanksgiving were fervently prayed almost every day during those early years here! (I'm still going to celebrate Thanksgiving in November.) :)

Christian Media Prototypes

While the early colony surely produced sermons and booklets on the faith, it was not until modern times that Tidewater produced two Christian media prototypes that have spread the Gospel nationally and worldwide.

On October 1, 1961, Pat Robertson's Christian Broadcasting Network ("CBN"), now based in Virginia Beach, became the **first Christian television network** in the United States, and probably the first in the world. After over 60 years, CBN is still one of the most original and fruitful Christian ministries on earth. It is a religious prototype of a high degree—for both qualitative and quantitative reasons.

Bishop John Gimenez founded Rock Church in Virginia Beach. He and his church created **Washington for Jesus** on April 29, 1980, to pray and repent for America's sins according to II Chronicles 7:14.[19] They picked April 29 because that was the day in 1607 that a Christian cross was first planted on the shores of the Jamestown Colony in what is now Virginia Beach.

With well over 200,00 in attendance, Washington for Jesus was *probably the largest single Christian gathering in America's history up to that time.* Bishop John & Anne Gimenez organized four more of these unique national events in 1988, 1996, 2004 and 2012.

These huge prayer rallies (much like the massive repentance meeting in Nehemiah 9-10), seemed to deeply encourage the evangelicals of America for more than a decade to seek God for America and turn from sin more fervently. This was something no Christian group had ever done before on that scale. They were telecast by CBN, TBN and the PTL television networks to global audiences. This was a **national prayer prototype** birthed in Tidewater.

GOVERNMENT PROTOTYPES

First Protestant Government in America

Since the King of England was also the head of the Anglican Church, church and state were one. This charter had both spiritual and political authority! All British kings and queens since Henry VIII are also the head of the Church of England! The Virginia Company's mission to found Virginia carried the authority and blessing of Great Britain and the Anglican Church. It was truly a mission for God and country. Every concern of the government was also the concern of the Church. Biblical principles and Christian church rules were everywhere in early America—even if enforced *in a very legalistic, ritualistic and often harsh manner.* For example, Under one governor, Lord De la Warr, the Jamestown colonists had to assemble for prayers twice a day and attend two services on each Sunday in the centrally-located chapel —or face painful discipline![20]

While this Christian culture sometimes led to abuses of power and abuses of certain Christian principles (similar to every other Christian group in history), there is no doubt that the first settlers of America attempted to be thoroughly Christian in beliefs, culture and laws.

Evidence of this was everywhere! Prayer, the reading of scripture in government meetings, teaching the Bible in schools, and even laws demanding attendance at church---all these were common practices in Tidewater for well over 150 years from its founding. To be a British colonist was to be a Christian colonist. Period!

The governments of future states and the federal government of the United States are deeply influenced by the prototype government of the Virginia Colony. The Virginia State Flag Salute even calls Virginia the "Mother of States."

The Virginia House of Burgesses[21] (later called the Virginia General Assembly) began on July 30, 1619, in the choir seats of the church in Jamestown.

As the first representative Christian government in the New World,[22] its laws were largely based on biblical truth. This body of legislators later became the model for the United States government. America's first  capital was in Williamsburg, at the northern end of Tidewater, and its first President was a Virginian. *Four of its first five presidents came from Virginia.* Eight presidents in total as of 2023. For that reason, Virginia calls itself the "Mother of Presidents".[23]

CONFEDERACY PROTOTYPES

This region seems to beget coalitions and alliances—especially for military purposes.

Indian

Tidewater birthed the first Native American confederacy of tribes under one leader in Virginia and perhaps on the entire East coast of America.

Led by Chief Powhatan[24] this confederacy may be unique in that period of American history. Powhatan (known as Wahunsonacock to other Indians) ruled up to 30 tribes but was not able to drive the British from his territory.[25]

French & American

Another God-given confederacy drove out the British 163 years after Powhatan's death just across the York River from his main camp: American and French soldiers and sailors (with help earlier in the war from German deserters[26]) won the battle of Yorktown against the British and German Hessians in 1781.

The British abandoned America as a colony shortly afterward! The coalition of American and French forces changed America's history—and probably the history of the world[27]

The Confederacy

As everyone knows, the capital of the Confederate States of America was in Richmond, just north of Tidewater, during the Civil War.

Modern-Day Confederacies in Tidewater

The American headquarters for the **North Atlantic Treaty Organization** (NATO) is in Norfolk, Virginia. This prototype "confederacy" of Western nations coordinates its joint military forces from this region.

The **American Joint Forces Command** is also stationed at Norfolk, not far from where mighty Powhatan ruled his confederacy of warriors. This command exercises control over all operations involving the joint forces of all the branches of the US military around the world.[28]

Supreme Allied Commander Atlantic (SACLANT) is also in Norfolk, commanding almost all US and NATO forces in the Atlantic Ocean regions.

EDUCATION PROTOTYPES

Henrico College, founded in 1619, became the first school of any kind in the United States and the first school commissioned to teach Native Americans—although they never did.[29]

The **College of William & Mary**, chartered in 1693, is the only college established by a British royal decree but Harvard University started first in 1636.

Founded as a Christian College by the Anglican Church (later the Episcopal Church) of Virginia, William and Mary was established to train ministers of the gospel: "that the Church of Virginia may be furnished with a Seminary of Ministers of the Gospel...that the Christian Faith may be propagated among the Western Indians."[30] Sadly, that royal degree has never been fulfilled even though it is engraved on a large bronze plaque next to the Wren Building on the campus. That God-given mandate to train Gospel ministers to spread the Gospel *is still valid for the Christian students of William and Mary!* May God give the Christian students there the grace to claim the Christian goals of the college's 1693 charter!

MEDICAL PROTOTYPES

The first hospital in North America was **Mt. Malady,** located in the "Citie of Henricus", north of Jamestown.

MILITARY PROTOTYPES

The Battle of the Ironclads

Naval history was made on March 8-9, 1862 when an iron-sided Confederate ship, the CSS Virginia (formerly a wooden Union ship called the USS Merrimac), defeated two wooden Union vessels and then fought a two-day battle with the iron-clad Union Monitor. An iron-clad ship had never fought a wooden ship, not to mention another iron-clad ship! Naval warfare was never the same.

Eugene Ely's Flight

Eugene Ely flew off the deck of the USS Birmingham (at right) on November 14, 1910, in Norfolk, Virginia. No one had ever flown a plane off a ship. Naval Aviation in America began in Tidewater.[31]

Ely could not swim but he did it anyway!

Conclusion

The Tidewater region of Virginia has given America many significant prototypes. This gift to birth prototypes is now part of America's gifts to the world—a gift that started in 1607 in the Virginia Colony.

Discussion Questions

1. What are your favorite Tidewater prototypes?

2. Name three Christian prototypes that started there.

3. How have these prototypes influenced America today?

4. Have any of these Virginia prototypes impacted your life? How?

---

1. http://www.m-w.com/dictionary/prototype (1 Dec. 2022)
2. https://www.biography.com/historical-figure/pocahontas (1 Dec. 2022)
3. https://www.biography.com/historical-figure/pocahontas (1 Dec. 2022)
4. https://en.wikipedia.org/wiki/Pocahontas (1 Dec. 2022)
5. https://en.wikipedia.org/wiki/Thomas_Rolfe (1 Dec. 2022)
6. Ibid.
7. Luke 10:6, alluding to the person whom God would use to bring the Gospel to a village through hospitality to missionaries.
8. https://en.wikipedia.org/wiki/Virginia_Beach_Surf_%26_Rescue_Museum (1 Dec 2022)
9. Fischer, 207 quoting *Ingram's Proceedings,* Virginia, 1676.
10. Picture of the concrete cross by the author
11. https://en.wikipedia.org/wiki/Pocahontas (19 March 2021)
12. John Dawson, Healing America's Wounds (Ventura: Regal, 1994), 37
13. https://en.wikipedia.org/wiki/Alexander_Whitaker (1 Dec 2022)
14. Marshall, 87.

15. Ibid., 96.

16. https://encyclopediavirginia.org/entries/first-charter-of-virginia-1606/ (1 Dec. 2022)

17. Not to be outdone, the **Berkeley Plantation on the James River,** many miles away from Norfolk's Berkeley section, also claims the first Thanksgiving *on the same day*! In their brochure, they state: "On December 4, 1619, early settlers from England came ashore at Berkeley and observed the first official Thanksgiving in America." They even have a painting depicting the event. It may have been one event that someone later mistakenly attributed to two locations called Berkeley.

18. Charles and Eleanor Cross, "It Happened Here" (Chesapeake: Norfolk County Historical Society of Chesapeake, 1964), 25 quoted in Toward a Spiritual Mapping of South Hampton Roads, Virginia, by Jerry Graham.

19. "If my people, who are called by my name, will humble themselves and pray and seek my face and turn from their wicked ways, then I will hear from heaven, and I will forgive their sin and will heal their land."

20. Fischer, 233

21. Picture from https://www.ushistory.org/us/2f.asp (19 March 2021)

22. This was the third oldest, continuous legislature in the world after England and Iceland.

23. https://www.virginia.org/presidents (19 March 2021)

24. John Smith, Picture from "Virginia, Discovered and Discribed by Captayn John Smith, 1606" ; map graven by William Hole, Library of Congress <http://lcweb2.loc.gov/cgi-bin/query/r?ammem/gmd:@filreq (@field(NUMBER+@band(g3880+ct000377))+@field(COLLID+dsxpmap)) (17 March 2020).

25. The **Powhatan Confederacy** was a group of Native North Americans belonging to the Algonquian branch of the Algonquian-Wakashan linguistic stock. Their area embraced most of tidewater Virginia and the eastern shore of Chesapeake Bay. Wahunsonacock, or Powhatan, as the English called him, was the leader of the confederacy when Jamestown was settled in 1607. The Powhatans are said to have been driven North to Virginia by the Spanish, where their chief, Powhatan's father, subjugated five other Virginia tribes. **With Powhatan's own conquests, the empire included, among some 30 peoples**, the Pamunkey, Mattaponi, Chickahominy, and others likewise commemorated in the names of the streams and rivers of eastern Virginia. They were a sedentary people, with some 200 settlements, many of them protected by palisades when the English arrived. They

cultivated corn, fished, and hunted. Of his many capitals, Powhatan favored Werowocomoco, on the left bank of the York River, where Capt. John Smith first met him in 1608. The English soon seized the best lands, and Powhatan quickly retaliated. **To appease him, he was given a crown, and a coronation ceremony was formally performed by Christopher Newport in 1609**. Peace with Powhatan was secured when his daughter Pocahontas married (1614) John Rolfe.

On Powhatan's death in 1618, **Opechancanough**, chief of the Pamunkey, became the central power in the confederacy, and he organized the general attack (1622) in which some 350 settlers were killed. English reprisals were equally violent, but there was no further fighting on a large scale until 1644, when Opechancanough led the last uprising, in which he was captured and **murdered at**

Jamestown. In 1646 the confederacy yielded much of its territory, and beginning in 1665 its chiefs were appointed by the governor of Virginia. After the Iroquois, traditional enemies of the confederacy, agreed to cease their attacks in the Treaty of Albany (1722), the tribes scattered, mixed with the settlers, and all semblance of the confederacy disappeared. **In 1990 there were about 800 Powhatan in the United States, most of them in eastern Virginia.** (Cited in The Columbia Electronic Encyclopedia, Sixth Edition Copyright © 2003, Columbia University Press. Licensed from Columbia University Press. All rights reserved. www.cc. columbia.edu/cu/cup/).

26. https://en.wikipedia.org/wiki/Germans_in_the_American_Revolution (19 March 2021)
27. Edward J. Lowell. The Hessians and the other German Auxiliaries Of Great Britain in the Revolutionary War. (New York: Harper and Brothers Publishers, 1884), Preface.
28. "Headquartered in Norfolk, Va., **U.S. Joint Forces Command** is one of nine unified commands in the Department of Defense. **It is the only command with both a geographic region and a functional responsibility to support the other four geographic commanders**. Among his duties, the commander-in-chief, USJFCOM, oversees military operations in the North Atlantic geographic area and supports the other commanders-in-chief in their geographic regions around the world." (http://www.globalsecurity.org/military/ agency/dod/jfcom.htm)
29. This was one of the first broken promises to Native Americans in Tidewater by our founders. The College of William and Mary later also reneged on its promise to evangelize and educate Native Americans
30. Godson et al., The College of William and Mary: A History, Vol. 1, 1693-1888 [King and Queen Press, 1993], (March 8-9, 1862)12. See the entire charter online in modern English at https://scrc-kb.libraries.wm.edu/royal-charter#Transcription+of+the+Royal+Charter (26 Dec. 2022)
31. https://airandspace.si.edu/stories/editorial/eugene-ely-and-birth-naval-aviation—january-18-1911 (17 March 2020)

CHAPTER 12

THE LOVE OF MONEY

THE MAIN SIN IN THE COLONY

"No servant can serve two masters; for either he will hate the one and love the other, or else he will be devoted to one and despise the other. You cannot serve God and wealth. " (Luke 16:13)

TRYING TO SERVE BOTH GOD AND MONEY

England had three main motives for sending settlers to the New World. Two were all about money and political power.

England's first motive was to **get its share of that New World wealth** and build an overseas empire as Spain and France had done. Spain, France and England were all in a mad dash to claim their piece of the newly discovered New World on the other side of the Atlantic. Spain had already brought back literally tons of gold and silver from South America and it also claimed Florida. France claimed what is now Canada and Nova Scotia.

England's second motive for founding a colony in North America was to find the fabled **Northwest Passage route** to the Orient so she could more easily trade with the Far East.

Thirdly, England wanted to know what happened to **the "Lost Colony"** of 1585 that Sir Walter Raleigh tried unsuccessfully to plant in present-day Manteo, NC.

Along the way, England settlers tried to fulfill one of their charter's goals "in propagating of Christian Religion to such People, as yet live in Darkness..."[1]

The most fundamental issue in the founding of Tidewater—and America—concerns the dangerous and often deceptive interplay between money and religion. *Both* were motives for all exploration of the New World by the "Christian" European nations like Spain, Portugal, France and England.

No motive seems more pervasive or powerful in the founding of Jamestown than the one Jesus sternly warned us about: the love of riches. It is the one thing Jesus said could radically compete with our serving God.

The one time we see Jesus truly angry in the Gospels involves the mixture of money and ministry: when He drove the money-changers out of the temple, beating them with a scourge of rope and over-turning their tables. Such extreme measures by *Jesus demonstrated His deep concern that the excessive pursuit of money could corrupt the spiritual lives and ministries of His people.*

It is no wonder that the Apostle Paul later writes, "For the love of money is *a root of all sorts of evil...*" (1 Timothy 6:10). The love of money certainly brought much evil to Jamestown.

Mixed Motives Are Normal

Most people would admit to having multiple motives for just about everything they do. We love and serve others because we love them, but we might also want them to love us in return or it might meet some personal needs to love and serve others. This is normal and not inherently a bad thing.

Even in Christian ministry, we serve to please God, but, as humans, we often also have some personal agendas to fulfill in serving God. It is **the ratio of these mixed motives** that makes all the difference. In the Virginia Company of senders and settlers, there is much evidence to say that in the early colonists up to **90%** of their motives focused on the accumulation of wealth and only 10% related to Gospel goals and values.[2] If that is true, it is easy to see why that ratio of motives created the framework for much that went wrong with the colony and eventually with America. [3]

"Sir Walter Raleigh, who orchestrated the earlier attempts to plant the Roanoke Colony in North Carolina, described the various motives people had for colonizing during this era: '...for religion, for wealth, for knowledge, for pleasure, for power and for the overthrow of rivals.'"[4]

Examples of Gold Over God

Captain John Smith summed up the focus of the first settlers well: "No talks, no hope, nor works, but dig gold, wash gold, refine gold, load gold."[5]

In September 1608, Newport—the admiral of the three-ship fleet that founded Jamestown—returned to Jamestown from England in disgrace. The load of ore that he had quickly collected in Virginia turned out to be largely the glittering iron pyrite, called "Fool's Gold." Now the Virginia Company had commanded him "not to return without a lump of gold, a certainty of the South Sea [the Pacific], or one of the "Lost Company" of Sir Walter Raleigh!" And if the colonists were not able to provide him with some sort of valuable cargo, they concluded ominously, *"they were to remain as banished men."*[6] There was no mention of the importance of evangelizing the natives or building a Christian community in the New World.

James Blair was prevented from evangelizing Powhatans

The primacy of money continued to compete with the love of God in the development of the College of William and Mary. The godly Scotsman, James Blair [7], as president-elect of the emerging college, asked England's Attorney General, Edward Seymour, for money. William and Mary's royal charter called for the training of clergy to reach the Indians with the Gospel. Seymour wrote back saying that he thought the college was a waste of money. Blair responded that there were souls that needed to be saved.

"Souls?" replied Seymour. "Damn your souls! Make tobacco!" [8]

Again, to summarize:

The founding of Virginia marked the beginning of a twenty-five-year period in which every colony in the New World was established by means of a joint-stock company. A variety of motives intensified the colonizing impulse—international rivalry, propagation of religion, enlarged opportunity for individual men—but none exceeded that of trade and profit.[9]

Governor Berkley's Embezzlements

Tidewater's genetic defect of love for money continued to show up even in the highest leaders of the colony. Governor Berkeley was the most powerful person in shaping Virginia for his 35 years in office from 1642-1676---very formative years for the colony. It was a terrible place to live in most respects. It was like a lawless, wild-west gold-rush town.

To his credit, Berkeley turned the colony around to become a very civilized and prosperous place to live. Yet, "he openly enriched himself from his offices and set a sad example of peculation [embezzlement] that long persisted in Virginia... In 1667, for example, he wrote directly to his superior, Lord Arlington, 'Though ambition commonly leaves sober old age, covetousness does not...' These were the vices of his age and Berkeley had them in a high degree."[10]

THE GREAT NICOTINE EMPIRE

While gold and silver spurred the birth of Spanish nations in Latin America, America became the first nation initially built on the sale of a highly addictive substance: tobacco— *Virginia's brown gold.*

John Rolfe, the husband of Pocahontas, first planted Caribbean tobacco seeds here in 1612, after he shipwrecked on the Island of Bermuda while en route to Jamestown in 1609. The Indian variety was not good for commercial purposes, so Rolfe tried seeds he brought from the Caribbean and found that people liked the tobacco that grew from them.

Growing tobacco became the foundation of the Virginia economy. Settlers planted tobacco as fast as they could because it sold furiously and produced a large profit. Many of the "Tobacco Coast" farmers along the James, York and Potomac rivers grew rich in the process.

This frenzy to produce tobacco was one reason it took twenty years before the settlers grew their first corn crop large enough to sustain themselves![11]

Historian T.J. Stiles calls it *"the great nicotine empire*—perhaps the first time in history that an economy rose purely on the export of an addictive drug."* The love of money found in tobacco drove the first settlers to do whatever they needed to farm and sell tons of tobacco.

Even then, leaders knew the planted "weed" was bad for people. Nine years before Rolfe exported his first tobacco shipment to England, King James himself wrote a strong denunciation in 1604 of tobacco use as detrimental to people's health in his famous *"Counterblaste to Tobacco"*.

The king warned his subjects in this tract that smoking led to depravity and stated that it is "a custom loathsome to the eye—hateful to the nose—harmful to the brain—dangerous to the lungs—and, in the black stinking fumes therof, nearest resembling the horrid Stygian fumes of the pit that is bottomless."[12]

Initially, all the authorities at home and abroad were against tobacco farming, largely because King James hated "the weed", but eventually, the lust for profits won the day and tobacco became king in Virginia and the king made tobacco a royal monopoly in 1624.

Coin of the realm

Tobacco was so central to the colony that it became the "coin of the realm" in Tidewater. You could buy a wife/servant with tobacco. In 1619, lonely, male settlers eagerly paid about 150 pounds of tobacco for each of the indentured women shipped to the colony as wives and servants between 1620 and 1624.

Anglican priests were also paid with bundles of tobacco! The Priest at St. Paul's Church in Norfolk (the one with a British Revolutionary War cannonball stuck in the wall) was paid in tobacco. The 50 acres of land on which the city of Norfolk lies was purchased in 1682 from Nicolas Wise for "ten thousand pounds of good merchantable tobacco".

Tobacco's Evil Legacy

In a real sense, tobacco laid **the foundation for slavery** in America. One evil led to another—far worse than anyone could have ever imagined, especially in "the land of the free and the brave." Larger profits from larger tobacco fields demanded cheap labor. That meant the importation of thousands of poor white men, women and children from England and later, Africans, as indentured servants and slaves for decades in Tidewater. **This was the beginning of human trafficking in America!**

The lust for tobacco profits **robbed the Powhatans of their land.** Eventually, the English colonists took almost all their land by force and by trickery—as white Americans did all across our new land. Our region created a **pattern of deceit and fraud** on the Native Americans that went on for generations, as the next chapter describes. 13

Finally, we have to admit that tobacco is **a drug that has addicted, sickened, and killed multitudes** of people all over the world. Growing and selling anything that harmful to people has to be a sin against others. How can we say we love our neighbor and make a profit from an addictive drug that is so dangerous to his health? This *sinful culture of addiction-for-profit needs to be confessed and renounced by the Church in America and Great Britain.*

SUMMARY

Throughout history, when business and religion clashed, the business usually won. Therefore, it is no great surprise that the love of money often trumped biblical behavior in the colonization of this nation, as it probably had in the establishment of almost every colony created by European Christians.

Peter Marshall, son of the former famous chaplain to the US Congress, wrote a well-researched book about the Jamestown and Plymouth colonies called The Light and the Glory. He concluded,

"The settlement of Jamestown was undertaken without Christ".[14]

Although that may be somewhat of an overstatement, it sadly seems close to the truth for many of the first colonists. God's Kingdom agenda took a backseat to money in Jamestown.

This is an ancient sin pattern. The first sin of Israel in the Promised Land was due to Achan's love of money when he stole forbidden things from Jericho.[15] That sin brought defeat to Israel in the next battle at Ai![16] The love of money has hindered the spread of the Gospel in similar ways for centuries. It has even hindered the spread of Islam!

Islam's Love of Money Protected Africa

Many know that God used Jamestown's Captain John Smith to defeat Muslims in Europe, but in a bizarre twist that also proves the power of money over religion, God used the love of money to thwart the missionary plans of Islam in Africa.

Muslim missionaries had the potential to win all of Africa to Islam a thousand years before Christian missionaries finally tried to go there. However, the Muslim mullahs would not evangelize regions of Africa where Muslim slave traders were successfully preying on tribes below the Sahara.

Deferring to the powerful Muslim slavers and the support of the Koran for slavery (Mohammed himself was a slaver), the Islamic mullahs decided to evangelize "only along the 4000-mile-long southern fringe of the Sahara from Senegal to Somalia...and on a crescent of coastline facing Zanzibar."[17] This saved sub-Saharan Africa from Islam and allowed later Christian missionaries to spread the Gospel there!

❧

Discussion Questions

1. When have you seen the love of money corrupt a Christian work or ministry?

2. Describe some biblical attitudes about money that protect us from the love of money?

3. Why can't we serve money and God? What does Jesus warn us that we have to choose?

4. What could the Jamestown colony have done to make their love of God more primary than their desire to make money?

4. How do you protect yourself from loving money more than God?

5. What specific things did our Christian forefathers do for money that we can confess and repent for to help break this sinful pattern in America?

---

1. The Virginia Charter of April 10, 1606 at https://avalon.law.yale.edu/17th_century/va01.asp (19 March 2021)
2. Healing America's Wounds Video Series, Part One, starting at 26:33 minutes
3. Ibid, starting at 25:17 minutes
4. Rev. Marty O'Rourke. "Community Transformation," (Unpublished Paper for Regent University, Virginia Beach, VA., 2001), 18 quoting Edwin S. Gaustad, Revival, Revolution and Religion in Early Religion (Williamsburg: the colonial Williamsburg Foundation, 1994) 1.
5. John Dawson, Healing America's Wounds (Ventura: Regal, 1994), 44.
6. Marshall , 94.
7. https://www.britannica.com/biography/James-Blair (17 March 2020)
8. Ibid., 104.
9. http://www.let.rug.nl/usa/documents/1600-1650/instructions-for-the-virginia-colony-1606.php (19 March 2021)
10. David Hackett Fischer , *Albion's Seed: Four British Folkways in America*, Oxford University Press, New York, 1989, 209 Many of Fisher's insights have been incorporated into this book. **Dr. Charles Wolfe**, head of the Plymouth Rock Foundation, Plymouth, MA. told me that he considers Albion's Seed a masterpiece of historical research and writing.
11. Marshall, 89.
12. https://www.laits.utexas.edu/poltheory/james/blaste/blaste.html (1 Dec 2022)
13. See Appendix A for a new congressional resolution aimed at apologizing to Native American's for centuries of fraud and abuse by the Federal government.
14. Peter Marshall and David Manuel. The Light and the Glory (Grand Rapids: Fleming Revell, 1977) , 105.
15. Joshua 7: 1-26
16. Joshua 7: 11-12
17. Don Richardson, Secrets of the Koran (Ventura: Regal Books, 2003), 202.

CHAPTER 13

ABUSE OF NATIVE AMERICANS
BEGAN IN JAMESTOWN

"Cursed is one who displaces his neighbor's boundary marker"
(Deuteronomy 27:17).

THESE JAMESTOWN SETTLERS HAD A TERRIBLE START WITH THE
Indians. Going well beyond the intermittent harshness that the
English showed the Indians in the earlier short-lived Roanoke Colony,[1]
the Jamestown settlers saw themselves as superior to the Indians and
treated them with much deceit and often with violence for years. The
cocky, pugnacious John Smith personified that attitude.

To be fair, Smith was only reflecting the attitude many English
leaders felt about our Native Americans. King James himself in 1604
described Native American people as "these beastly Indians, slaves to
the Spaniards, refuse to the world, and as yet aliens from the holy
Covenant of God."[2]

Smith and Chief Powhatan played, as historian Timothy Stiles says,
"a deadly game of smiling deceits and open attacks"[3] between the
colony and the Indians. But remember that we have to judge the
colony by God's holy standards—not the culture of the day to find out
the roots of sin that began there.

Both sides gave as much as they received, but the English, always more desperate initially, even violated the basic rules of Powhatan warfare by destroying entire villages—including the women and children—like the village of Paspahegh.[4]

These English atrocities only escalated the tensions and intrigue between the Indians, whom the English supposedly came to Christianize, and the very vulnerable colony. This picture depicts Smith in battle with a local tribe to steal their food— a very common event in the early years of the colony.[5] The treachery of the Indians in the 1622 massacre of the colony may seem more justified in light of these many years of English war crimes, predations and deceptions.

*"C. Smith takes King of Pamunkey prisoner, 1608"
near Jamestown*

MODERN ABUSE OF VIRGINIA'S TRIBES

The Racial Integrity Act

> Woe to those who enact evil statutes and to those who constantly record unjust decisions (Isaiah 10:1).

These abusive and deceitful attitudes towards our Native Americans have carried down to modern Virginians—as spiritual DNA often does!

In the August 11, 2003 edition of the Virginian-Pilot on page A10, there was a story outlining the continued legal fight of Virginia's remaining eight tribes to get federal recognition. **Virginia waited until 1983 to officially recognize them as Native American tribes**. The Federal government waited until **2018 to officially recognize** seven Virginia tribes: the Pamunkey, Chickahominy Providence Forge, Eastern Chickahominy, Upper Mattaponi (Formerly called Adamstown Indians [6]), Rappahannock, Nansemond and Monacan. Several other Virginia tribes are still seeking federal recognition, including the Mattaponi on the Mattaponi Reservation[7] near West Point, Virginia.

This was a tragedy for those seven tribes. **Over 550 other tribes in America had federal recognition and all the financial benefits that go with it for over 150 years.** The federal delay was due to an obscure *British law* from the 1600s which was finally overruled by the US Congress in 2018.

In fact, unlike many other states with Native American populations, Virginia has tricked and deprived its Native Americans repeatedly. The Virginian Pilot newspaper wrote that Virginia has:

Long denied education and employment opportunities to Indians. Later, the Virginia General Assembly tried bureaucratically to eliminate Indians by passing the **Racial Integrity Act of 1924**. The law mandated that only two races be recorded on state birth records: **White and Negro**.

The Act also would not allow anyone to get a marriage license until they could prove what race they belonged to. Therefore, it was easy to force Indians to claim being Negro since they often could not prove their Native American roots on paper. Somehow, many of the courthouses where those Native American records were kept had *burned down over the years.*

This infamous Act also prohibited whites from marrying Indians or any other racial group.

It shall hereafter be unlawful for any white person in this State to marry any save a white person or a person with no other admixture of blood than white and American Indian.[8]

This was a **very hypocritical law** for a state that prides itself on the marriage of Pocahontas to John Rolfe!

The Racial Integrity Act was zealously enforced by a devout Presbyterian named **Walter Ashby Plecker,** Virginia's first Registrar of the Bureau of Vital Statistics, who, "starting in 1912, forced Indians to classify themselves as black," He worked with a vengeance.

Plecker was a white supremacist and a zealous advocate of eugenics—a now-discredited movement to preserve the integrity of white

blood by preventing interracial breeding. "Unless this can be done," he once wrote, "we have little to hope for, but may expect in the future decline or complete destruction of our civilization" The tribes, according to Plecker, had become a "mongrel" mixture.[9] "Plecker's icy efficiency as racial gatekeeper drew international attention, including that of **Nazi Germany**. In 1943, he boasted: "Hitler's genealogical study of the Jews is not more complete."[10]

Plecker systematically changed the race recorded on many birth, death and marriage certificates from "Indian" to "Negro" until his retirement in **1967** when the Racial Integrity Act was struck down by the U.S. Supreme Court. But by then, it was too late for thousands of Native Americans to recover their real identity and the benefits that went with it. The State of Virginia, with a great deal of help from Plecker, committed ethnic cleansing of Native Americans by systematic, massive identity theft.

Pamunkey Museum in Virginia

As one Native American who lost her identity as an Indian through Walter Plecker remarked, "I thought Plecker was a devil...I still do."[11] If he could have responded to her, Dr. Plecker might have quoted a line he wrote in a 1925 essay, "Let us turn a deaf ear to those who would interpret Christian brotherhood as racial equality."[12] One of his co-workers said of Plecker, "I don't know of anyone who ever saw him smile."[13] Small wonder.

"We were victims of statistical genocide," said William P. Miles, chief of the Pamunkey.[14]

Virginia Congressman Jim Moran confirmed this shameful treatment of Virginia tribes in his June 2004 article in the Falls Church News Press:

> During our country's early history, the Virginia tribes were subdued, pushed off their land, and up through much of the 20th Century, denied full rights as U.S. citizens. In more recent times, racial hostility culminated with the enactment and brutal enforcement of Virginia's Racial Integrity Act of 1924...To call yourself a "Native American" in Virginia was to risk a jail sentence of up to one year. Married couples were denied marriage certificates and were even unable to obtain the release of their newborn child from a hospital until they changed their ethnicity on the state record. For much of the 20th Century, admission to public school education was denied. These and other indignities are part of a shameful legacy experienced in our lifetime.[15]

The Virginian-Pilot article continues to tell of the "devastating impact" this law had on the Indians who could now not prove who they were. They were, consequently, not able to get the federal assistance that all the other tribes in America do for food, shelter and school scholarships.

What can we learn? The early European settlers mistreated the very people whose native ancestors kept our Jamestown settlers alive with donations of food. Virginians broke many treaties with them and stole their land.

Then, Virginians stole their identity to deprive them of the very benefits our state and federal government might have given them for taking their land away from them. What appalls me, even more, is that **many other Virginia politicians and pastors knew of it**...for over 40 years! This is a great shame on Virginia! Sins of massive discrimination like these have probably brought **God's curses** on Virginia.

Native American Anointing

Many Christian leaders agree with what well-known prophetic leader, Chuck Pierce[16] has said about the huge importance of Native Americans in God's plans for America and the world. God is already using Native Americans to reach the world with the Gospel in places where other racial groups would not be easily accepted. Native Americans also carry a special anointing from God as the Host People of North America to evangelize the immigrants who came here in the last 400 years! The Church needs our Native Americans to bring full revival to America!

Few Native Americans Are Christians

While in Washington, DC in 2004 for the opening of the National Smithsonian Museum for Native Americans, my wife and I met some wonderful native Americans from all over the Western hemisphere. It was the largest gathering of native peoples in the history of our hemisphere: Aztecs from Mexico, Incas from Peru, Hopi, Navaho, Apache, Sioux, and others from North America. It was thrilling to see them so honored and so sad to hear their stories as we talked to them while watching the parade that warm October day on the Mall. I am proud that our family name is engraved on the walls inside the museum as a contributor.

Native Americans at the Dedication of the National Museum of he American Indian in 2004

These once great people are still being treated shamefully by our government *into the 20th century*. One older gentleman from California told me that **his mother had been taken from her family by the Federal government** and forced to attend a school for whites far away, and against the will of her parents. She never saw her parents again. "Why did our government do that to Indian children?" I asked. "Because they wanted to break up the Indian way of life and force them to assimilate into white America," he quietly replied. I was amazed at his gentleness and apparent forgiveness to whites for such ruthless behavior by our federal government—even in the last 100 years.

After 400 years of exposure to the white man's churches and "Christian" government, only about **3 %** of Native Americans are born-again Christians!

Could our treatment of Native Americans—past and present—have anything to do with that? I think so!

There is still time for the Church to confess, repent and make restitution for the crimes our government and our Church have committed against them. As current Indian leaders declare, "It has been said that America will never be right until they right themselves with the American Indian."[17] The full blessing and protection America longs for may depend more on securing the blessing of our Native Americans than we realize!

Again, II Samuel 21 is instructive: If Christians break covenants—even with unbelievers— God is not pleased and will often punish that land for those broken treaties and covenants.

Could there be just *curses on America from God* because America, and especially on the Church in America who should have known better, has not dealt honestly and lovingly with our Native Americans? The silence of the American Church on these injustices is *deafening*.

It cannot be overstated that America needs the blessing of its native tribes for God to heal America!

⚜

Discussion Questions

1. Describe how King James I and Capt John Smith viewed the Powhatan natives?

2. Why do you think our Christian forefathers in the colony treated the natives so harshly?

3. How could our ancestors in the colony have loved the natives as their neighbors, as God commands?

4. How did the racial Integrity Act damage Virginia's tribes?

5. What does Isaiah 10:1 warn us not to do?

5. Name the seven Virginia tribes that were finally recognized by the federal government in 2018.

5. What does II Samuel 21 tell us about how God views the breaking of treaties by His people?

6. What specific sins of our forefathers against our Virginia tribes do we need to confess to break God-given curses that may be on Tidewater, Virginia and America due to those sins?

7. How can we appeal to the tribes of Virginia to forgive and bless Virginia and America despite all that they have endured at the hands of our Christian forefathers?

---

1. Harriot, 28.
2. https://www.laits.utexas.edu/poltheory/james/blaste/blaste.html
3. Stiles, T.J., ed *In their Own Words: The Colonizers*
4. Marty O'Rourke, "Community Transformation" (Unpublished paper for Regent University, Virginia Beach, VA. 2001), 19.
5. http://npshistory.com/publications/colo/moretti-langholtz/appa.htm (17 March 2020)
6. https://accessgenealogy.com/virginia/adamstown-indians-upper-mattaponi-band.htm (29 Dec 2022)
7. https://www.mattaponination.com/ (29 Dec. 2022)
8. http://www.vcdh.virginia.edu/lewisandclark/students/projects/monacans/Contemporary_Monacans/racial.html (1 Dec. 2022)
9. Warren Fiske, The Virginian-Pilot, *The black-and-white world of Walter Ashby Plecker,* August 18, 2004, including the picture of Plecker.
10. Ibid.
11. Ibid.
12. Ibid.
13. Ibid
14. Virginian-Pilot, 10
15. https://www.legistorm.com/stormfeed/view_rss/385983/member/386.html (19 March 2021)
16. Healing America's Wounds Video Series, Part Two, starting at 1:21 minutes
17. See Appendix A. Also, the entire Healing America's Wounds Video Series says this many times.

CHAPTER 14

ABUSE OF BLACKS

THE ROOTS OF HUMAN TRAFFICKING IN AMERICA

"Is not this the kind of fasting I have chosen: to lose the chains of injustice and untie the cords of the yoke, to set the oppressed free and break every yoke? (Is. 58:6-7)"

LIKE THE NOBLE CLASS IN ENGLAND FROM WHICH MANY WERE descended, Tidewater's farmers and elite families had an insatiable appetite for servants to make them richer and to take care of them. Initially, they bought white men, women and children for several years of service and then released them to live their own lives. Later, that system morphed into purchasing men, women and children from the Caribbean and Africa to serve as slaves for life.

Historian Philip Morgan from Hampton University in Tidewater explains this process of what we would now call **human trafficking** —and it began in America in the Jamestown Colony:

This system of indentured servitude served as a good training ground for the later expansion of a full-fledged slave system. For one thing, Virginia planters learned to treat their white laborers as commodities, buying and selling their contracts on the open market. The contracts of indentured servants were sold on the open market. For another, they learned to treat their servants brutally, beating them cruelly for disobedience or insufficient work, extending the terms of their contracts should they run away.[1]

Abuse Against Blacks

This is probably the single most defective part of our regional and national DNA as Americans.

It is a story that is well known, but rarely told publicly in any detail until the last 30 years.[2] Thank God for the United States National Museum of African American History and Culture in Washington DC which describes this terrible chapter of our nation's life.

Black slaves being branded

Most adults today in America grew up in schools that only touched on the unbelievable evils accompanying slavery in America for 241 years, not to mention the severe persecution of Blacks after President Lincoln emancipated them.

The first Africans came to America in 1619 off the *White Lion,* an English privateer ship, at Old Point Comfort (later called Ft. Monroe), just south of Jamestown. There, Governor George Yeardley and his head of trade, Cape Merchant Abraham Piersey, bought the "20. and odd Negroes" aboard in exchange for "victuals" — meaning, they traded food for slaves. [3]They became indentured servants to the Jamestown farmers.

Seventy-five percent of the colony, white and black, came as indentured servants. *Some black servants became free people who, in turn, had their own indentured black and white servants.* Gradually, the system of indentured servants evolved into the system of full-fledged slaves for life.

In 1662, Virginia legally recognized slavery as a hereditary, lifelong condition. Even before this statute appeared, however, many blacks were being held as slaves for life, and as black laborers gradually replaced white indentured servants as the principal source of agricultural labor...[4]

The U.S. Constitution outlawed the importation of slaves in 1808, yet slaves were not granted freedom by the Constitution until 1865.[5] Undaunted by such moral legislation, some southern plantations started to breed slaves like so many head of cattle to supply the demands of Southern farmers.[6] Truly, the love of money is a root of many, many evils.

Even Freed Blacks Owned Slaves

The first judicial support of slavery in Virginia, except for criminal punishment, happened in 1654. Ironically, *the case involved a free Negro planter who sued to have a Negro servant returned to him*, saying that 'hee had ye Negro fro his life,' to which the court agreed."[7] Blacks owning blacks was not uncommon: "In the official U.S. Census of 1830, there were 3775 free blacks who owned 12,740 black slaves. The first slave owner was Anthony Johnson of Northampton, Virginia. His slave was John Casor. *They were both black.*"[8]

Virginia Laws About Slaves

"In the 1830s, Virginia's Legislature passed a law that *made it illegal for any blacks — slaves or free — to preach at a religious service.* In 1860, it ordered that any free black who was sentenced to prison for a crime could, at the court's discretion, be sold into slavery". [9]

By "1662, a Virginia law stated that a newborn was or was not free depending on the status of his mother."[10] That law applied even if "any Englishman" should be responsible for the pregnancy.[11] However, during the 1600s, Virginia used mostly white indentured servants with just a few slaves.[12]

In 1669, the Virginia House of Burgesses passed a law about the "casuall killing of slaves"; if a slave died because of a beating from his master for insubordination, the master was not to be charged with a crime "since it cannot be presumed that...any man [would willingly] destroy his own estate."[13] Sadly, cats and dogs have more protection under the law today than the slaves then!

Cruelty to Slaves

Both indentured servants and slaves were cruelly abused. Misery breeds friendship, and in Bacon's rebellion in 1676 against the harsh masters who owned them, both black slaves and white indentured servants fought together![14] As economic conditions in Britain got better, fewer whites came here as indentured servants. This coincided with the British businesses entering into African slave trading.[15]

Church Response to Slavery

What did the Anglican Church have to say about these blatant human rights abuses? What did the pastors teach their wealthy parishioners about loving slaves like our neighbors? Did they ever preach on Job 31:13-14: "If I have despised the claim of my male or female slaves when they filed a complaint against me, what then could I do when God arises? And when He calls me to account, what will I answer Him?"

By 1710, the Church of England owned hundreds of slaves in Barbados, in the Caribbean.[16]

The Anglican Church refused to liberate them until English law forced them to in 1833, but only after paying huge sums of money to their masters, the Anglican bishops![17]

More research needs to be done on the Anglican response to slavery as well as to these other terrible abuses of people in the colonies. At first glance, it does not appear that the Anglican Church in Tidewater did much to oppose any of these abuses, and may have encouraged them in some ways, at least by silence.

An old Latin proverb says, "Silencio dabit consentio", meaning that silence gives consent. That silent consent of Christian pastors for abusive slavery has not been widely acknowledged in American congregations. This is a serious sin for our corporate identity as American Christians.

The Love of Money

The insatiable love of money was the engine and the rudder of this colony. **Slavery was started to make money,** not primarily to express racist ideas. Sadly, Virginia led the way for all this in America.

In the three-and-a-half centuries of the Atlantic slave trade, around 10,000,000 African slaves were brought to the New World—by Portugal first, then by Spain and England.

To sustain the tobacco and cotton farmers' greed for larger profits, indentured servants, and later slaves, were bought, sold, and handed down to the farmer's children like property upon the death of their father. As the 1705 Virginia Legislature declared, "All Negro, mulatto and Indian slaves within this dominion ... shall be held to be real estate."[18] Some slaves were even branded like cattle by their masters.[19]

A Glaring Hypocrisy

How could good people be so hypocritical and mean-spirited to so many for so long? Many of America's great leaders in the Revolution of 1776 came from Virginia. Those Virginia leaders were passionate about liberty and justice for all...yet they pioneered slavery in America.

This irony was not lost on others outside Virginia. A famous leader in England wrote, "How is it," Dr. Samuel Johnson asked, "that we hear the loudest yelps for liberty among the drivers of negroes?"[20]

How did our colonial leaders ever sign a document declaring that "all men are equal and created by God with inalienable rights and that among these are life, liberty and the pursuit of happiness?"

The reason was simple: Southern leaders with slaves did not want to lose the income their slaves produced.

To get them to sign the Declaration of Independence, Jefferson **had to omit any reference to the slaves.** As he wrote in his autobiography about the writing of the Declaration: "The clause too, reprobating the enslaving the inhabitants of Africa, was struck out in complaisance to **South Carolina and Georgia**, who had never attempted to restrain the importation of slaves, and who on the contrary still wished to continue it."[21]

In Virginia

As we all know, many of our states had slaves before the Civil War, but Virginia was at the center of American slavery. "Virginia was the largest of the new United States—in territory, in population, in influence—and slaveholding. Virginians owned more than 40 percent of all the slaves in the new nation."[22] Remember, Virginia's actual political rule operated as far as the Mississippi River and the Great Lakes by 1774.

> By 1700, over half of all blacks inhabiting mainland North America lived in Virginia...Even though this proportion declined gradually over the course of the eighteenth century, **the Old Dominion was by far the most formidable slave state in the new nation** and to a large extent Virginia defined the nature of American slavery.[23]

In Tidewater

In Tidewater, the legacies of slavery lasted well into the Twentieth Century. Starting in the 1890s, states throughout the South passed laws designed to prevent Black citizens from improving their status or achieving equality. These statutes were called Jim Crow laws. They were enforced until the 1960s.[24] Discrimination, segregation and many injustices were perpetrated against blacks by the white majority—especially in Norfolk.

Black neighborhoods were neglected by the city of Norfolk. Healthcare for Blacks was very poor. Blacks had to start their own hospitals to get medical treatment since whites who would not treat Blacks privately owned most of the Southern hospitals![25] Whittaker Memorial Hospital in Newport News was founded in 1908 because of discrimination in healthcare against Blacks.[26]

How many black mothers died in childbirth, how many black children died from injuries, and how many black men lost limbs simply because they were refused emergency medical care at white-owned hospitals?

This sad, sick, sinful story goes on and on. City jobs in Norfolk were closed to Blacks during the Depression. Norfolk's resistance to the desegregation of schools was widespread and made national headlines.

To "defend" Virginia schools against black students entering white schools, "Governor J. Lindsay Almond, Jr. of Virginia, on September 8, 1958, closed all the schools in Warren County rather than integrate them! Meanwhile, in the hopes of finding a solution, Charlottesville and Norfolk postponed the opening of their schools. But, on

September 19, Almond closed two schools in Charlottesville, and on September 27, he closed another six schools in Norfolk."[27] *Is it any wonder why many Blacks don't trust Whites?*

The Church in Tidewater

How did the pastors and Christians of Tidewater respond to the tragic needs of black people all around them in the 20th century? Was there any church resistance to the sinful government and business practices outlined above? Or will we find compliance and even encouragement from the pulpit for what were grievous sins against humanity, not to mention against fellow Christians?

in the 1990s, I visited a Baptist Church near Valentine, Virginia that excluded Blacks from membership. An Episcopal Church in Portsmouth did not take down its large Confederate flag hanging prominently *in the sanctuary* until about 1997 despite the obvious offense it was to local Blacks. I saw that flag there before it was removed.

If the gold rusts, what will the iron do? No wonder our region and our nation have sinned so severely in slavery and racial discrimination: The Church has been silent or compliant, instead of prophetic and compassionate. If Christians will act like this, what can we expect of non-Christians in America?

This persistent willingness to abuse Blacks for personal financial gain[28] is a great stain on Virginia's conscience...and on our national conscience.

I believe the Lord is saying that **any ministry in America that wants God's full endorsement needs the blessing of the Black community in that region.** As followers of a Savior who came to set the captives free,[29] let the American Church repent for this terrible sin against Blacks and work to build godly relationships with them now, as individuals and as groups.

A TIDEWATER VICTORY

Here is a story few know about: the African tribes who sold other African tribes to the British and later, to American slave ships. Even the United States National Museum of African American History and

Culture does not have any displays about this part of the slave story in America.

But a humble black pastor from Portsmouth, Virginia at Calvary Evangelical Baptist Church named **Jack Gaines** knew this story—and God used him to do something that had never been done to help heal the lands of Africa and America. It's a long story you can read about here: https://bobfox.org/the-apology-that-shook-a-continent/

Briefly, God gave Pastor Jack Gaines the vision for a conference of reconciliation for the African slave trade from Africa and the born-again President of Benin, Mathieu Kérékou agreed to help. US Representative Tony Hall was there, and Senator  James Inhofe. Michael Fenton-Jones, president of the International Christian Chamber of Commerce (ICCC), also attended.

 For the first time in history, a national leader of Africa **publicly apologized to representatives of African Americans** for the sins of their ancestors who sold the ancestors of the African-Americans into slavery from the shores of Africa. In the picture above, African intercessors knelt before African-Americans to confess the sins of their forefathers in selling other tribes to white slave traders. *There was not a dry eye in the house!*

This is a beautiful and powerful example of identificational repentance! *And it started in Tidewater, Virginia!*

Let's do more of that so God can heal Tidewater and America!

Discussion Questions

1. Slavery was permitted in the Bible, so what was sinful about slavery in Virginia?

2. How could our Christian forefathers who owned slaves obey

God's command "to love their neighbor as themselves" in their treatment of their slaves?

3. What could pastors in slave states have done to love the slaves in that region? Did any pastor or church leader speak against cruelty to slaves?

4. How can you encourage white churches to build relationships with black churches? What good would that do to heal America?

5. Should African pastors in America apologize to African-Americans for the sale of their ancestors to white slave traders?

---

1. Philip Morgan, Editor et al, "Don't Grieve After Me: The Black Experience in Virginia, 1619-1986" (Hampton: Hampton University, 1986), 15.
2. https://nmaahc.si.edu/
3. https://time.com/5653369/august-1619-jamestown-history/ (7 Dec. 2022)
4. https://www.thirteen.org/wnet/slavery/experience/legal/history.html (19 March 2021)
5. https://nmaahc.si.edu/ (17 March 2020)
6. Johnson, 311
7. Ibid., 393.
8. https://nmaahc.si.edu/ (17 March 2020)
9. http://www.usatoday.com/news/opinion/columnist/wickham/2007-02-05-wickham_x.htm (17 March 2020)
10. https://nmaahc.si.edu/ (17 March 2020)
11. http://www.usatoday.com/news/opinion/columnist/wickham/2007-02-05-wickham_x.htm (17 March 2020)
12. Morgan, 15.
13. Ibid.
14. Ibid., 15.
15. Ibid., 16.
16. http://en.wikipedia.org/wiki/Society_for_the_Propagation_of_the_Gospel_in_Foreign_Parts (17 March 2020)
17. https://www.theguardian.com/uk/2006/feb/09/religion.world (17 March 2020)
18. Ibid.
19. Ibid.
20. Fischer, 410.
21. http://tjrs.monticello.org/letter/54 (17 March 2020)
22. https://nmaahc.si.edu (17 March 2020)
23. Morgan, 15.
24. https://www.history.com/topics/early-20th-century-us/jim-crow-laws (19 March 2021)
25. https://www.ncbi.nlm.nih.gov/pmc/articles/PMC2690142/ (17 March 2020)
26. https://www.dailypress.com/news/dp-xpm-20110221-2011-02-21-dp-nws-blackhistory-0222-20110221-story.html (17 March 2020)

27. https://en.wikipedia.org/wiki/Massive_resistance (17 March 2020)
28. Tidewater almost became the first place in the nation to breed human embryos for lethal medical experiments involving stem cell tissue. In 2001, the Jones Institute for Reproductive Medicine in Norfolk announced that it had already begun this process. I argued in a long Op-Ed article in the local newspaper that Hampton Roads pioneered the abuse of black slaves in America. We should know better than to now "lead the way in breeding fetal slaves." Our prayers were answered when the Jones Institute cancelled the experiments.
29. Isaiah 61:1

CHAPTER 15

ABUSE OF WOMEN
FLOURISHED IN JAMESTOWN

Treat "the older women as mothers, and the younger women as sisters, in all purity" (1 Timothy 5:1-2).

THE FIRST SINS OF OUR BRITISH FOREFATHERS AGAINST WOMEN IN America began in Tidewater, Virginia. Women were physically, emotionally and sexually abused here for many decades by men who attended Anglican churches! Tragically, colonial pastors seemed to be generally silent on these abuses! The evil effects of this pattern of abuse are still with us in America.

> Sexual and spousal abuse of women, trafficking of women plus egregious sexism and gender discrimination in America all have roots in the Jamestown Colony in the 1600s.

Unlike the Plymouth colony in Massachusetts which began with women and men, no woman arrived in the first landing in 1607 in the Chesapeake colony. A couple of wives came in another boat in 1608. In the "starving time" of the 1610's winter, one man killed his wife, salted her down and began to eat her before he was caught and executed.[1] Note Captain John Smith's gallows humor about this heinous crime:

And one amongst the rest did kill his wife, powdered her, and had eaten part of her before it was knowne, for which hee was executed, as hee well deserved; now whether shee was better roasted, boyled or carbonado'd, I know not, but of such a dish as powdered wife I never heard of.[2]

Trafficking of Women

Few women freely decided to go to Virginia. The word on the streets of England about the colony was very bad...and very true. It was like a "wild west" town, full of violence, danger, disease, hard work and poverty. The ratio of males to females was 4:1 and sometimes up to 6:1.[3] But the Virginia Company knew that without wives, the men would not stay in the colony. They would make a bundle of money and go home to England and settle down there. As that continued to happen, the future of the colony would be in jeopardy.

"In 1619, Sir Edwin Sandys, Treasurer of the Virginia Company, began to recruit English women to settle in Virginia. Knowing that no women would come if they knew how bad Virginia really was, Sir Edwin used trickery and deceit to get them to consent to come. He gave them the picture that going to Virginia would be an "adventure."[4] Here is how the investors in the Virginia Company lured mostly *poor women* to a dangerous place that few women wanted to go.

The Virginia Company offered substantial incentives to the women who signed up to leave England for Jamestown. They were provided a dowry of clothing, linens, and other furnishings, free transportation to the colony, and even a plot of land. They were also promised their pick of wealthy husbands and provided with food and shelter while they made their decision.

The women were later shipped to the colony in 1620 basically as "mail-order brides" to be bought by the men who had never seen them for about 150 pounds of tobacco, hence the name "Tobacco Wives" became attached to them.

Another 56 came over in late 1621 and early 1622—all to be sold to the men for the exorbitant sum of 150 pounds of tobacco—about

$5000 in today's terms.[5] Some were purchased as wives to be loved, but others were used as *indentured servants* to work the fields.[6] It is safe to assume the Virginia Company sold every one of those ladies and that any man who paid $5000 for a woman saw her *as his property* for at least the normal seven years of indentured service which was widespread in the colony.

In fact, almost every man and woman who came to Virginia in the first few waves of ships came as indentured servants to the Virginia Company to pay back their sea passage to the colony.

One redeeming feature of this arrangement was that the women were given 50 acres of land in Virginia which they could keep for themselves even if they married. This was never allowed in England. It was a powerful incentive to convince women to immigrate to Virginia. [7]

Some argue that this was really trafficking since the women consented to go to Virginia.

So, while this version of trafficking may not be as evil as know it today, it set the pattern for trading women for money in a colony that had already purchased nineteen blacks as indentured servants in 1619 from the *White Lion* and 100 boys for about $5 each. These "Migrant Children" were *forcibly* taken off the streets of London or from orphanages by the government and shipped to Virginia to help establish the colony. See the story of those boys in the next chapter.

A DISASTROUS LAW

On November 18, 1618, the Virginia Company passed a set of laws that included a "headlight" law.[8] This law stayed in force until 1779! While this was a wise law to encourage immigration to Virginia, the law had unintended and disastrous effects.

Under this new arrangement, called the headright system, settlers who financed their own passage to the Virginia colony received 50-acre tracts of land. The same amount of land was offered to anyone willing to sponsor the passage of a new settler. Speculators and planters were eager to take advantage of the latter offer, but they had difficulty finding willing recruits. Paying men and women to kidnap settlers solved this problem. By mid-century, **thousands of unwilling immigrants were being shipped to the colony as indentured servants every year.** One particularly prolific kidnapper was rumored to have abducted more than 6,000 victims. [9]

This law was a human trafficker's dream: Each kidnapped person gave the greedy master who bought them another 50 acres of land and cheap labor to work it. And English leaders winked at all this.

Penalties for kidnapping people sent to Virginia were very lenient in England. In 1684, a couple was fined only 12 pence for kidnapping and selling a 16-year-old girl. In comparison, a horse thief in England would have been hanged. [10]

A folk ballad from that era called "The Trappan'd Maiden" describes the fate of many such indentured women who were tricked or kidnapped into going to Virginia:

> Give ear to a Maid , that lately was betray'd
> And sent into Virginny, O
> In brief I shall declare,
> what I have suffered there,
> When I was weary,
> weary, weary, weary, O...
>
> Five years I served I, under Master Guy
> In the land of Virginny, O,
> Which made me know
> sorrow, grief and woe,
> When that I was weary,
> weary, weary, weary, O...
>
> I have played my part
> both at Plow and Cart,
> In the land of Virginny, O,
> Billets from the Wood
> upon my back they load,
> When that I am weary,

weary, weary, weary, O...

Then let Maids beware, all by my ill-fare,
In the land of Virginny, O;
Be sure to stay at home,
for if you here do come,
You will all be weary,
weary, weary, weary, O..... [11]

Between 1620 and 1621, "150 women arrived in Virginia. Since they were poor, Most came by choice, knowing that since they were poor, they were to be servants in this new land.

Incredibly, some women were *sold by their English husbands* and were sent to be married to the men in Virginia— a land of "adventure."[12] "Another ballad sings about the 'honest weaver' who sold his wife to someone in Virginia. This terrible practice of selling wives existed in 17th century England!"[13] *And in the same land where Shakespeare was still writing his famous sonnets and books!*

Sadly, the deceit and betrayal that got women to come to Tide-water was only the beginning of misery for many; the worst was yet to come.

Rachel Upton (wife of Christian musician, Jason Upton) writes:

Because the main concern of these Chesapeake men was rapid pros-perity through the growing and selling of tobacco, there was a shortage of workers to tend to the farms. So, the women worked beside the men in the severest farming conditions.[14]

Due to the poor and dangerous conditions of Virginia in these early years, by 1625 three-quarters of the 150 women who had come to Virginia *had died.* There remained a great shortage of women in this area up until the early 1700s.[15] This shortage of women left those few women who did live here very vulnerable to sexual exploration and exploitation by the men of their day.[16]

SEXUAL SINS AGAINST WOMEN

Let's now take a look at this sordid and almost unbelievable spiritual DNA that our first settlers have left us: sexual sins, sexual abuse and gross legal discrimination against women in sexual matters.

This pattern of sexual sin is found in every Christian society where immature, nominal or rebellious Christians are found and it creates great damage. Unfortunately, sexual sin in the American Church today *is the elephant in the room*—it is rampant and usually *not challenged* from the pulpit in many churches. This combination of widespread fornication even among Christians often creates fatherless homes that often doom those children to lives of failure and decades of pain. Our prisons today are full of men who never knew their fathers.

NATIVE AMERICAN ROOTS OF SEXUAL IMMORALITY

Native dance with women

To begin with, as in many other non-Christian cultures, Indian men used women as sexual gifts for their guests; it was considered an honor by an Indian maiden to be used in this manner. After a feast, the Indians customarily gave lodging to visiting colonists. The lodging included "a young woman fresh painted red with pochone and oil, to be his bedfellow."[17]

Concubines were common for leaders. "They have one wife, many loves and are also Sodomites," Edward Wingfield writes. Even homosexuality existed among the Native Americans.[18] Capt. Smith notes 20 concubines around Powhatan at one feast[19] where bare-bottom dancing was common.[20] Female prostitutes were also common, according to Smith.[21]

William Strackey gives the most amazing description of the sexual climate among the Powhatans: "They are people most voluptuous, yet the women are very careful not to be suspected of dishonesty without the leave of their husbands. But giving his consent, they are like Virgil's scrantiae[22] and may embrace the acquaintance of any stranger for nothing, and it is accounted no offense." [23]

Strachey goes on to say that the sexual appetites of both Indian men and women were "incredible" and that they contracted many sexually transmitted diseases (STDs) for which they have devised cures from local herbs and roots.

Given all that, it is highly probable that the English settlers were often sexually active with Indian women during their visits to their camps. Sermons were preached in England about the "sexual availability of the Indian women."[24]

According to one eyewitness, one night while waiting to meet Powhatan, Capt. Smith and about 40 men were easily seduced by a group of Indian women who had danced for them around a fire.[25] It should be noted that native women at that time did not clothe themselves above the waist.[26] [27] This immorality with the Native Americans was almost totally absent in the earlier Roanoke colony and was certainly not in the Massachusetts colony. The American DNA of sexual immorality started in Jamestown.

Not a New Problem

This immoral behavior is, of course, prohibited in scripture for believers and yet even the founders of Israel fell into such sin. Speaking of the Israelites en route to founding the first permanent "Jewish colonies" in the Promised Land, the Bible says: "Nor let us act immorally, as some of them did, and twenty-three thousand fell in one day" (1 Cor. 10:8). Note that such immorality of God's people with pagans led to the death of thousands of Israelites at God's hand! "Now these things happened as examples for us so that we would not crave evil things as they also craved."[28] How could God bless and protect the colonists as He wanted to when they acted so immorally with the pagan Indians?

Colonial Roots of Sexual Abuse against Women

There is a stark contrast between the way sexual activity was regulated in the Chesapeake colony and the Plymouth colony. To begin with, the rate of pre-marital pregnancies was high in the Chesapeake colony—much higher than in the Plymouth colony, especially among indentured servants, as could be expected.

In Somerset County Maryland, a part of the Chesapeake region, about one-fifth of all women, immigrant and native settlers, were carrying a child before they were married.[29] One-third of all immigrant brides were pregnant before marriage in that county.[30] Fornication was a crime, but it was not often tried in court. When it was, the woman was severely punished, usually by whipping. The man involved usually got off with a fine or no punishment at all![31] In contrast, the man was more severely punished than the woman for fornication in New England.

Having a child out of wedlock was the worst thing that could happen to a woman in the Virginia colony! Please forgive the graphic nature of this next quote, but it is necessary to understand the unbelievable abuse the Anglican authorities used on hapless women who were extremely vulnerable almost constantly in this colony full of sexually immoral men:

> When an unmarried woman gave birth outside of wedlock, a heavy fine was imposed upon her. If the fine could not be paid (as often happened), she was trussed up like an animal, her dress was ripped open to the waist, and she was publicly whipped in the sight of a shouting mob until the blood flowed in rivulets down her naked back and breasts. Further, if she were a servant, she was required to compensate her master for the time lost in her pregnancy by serving an additional term, even in some cases where he was the father of the child![32]

There is some evidence that some masters **deliberately got their servant girls pregnant** to force the extension of their contracts![33]

Bastardy was considered one of the worst offenses in the colonies, but not for Christian reasons: because it might place a financial burden on the parish rolls to support a child without a father and because it kept the servant from working full-time for her master! The love of money, again—the primary motive behind almost everything the

Virginia Colony did—is the evil source of Tidewater's spiritual DNA in almost every case.

The English Anglican's sense of justice was equally skewed when dealing with adultery: "Women were flogged severely or dragged through the water behind a boat until they nearly drowned. Men were treated leniently."[34] By contrast, the Algonquians would execute any male Indian caught in the act of sleeping with another brave's wife.[35] The wife could also be killed if caught in the act.

The Virginia Gentlemen: Sexual Predators!

Even more bizarre are the almost unbelievable customs in Virginia regarding the sexual lives of gentlewomen and gentlemen. While gentlewomen were required to act as pure as possible in behavior, Virginia's fine gentlemen (what a misnomer in this case) were encouraged by common custom to be sexual predators on women!

One of the most famous examples is *William Byrd, II.* His diary is quite different from any diary in New England.[36] "With mixed success, he attempted to seduce relatives, neighbors, casual acquaintances, strangers, prostitutes, the wives of his best friends, and servants both black and white, on whom he often forced himself, much against their wishes."[37] Sexual predators appear in every culture, but some cultures promote that

William Byrd, II

activity more than others, and Chesapeake's colony saw this kind of decadent behavior as proper for a gentleman! Male supremacy and English machismo were in full bloom in the colony.

An old Tidewater saying jokingly defines a virgin as "a girl who could run faster than her uncle."[38] "This kind of behavior differed only in degree from Thomas Jefferson's relentless pursuit of Mrs. Walker... These men represented the best of their culture; the sexual activities of the other planters made even William Byrd appear a model of restraint."[39]

These gentlemen sexual predators of Virginia found easy marks among the poor, illiterate indentured servant girls and later among black female slaves. And why not? There was no penalty for such wicked gentlemen...only for the hapless women—especially if she bore a bastard child.

Abolitionists rightly accused slavery of encouraging the sexual exploitation of black women...even by the teenage sons of white masters.[40] Even rape was trivialized in the Chesapeake colonies. On the other hand, in New England's colonies, rape was a hanging offense. In Tidewater, it was joked about in the diaries of gentlemen and often punished less severely than petty theft.[41]

Is it any wonder that most of America is now saturated and defiled with inappropriate sexual content in every kind of media?

Even US Presidents have been sexually immoral while in office. President John Kennedy was a serial adulterer. President Bill Clinton also exhibited gross sexual immorality. The recent #MeToo movement is just one expression of the damage of sexual sins that first began in Jamestown and now still plague America *and the American Church.*

Discussion Questions

1. Describe the abuse of women in the colony.

2. What sins of the colony against women do you see in America today?

3. What could Anglican pastors have done to protect women in the colony from abuse?

4. What can pastors today do to protect women in their church and community from abuse?

5. What percentage of Christians are using pornography now? What percentage of pastors and church staff?

6. Why do you think sexual sin and sexual abuse of women are not preached against much in American churches today?

---

1. John Smith, "The Generall Historie of Virginia" quoted in The Colonizers, by T.J. Stiles, 146
2. Ibid, Book IV, 106, also cited in: https://college.cengage.com/history/ayers_prima ry_sources/john_smith_starving_time.htm (19 March 2021)
3. Fischer, 229.

4. Rachel Upton, *"History of the Suppression/ Oppression of Women: Tidewater Virginia,"* (Virginia Beach: Unpublished paper for Regent University), quoting The Young Oxford History of Women in the U.S.—1600-1760. 1995. 30-40.
5. https://www.history.com/news/jamestown-colony-women-brides-program (28-03-2023)
6. Rachel Upton, Ibid, 40-46.
7. https://www.theatlantic.com/business/archive/2016/08/the-mail-order-brides-of-jamestown-virginia/498083/ (329-23)
8. https://www.lva.virginia.gov/public/guides/va4_headrights.htm (3-29-23)
9. https://www.theatlantic.com/business/archive/2016/08/the-mail-order-brides-of-jamestown-virginia/498083/ (4-1-23)
10. https://www.theatlantic.com/business/archive/2016/08/the-mail-order-brides-of-jamestown-virginia/498083/ (3-29-23)
11. Ibid, 229.
12. Ibid., 30-40.
13. Ibid., 231.
14. Upton, 40-46.
15. Ibid., 30-40.
16. Ibid., 55.
17. Edward Wright Haile, *Jamestown Narratives: Eyewitness Accounts of the Virginia Colony*, (Roundhouse, Champlain, Virginia, 1998). p. 642 quoting William Strachey, secretary to the colony.
18. Ibid., 202.
19. Ibid., 245.
20. http://www.virtualjamestown.org/images/white_debry_html/jamestown.html (29 May 2006) for picture.
21. Ibid., 210-211.
22. Offensive Roman term for all prostitutes, meaning "chamber pot".
23. Haile, 670.
24. https://www.history.com/news/jamestown-colony-women-brides-program on 3-29-23
25. Thomas Harriot, Engraving of Indians Dancing in the ill-fated Roanoke colony of North Carolina taken from A Briefe and True Report of the New Found Land of Virginia (New York: Dover Publications, Inc., 1972). The 1590 edition by Theodor de Bry.
26. George F. Willison, *Behold Virginia: The Fifth Crown*, Harcourt and Brace & Co., NY, 1952, 71.
27. It is still one of the trademarks of false religions that they encourage sexual promiscuity among its members. Roman & Greek and Hindu temple prostitutes, Tibetan Buddhism and many Native American cultures used sex outside of marriage in a variety of religious and social contexts that were totally opposed to Biblical teaching.
28. (1Corinthians 10:6).
29. Fischer, 298.
30. Ibid.
31. Ibid.
32. Ibid., 299.
33. Ibid., 303.

34. Ibid., 300.
35. Henry Spelman, "Relation of Virginia, 1609," quoted by Edward Wright Haile, editor, Jamestown Narratives: Eyewitness Accounts of the Virginia Colony, (Champlain: Roundhouse,1998), 491.
36. Fischer, 300.
37. Ibid., 300.
38. Ibid., 303.
39. Ibid., 303.
40. Ibid., 304.
41. Ibid., 304.

CHAPTER 16
ABUSE OF ENGLISH CHILDREN
CHILD TRAFFICKING STARTED IN JAMESTOWN

"Religion that is pure and undefiled before God, the Father, is this: to visit orphans and widows in their affliction" (James 1:27).

BRITAIN IS PERHAPS THE ONLY COUNTRY IN THE WORLD TO HAVE exported vast numbers of its own children overseas without their parent's knowledge or consent to serve the needs of its new colonies!

From 1618 to the late 1980s, an estimated 150,000 children—*some as young as two*— were sent over a 350-year period—first to the *Virginia Jamestown Colony*— then Australia,[1] New Zealand, Canada, and what was then Southern Rhodesia, now Zimbabwe.[2]

By the 1600s, British orphanages were overflowing with children born out of wedlock and British streets were full of poor children roaming the streets, many committing petty crimes. So, the British government decided to kill two birds with one stone: send the children to their new colonies to boost the labor force of the colonies and reduce the state's burden to care for orphans and street children.

So, **in 1619, t**he same year as the first Africans were sold to the colony as indentured servants, a boatload of white, English children arrived also as indentured servants! Most history books do not mention this!

> On "November 17, 1619, the first group of one hundred children, aged between eight and sixteen, arrived in Jamestown. Another group of one hundred was sent in 1620, and then another in 1622. Of these three hundred children, **very few seem to have survived**"...In the 1630s, **only three of the boys appear in colony records.**[3]

As long as there has been an English empire, children have been an important part of building it. Virginia was England's first colony and this is where orphaned children were first sent.

> John Smith named Samuel Collier, Nathaniel Pecock, James Brunfield, and Richard Mutton, all "Boyes," as among the original 104 Englishmen to travel to Jamestown in 1607.
>
> Boys initially worked as servants and laborers in the struggling colony but some soon served the much more important role of part peace offering, part translator. At least three boys were given over to various members of the Paspahegh tribe during the early years of the colony in order to show the settlers' good intentions toward Powhatan and so the boys could learn Algonquian.
>
> One of the boys, Thomas Savage, arrived in Jamestown in 1608 at about the age of thirteen as a poor laborer but worked as a translator after he was given to Powhatan in exchange for one of Powhatan's men and a bushel of beans. Savage frequently moved back and forth between the Paspahegh and the English, and he eventually found a considerable source of wealth in the fur trade.[4]

Many children probably came against their will. How can a child of eight make that decision to leave England and go to another continent? After all, the forced emigration of children was is especially desirable to the Virginia Company which was making lots of money on these child shipments and the city fathers of London were eager to clear its streets and orphanages of such burdensome children.

Only God knows the hardships, abuse and dangers those children faced in the Jamestown Colony. They lost their childhood, their parents, their freedom and their emotional health at the hands of Christian British leaders who forcibly sent them overseas.

But **selling children for labor** in Virginia was still a profitable trade, even in the private sector. "In 1645 Parliament heard evidence of gangs who 'in a most barbarous way steal away many little children for service in the Chesapeake colonies."[5]

Most of the orphans were told that their parents were dead or could not be located. To make matters worse, the British government never allowed the children to reconnect with their parents— and their parents

Child slaves in English coal mines in the 20th century

were told that someone had adopted their children. *Lies all around.* Many of these children are up with terrible emotional scars.

I suppose that for some of the 150,000 migrant children, it might have been a good experience. They had opportunities to travel, learn new skills and perhaps make a much better living than possible in impoverished Great Britain at that time.

A play called *Zara* was performed in 1759. The Prologue describes the benefits of sending homeless or children born of unwed mothers to the colonies.

> How strong must be our feelings of delight Where Int'rest & humanity unite, And Briton's Glory crowns the point of sight. Ye sons of Freedom! view this little band, They owe their safety to your fost'ring hand, Snatch'd from the paths of vice & branded shame, You point the road to honesty & fame, This small plantation which your hands first laid May rise in time your ornament & shade.[6]

I have a good friend whose father was a Migrant Child sent to Canada. My friend is a nationally known Christian leader today, but his father deserted him when he was a child—a somewhat understandable response by a father who had been traumatized by being forced to

leave his family in England. *Hurt people hurt people.*

FINALLY EXPOSED

Finally, in 1987, a British social worker named **Margaret Humphreys**[7] exposed this horrible, clandestine government system of forcibly relocating poor British children around the world to help British Commonwealth nations, often without their parent's knowledge. Humphreys

England abused children in many trades for centuries

proved that deported children were promised "oranges and sunshine" but they got hard labor and life in institutions—Many were given to the Congregation of Christian Brothers, where they suffered physical and sexual abuse. This website[8] called Child Migrant Trust has the most information about this incredible systematic abuse of English children.

DOCUMENTARIES

[9] A movie called Oranges and Sunshine[10] was made about her battle to uncover this terrible trafficking of children by the British government. Recently, hundreds of migrant children have given accounts of poor education, hard labor, physical beatings and sexual abuse—often at the hands of religious leaders in Catholic or Anglican schools.

Child Migrant Trust Website

The 2009 Australian documentary called *The Long Journey Home* aired on ABC Television is full of heart-wrenching testimonies from former child migrants. [11] In 2009 and 2010, the prime ministers of Great Britain and Australia made national apologies for these atrocious sins against children that were mentioned in Chapter Five.

Today, child trafficking for work or sex is a multi-million dollar industry in America and a multi-billion dollar industry worldwide.

One in five girls and one in thirteen boys are sexually abused before the age of eighteen in the United States.[12] Many are kidnapped into sex trafficking rings or forced labor systems.

Our Christian forefathers that birthed America started this in the Jamestown Colony. This sin against children by our Christian forefathers has not been addressed in the American Church.

⚜️

1. Describe the Migrant Children system that Britain began in Jamestown in 1619 and ended n 1970.

2. Describe the benefits and dangers of this system.

3. What motivated England to do this for 350 years?

4. What sin patterns do you see in America today that may be connected to this systematic abuse of children?

---

1. https://www.bbc.com/news/uk-39078652 (3 Dec. 2022)

2. https://www.bbc.com/news/uk-39078652

3. Kristen Grace Lashua, *"Children at the Birth of Empire, c.1600-1760"* , page 168.
   A Dissertation presented to the Graduate Faculty of the University of Virginia in Candidacy for the Degree of Doctor of Philosophy, Department of History, University of Virginia May 2015

4. Kristen Grace Lashua, *"Children at the Birth of Empire, c.1600-1760"* , page 2.
   A Dissertation presented to the Graduate Faculty of the University of Virginia in Candidacy for the Degree of Doctor of Philosophy, Department of History, University of Virginia May 2015

5. David Hackett Fischer, Albion's Seed: Four British Folkways in America (New York: Oxford University Press, 1989), 227.

6. Kristen Grace Lashua, *"Children at the Birth of Empire, c.1600-1760"* , page viii.
   A Dissertation presented to the Graduate Faculty of the University of Virginia in Candidacy for the Degree of Doctor of Philosophy, Department of History, University of Virginia May 2015

7. https://www.childmigrantstrust.com/our-work/about-us (23 Dec. 20222). See her interview about this at https://youtu.be/7FcIguf3mJo (3-29-23)

8. https://www.childmigrantstrust.com/

9. https://en.wikipedia.org/wiki/Oranges_and_Sunshine
10. Available on Amazon
11. https://en.wikipedia.org/wiki/The_Long_Journey_Home_(2009_film)
12. https://www.cdc.gov/violenceprevention/childsexualabuse/fastfact.html (26 Dec. 2022)

CHAPTER 17

ABUSE OF OTHER DENOMINATIONS

DIVISION AMONG AMERICAN CHRISTIANS BEGAN HERE

"I am giving you a new commandment, that you love one another; just as I have loved you, that you also love one another" (John 13:34).

ANGLICAN PERSECUTION OF NON-ANGLICANS

This began at Jamestown and continued for many decades. This abuse laid the foundations of division between Christian groups in America which is still so strong today.

Denominational Wars

Since the Protestant Reformation began in 1517, denominational affiliation was taken very seriously, since that affiliation often was usually connected to political submission to a government that promoted a particular denomination. Up to 50 million Christians died at the hands of other Christians in the Wars of the Reformation that followed after 1517. The Catholic Church's brutal and bloody persecution of Protestants in Europe during that period is hard to comprehend. Besides Catholics, many groups were involved in religious mayhem. For instance, Presbyterians in Switzerland killed Anabaptists for not believing in infant baptism.

The abusive nature of the Anglican Church goes right back to its founders—the proud, adulterous and cruel Henry VIII and his hench-men, Archbishop Cranmer and Thomas Cromwell. Their spiritual DNA in the Anglican Church allowed little room for dissenters. The religious culture they developed paid little attention to the command of Jesus to love all Christians as Jesus loved them.

Oddly enough, *even the Puritans who broke off from the Anglican Church carried this abusive spiritual DNA* into Massachusetts when they settled there as the northern colony of Virginia.

Despite coming here for freedom of religion, the Puritans in the northern Virginia Colony of Massachusetts were as narrow-minded and restrictive about other denominations as the Anglicans of the southern colony in the Tidewater area.

In the minds of the Puritans, religious liberty was thought to be consistent with the persecution of Quakers, Baptists, Presbyterians, Anglicans and indeed virtually everyone except those with a very narrow spectrum of Calvinist orthodoxy.[1] Religious intolerance was one of the great sins of that age.

Religious Legalism Encouraged Intolerance

Christian life in Anglican Virginia was highly regulated and ritualis-tic. No one was allowed to improvise on the King's religion. **That British rule is exactly why the Puritans and Pilgrims came to the northern Virginia colony in 1620**: they desired the freedom to practice British Protestantism differently than established Anglican practice in the Church of England.

From the beginning of colonial planning in 1603, Lord De La Warr and others advocated *a uniform and strict church government* in the soon-to-be-founded colony. Later, as governor, Lord de La War ordered chapel services twice a day with much ceremony. In 1632, tithes to the Church were *mandatory*, and it was forbidden to "disparge their ministers."[2]

Harsh Christianity ruled the colony

Persecution by Anglicans

After 1642, Governor Berkeley added laws that required "all non-conformists...to depart the colony with all convenience."[3] Some Puri-tans had already settled here with Puritan ministers before Berkeley arrived, but he did his best to scatter and banish them from Virginia. Anglicans tried to blame the 1622 massacre by the Indians on the harboring of dissenters by some settlers! [4]

In 1658, all Quakers were ordered by law to leave Virginia.

One Quaker lady was ordered to be whipped 20 strokes on her bare back by a good Anglican brother for refusing to be Anglican! She finally agreed and the whipping stopped.

Is it any wonder why so few Powhatans became followers of Jesus when they saw Christian behavior like that? Hatred for Quakers by Anglicans was so severe that they passed *a law punishing Anglicans who were merely "loving to Quakers."*[5]

Anglican efforts to cleanse the colony of all non-Anglicans worked. By the end of the 1600s, **the entire state of Virginia could boast that it was uniformly Anglican.**

In 1705, only three small congregations of Quakers and two tiny Presbyterian churches could be found in Virginia, while Anglican churches were full and robust. [6] This strong, uniform religious life shaped Virginia's culture much in the years to come.

Yet, despite the Christian values of the founders, the Anglican government and clergy allowed and apparently—for the most part—supported the severe abuses of non-Anglican Christians for generations!

Against Catholics

England was in a "lukewarm" war with Spain in the 1600s. They had ceased fighting military battles but they were also not in a "cold war". Although England had won the pivotal sea battle of 1588, ending their armed hostilities,[7] the two nations were sworn enemies in the race to claim and plunder the New World for "God and the Crown." Since all Spanish were Catholics, **the Virginia Charter would not allow any Catholic to immigrate to the Virginia Colony.** Every settler had to take an oath of Supremacy to the Church of England as his or her spiritual authority. Finally, in 1634, Cecil and George Calvert founded Maryland as a refuge for Catholics persecuted by Protestants in England. But the conflict between Protestants and Catholics continued there off and on until 1776!

To my knowledge, **no apology** has ever been made by Anglicans to Catholic Christians for those 140 years of intermittent persecution.

Against Baptists

Some years ago, I visited a Baptist church in Chesapeake near my home. Right at the entrance to the sanctuary was a large portrait of a Baptist preacher in jail. The bronze plate below the picture read: "Jailed for preaching without a license." Anglicans jailed him and that Baptist church in Chesapeake has not forgotten. From the looks of it, *they may not have forgiven, either.* Forgiveness needs to flow in both directions for all the offenses committed by Anglicans against other faith groups in the colony.

Pastors Are the Key to Church Unity

After being a pastor for over 35 years in America and after meeting pastors in several nations overseas, I see pastors holding the key to unity and collaboration among churches. Church members love praying and working together with members of other churches. The pastors, however, are usually very reluctant to do that. This is a global problem.

Why? Usually, the pastor fears that he will lose members to another church if he allows them to mingle with another church. That loss of members could hurt his church financially. In small churches, this is a bigger concern, a pastor in India told me. **The loss of "nickels and noses" is a common fear among pastors worldwide.**

A secondary fear of pastors may be that they will feel emotionally rejected by the loss of members. Many pastors are lonely and somewhat insecure so they look to their church membership as a validation of their self-worth. *I know I often did.* It is hard not to feel bad when someone you have loved for years suddenly leaves your church for another church nearby. I have seen pastors suffer this way—and I have, also.

There are probably other reasons, but the result is what I call *the strongest, most common stronghold in the Church worldwide:* the unwillingness of most pastors to love, serve, encourage and bear the burdens (Gal.6:2) of Christians who are pastors.

We pastors teach our flocks to obey God's commands to love one another, but *competition among pastors is much more common than compassion.* The result is a greatly weakened Body of Christ in that region because we are grieving the Holy Spirit.

Years ago, as a pastor of a small non-denominational church, I decided to show love to churches of different traditions in my region. I invited them to send a deacon or elder to our church to tell us about their church and lead us in prayer for their church in our Sunday service. Many would not. They kept asking why we were doing this. They were suspicious of our motives. So sad.

God is very interested in healing the effects of these colonial sins between Anglicans/Episcopalians and the denominations they persecuted. The story in the Foreword of this book involving Pastors Marty O'Rourke and Ken Gerry is a dramatic example of how God blesses that kind of reconciliation.

More recently, a group of pastors in Tidewater from many different kinds of churches have formed a group they call Revival Alliance. This group of pastors is committed to helping each other when revival comes by sharing facilities, worship leaders and prayer teams. They also collaborate on outreach projects. Two pastors have even decided to share a building to hold their church services. This is one simple model for loving and serving one another.

May the spiritual descendants of those colonial Anglican leaders in America publicly repent for the abuse of non-Anglican Christians that began in Jamestown.

Jesus commands us to love each other. He is coming back for one, pure and spotless Bride who walks in love and unity with one another. He is not coming back for a harem of squabbling wives!

According to Jon 17:21, our unity as believers is a powerful witness to the world that God sent Jesus to earth!

That they may all be one; even as You, Father, *are* in Me and I in You, that they also may be in Us, so that the world may believe that You sent Me.

Our lack of compassion and unity among believers in different churches shows the world the opposite. The unsaved have a right to wonder if we really are disciples of a loving Jesus, as John 13:35 says:

> By this all *people* will know that you are My disciples: if you have love for one another.

Pastors and denominational leaders need to get this right if they want the full blessing of God on their ministries and their region.

Discussion Questions

1. Describe the treatment of non-Anglicans by the Jamestown colony?

2. How would you describe the relationships among pastors in your area? How often do they collaborate to reach the community or to help each other's congregations?

3. Why would pastors normally feel reluctant to allow their people to collaborate with other churches in local ministry?

4. Why advantage is it to the enemy if churches do not work together to reach the community with the Gospel?

5. How can you and your church speak and demonstrate kindness and respect to other churches and pastors in your area?

6. In John 17, what does Jesus say will happen when Christians walk together in unity? Is that worth the "risks" of collaboration and partnership with other churches?

1. Fischer, 203.
2. Ibid, 234.
3. Ibid,
4. Picture of cross from http://www.persecution.net (16 January 2006).
5. Fischer, 234.
6. Ibid, 234-235.
7. That battle tragically delayed John White's return voyage to doomed Roanoke Island and to his grandchild, Virginia Dare—the first English baby born in the New World. He never saw them again.

CHAPTER 18

TREACHERY & VIOLENCE

There are six things the Lord hates, seven that are detestable to him: haughty eyes, a lying tongue, hands that shed innocent blood" (Proverbs 16:16-17).

DECEIT AND TREACHERY ARE EVERYWHERE IN HUMAN HISTORY— especially where money, power and survival issues are at stake. Jamestown is no exception. The abuses of people detailed in previous chapters were often perpetuated through deceit and treachery.

SPANISH & ENGLISH DECEPTION

Both the English and the Spanish **had come to deceive and conquer the Native Americans** so that they could take over their land by force, under the pretense of just wanting to live among them and perhaps save their souls.

Neither nation told the Indians the truth about why they came to settle in Indian lands. Deceit was the foundation of the Jamestown colony's relationship with the Indians—although the Indians initially kept the colony alive by freely and repeatedly sharing their corn with them when English supplies ran out.

Here are more details about the roots of this sin pattern that continues to make the soul of America sick with sin.

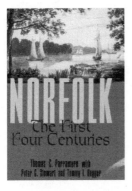

The first chapter of Thomas Parramore's well-known book, *Norfolk: The First Four Centuries*, tells a story of treachery by the Powhatans against the Spanish story in detail.

"The French under Verranzo and the Spanish under Estavan Gomes sailed past here in 1524. Chesapeake Bay was first named Bay of St. Mary (Bahia de Santa Maria) by Pedro de Quero in 1525. Later, John Rut, from England passed by here in 1527."[1]

Finally, in 1561, a Spanish ship under Pedro Menendez de Aviles visited the Indians here and sailed off with a bright, high-born Indian boy named **Paquiquino** and his servant to Spain.

The Spanish claim he went willingly, but the rest of the story makes it easier to believe that he was abducted by the Spanish—something they had refined to a fine art by this time after invading and looting the lands of Indians in South and Central America. Paquiquino converted to Catholicism while in Spain, lived in Cuba for a season and later was baptized in Mexico as a Catholic.

Nine years later, the Spanish Jesuits, led by **Father Juan Baptista de Segura** brought back Paquiquino, named Don Luis by the Spanish.[2] He was fluent in Spanish and had promised to help the Jesuits convert his entire tribe to Christianity.

While the Jesuits were sincerely zealous to save the souls of the Indians, Spain used conversion also as a political method to subdue the natives so they could invade and plunder the land for Spain and keep out the French and the British.

This strategy was not lost on Paquiquino. During his time in Mexico, he saw thousands of "converted" Indians harshly enslaved to serve the Spanish Empire machine. His exposure to the cruelties of the Spanish in Mexico, plus the post-hypnotic effect on Paquiquino of the drug-induced Huskanaw Warrior Ritual [3]probably played a big role in what was about to happen.

Shortly after arriving home, Paquiquino disappeared into the woods, only to return weeks later to his worried Jesuit brothers and priests claiming that his party of Indians came to help build a chapel, thus needing all the axes and other tools the priests had.

The next morning, on Friday, February 9, 1571, Paquiquino led his men to the cabin where the Jesuits were saying Mass and slew the unarmed eight adult worshippers[4] with their own Spanish tools and weapons.[5] These brave men became the first Christian martyrs in Virginia —a fact the Church in Virginia needs to recognize more.[6]

Paquiquino and warriors massacre priests

This ended the last serious attempt of the Spanish to settle in Tidewater. The Spanish never tried again to settle here. Their only remaining legacy here was the Spanish Thorn Apple, later called Jamestown Weed (Jimsonweed)—a hallucinogenic drug, mentioned earlier, that was to become part of the DNA for addictions in Tidewater.

There were two other amazing Spanish setbacks:

1. A very similar betrayal by a Spanish-trained Indian interpreter-guide had ruined the attempted Spanish colony at Roanoke in 1526![7]
2. The location of the Spanish defeat along the banks of the York River is *almost the same location* where the British were defeated in the concluding battle of the Revolutionary War in 1781 at Yorktown, Virginia.

It is eerie that one place could be the site where two nations were defeated 210 years apart! Furthermore, that that site was very close to the great Powhatan's headquarters!

It is almost as if the forces of darkness operating within the Powhatan's religion had a special authority in that area to defeat the hated British who surrendered at Yorktown, never to rule in America again.

Treachery and Deceit among the Colonists

Early Jamestown had a well-deserved reputation for being a place where a respectable person did not want to be. The settlement had a very bad reputation for laziness, disunity, fighting and even treachery among themselves right from the start of the voyage in 1607. Capt. John Smith's life in the colony is a good example of the treachery among the colonists.

The conflict in the colony started during the voyage from England! Colony leaders *jailed Captain John Smith*, who later became president of the colony, shortly after leaving the Canary Islands on suspicions of treachery. Captain Newport and others believed that Smith "intended to usurp the government, murder the council, and make himself king, that his confederates were dispersed in all the three ships, and that divers of his confederates that revealed it, would affirm it..."[8]

Smith [9] was later made president of the colony after other leaders died or left. Councilor George Kendall was shot to death for causing discord.[10]

Smith could be the "poster child" for all that went right at Jamestown and all that went wrong. Smith was easily the ablest leader at Jamestown among the first settlers. He possessed "a quick mind and more physical courage than was good for him." [11]As an explorer, negotiator with the Indians and rough-and-ready leader, there was none equal to him at

Capt John Smith

Jamestown. His mapping expeditions of the Chesapeake Bay were extraordinarily good. He had learned many such survival skills as a mercenary soldier of fortune in previous European wars where he won fame for his defeats of Muslim Ottoman Turks, who once captured him.

Smith captured by Turks

But Smith was also one of the most ruthless and arrogant men to live there. [12] He was "a cocky swaggerer who was forever making extravagant boasts and generous promises, only to go back on them the moment it was more convenient to do so."[13]

George Percy, one of the original leaders at Jamestown calls Smith "an ambitious, unworthy and vainglorious fellow, attempting to take all men's authorities from them."[14] *He was everything that Rev. Hunt was not.* He was a braggart, loved to start fights with the Indians, conned them out of anything he could—, especially corn—and killed them whenever he could, even killing women and children! It should not surprise you that his favorite author was Machiavelli—the paragon of deceit and treachery. [15]

In light of Smith's attitude and conduct, it was a miracle that the settlers were able to obtain any corn at all. For, as modern historian Edmund Morgan points out, **'Smith was sure that kindness was wasted on savages**...that the Spanish had shown the way to deal with the Indians.' Smith later wrote that, like the Conquistadors, the Jamestown colonists should have 'forced the treacherous and rebellious infidels to do all manner of drudgery work and slavery from them, themselves living like soldiers upon the fruits of their labors.' [16]

Smith's cruel wishes were more prophetic than he realized. Virginia birthed the infamous slavery prototype for the United States—only with whites and blacks instead of with Indians. The Virginia country gentlemen lived lives of luxury on the sweating, often bleeding, backs of indentured servants and slaves for hundreds of years.

It should be said that in Captain John Smith we see "a paradox so typical of the Virginia Colony:"[17]**great leadership ability combined with poor character**. Smith was just the first of several such Virginia leaders. As a counselor,

Violence in Jamestown

The enforcement of discipline at Jamestown was often like being in a war zone. People were shot, tortured and brutally treated just because they were trying to escape from "chronic hunger and disease, from servitude and savage martial law."[18] "Sick, Starving, Quarrelling: The Jamestown colonists nearly wiped themselves out, without any help from the Indians."[19]

Conditions were so bad in Jamestown that the Virginia Company passed a law that would effectively muzzle anyone from spreading bad reports about the colony in England. According to two settlers, Richard Pott and William Phettiplace, some Dutchmen among the colonists joined the Indians and schemed to steal tools, weapons and food from the colony. They then taught the Indians how to use English weapons against their own colony.[20] Betrayal, treachery and deceit grew in the first few years at Jamestown.

Eyewitness accounts from the colony bear that out. Well-connected gentlemen like Percy and West would only get a slap on the wrist after sailing back to England from Jamestown in ships full of food while the colony starved. Percy even returned to Jamestown to later become one of its governors—without ever being punished for deserting and taking critical food supplies with him! Yet, for similar offenses, ordinary settlers were punished like animals—especially by Governor Dale.

Though some collapsed and died from sheer despair, bolder spirits resolved to escape at any cost. Many fled to the Indians and were seen no more. Those unlucky enough to be caught [running to the Indians] were executed "in a most severe manner." Dale had some hanged; "some burned; some, to be broken upon the wheel; others, to be staked; and some, to be shott to death;...and some who robbed the store, he caused to be bound faste unto trees and so starved them to death.[21] Other deserters were even tracked and killed by Indians hired by Dale. **These were some of the founding fathers of America!**

When Sir William Berkley reached Virginia in February 1642, it was a sickly settlement of barely 8,000 souls. The colony had earned a very bad reputation. Berkley wrote, "that none but those of the meanest quality and corruptest lives went there."[22]

The quality of life in early Virginia was more like a remote military outpost or wild-west town than a permanent society. Its leaders were rough, violent, hard-drinking men. Berkeley's predecessor, Governor John Harvey, had knocked out the teeth of a councilor with a cudgel, before being "thrust out" himself by the colonists in 1635 ...The colony was in a state of chronic disorder.[23]

Like many other frontier towns across the globe, Jamestown could best be described in the words of Galatians 5:19-21:

> Now the deeds of the flesh are evident, which are: immorality, impurity, sensuality, idolatry, sorcery, enmities, strife, jealousy, outbursts of anger, disputes, dissensions, factions, envying, drunkenness, carousing, and things like these, of which I forewarn you, just as I have forewarned you, that those who practice such things will not inherit the kingdom of God.

Modern Proof

William Kelso, the archeologist who started and headed the dig at Jamestown in 1994, says of the 70 bodies he has unearthed, "*Homicide* seems to have been a cause of death as well."[24] New archeological and forensic evidence at the Jamestown site also suggests the possibility that many died from arsenic poisoning—perhaps from a Spanish operative among the settlers. Such treachery would not be uncommon between Spain and England, who were in fierce competition for rights to the New World. In addition, England humiliated Spain by defeating her armada in 1588 in the English Channel. "It was definitely a rough place."[25]

In partial defense of these atrocious acts by the English, remember that we have yet to probe the dark side of the spiritual world in Tidewater. The next chapter will help explain perhaps why such things happened to and through Christian men claiming to follow a merciful God.

Deceit and Hypocrisy in the Virginia Company Owners

When folks in England began to hear leaked reports of the carnage in the colony by returning ships crews and escaped colonists, the businessmen leaders of the Virginia Company had some fast explaining to do so that their financial supporters would keep investing in this badly failing colony. They tried with every means available to sugar-coat the terrible truth of the colony's agonies. They published sermons extolling the great Christian work the colony was doing and, in general, tried to dupe its investors into staying with the ship. They needed more money and felt the truth would ruin their investments in the colony. So, they lied...often and loudly.[26]

Finally, to his great credit, when John Smith exposed this deceit in his book in 1612 called A *Map of Virginia,* the Virginia Company Partners published a rebuttal called *A True and Sincere Declaration* claiming that

> Our principal and main ends...were first to preach and baptize into Christian religion...a number of poor and miserable souls...and to add our mite to the treasury of heaven...[27]

Smith's 1612 book was a sensation. He nailed the Partners with the astute observation that if evangelization was their chief goal, why did they send over so many "refiners, goldsmiths, jewelers, lapidaries, stone-cutters...so doting on mines of gold and the South Sea, that all the world could not have devised better courses to bring us ruin than they did themselves."[28] Smith had it right when he wrote that the Partners were making "Religion their color, when all their aim was nothing but present profit..."[29]

Later, the Virginia Company Partners (also called "adventurers") asked supporters for more money to send another ship over with Thomas West, Lord de La Warr, so he could be governor for life. But things in Jamestown were so bad that he only stayed for one year.

> Money was coming in slowly, so the Partners admitted that there had been "some distresses" but that was all behind them for the "extemitie in which they were is now relieved. This was a brazen and quite unprincipled lie as the adventurers well knew from the reports that their ships had just brought in. What a travesty of truth it was, they had no idea. At that very moment their True and Sincere Declaration

appeared, Virginia lay almost at last gasp, writhing in the agonies of the Starving Time."[30]

Shortly thereafter, the Virginia Company had to resort to raising funds via "a public lottery and direct mail campaign to mayors of small rural towns, urging them to invest from their municipal treasuries." [31]The love of money had driven the leaders of the Virginia Company to great dishonesty—under the cover of religion, a sin that still plagues the American Church today.

The 1622 Massacre

This story of treachery could make the most wicked person smile with envy. It was brilliantly conceived and carried out over a period of years by Powhatan warriors who saw the handwriting on the wall: their way of life would soon be extinct.

Futile battles with the British, and even more so, contact with European diseases, decimated the Indian population. Little by little, the British were taking over their ancestral lands without paying for them in any way. It was as if the Indians were watching a slow-motion video of their lives and lands taken over by more and more strangers who took what had belonged to the Indians for centuries.

Sometime during the next four years, this new chief devised a plan to exterminate the entire British colony of about 1,250 settlers.

Opechancanough decided that diplomacy had failed, and the Powhatans should not passively submit as the English occupied Virginia. He led two attempts to force the English to abandon Virginia, which resulted in hundreds of settlers being killed in two surprise attacks, one on March 22, 1622, and again in 1644.[32]

Opechancanough probably knew how the Spanish had brutally subjugated Mexican Indians from the stories Paquiquino had told after his return to the tribe in 1571. Understandably, Chief Opechancanough was not about to let the English do that in his land!

But what British leader would have thought that "savages" would have the patient cunning to build such trusted relationships with the white people that the colonists would teach them how to use their guns, and their riverboats and invite them into their homes for dinner? Settlers stopped carrying weapons, locking their doors or fearing any attacks from Indians. Settlers were encouraged by some leaders to build close friendships with the Indians to convert them to Christianity. Peace had come to the English—or so they thought.

Just as Paquiquino's war party had done in 1571, warriors again crept up on unsuspecting Christians *on a Friday*! Ironically, this Friday in 1622 was Good Friday— a day devoted to remembering the treacherous crucifixion of Jesus by his enemies. Again, as in 1571, the Powhatans used the settlers' own weapons against them.

So, on Good Friday,[33] March 22, 1622, at 8 in the morning, using the sun as a timepiece, hundreds of naked warriors descended upon the homes where they had often eaten and laughed with the children.

They knew where the location of every axe and every firearm. The settlers had shown them so the Indians could use them if they needed to hunt and farm for themselves. The Indians could have wiped out the entire colony, except that one Indian broke the silence just before the attack.

By God's grace, **Chanco,** a young Christian Powhatan boy, broke his allegiance to the tribe to save the Pace family who had loved him like a son. "Late on March 21, 1622, Chanco revealed the plans to Richard Pace. As John Smith later described it: 'Pace, upon this [warning], securing his house, before day rowed to James Towne, and told the Governor of it...'"

1622 Massacre

His warning saved hundreds from certain death. As it was, about 350 to 400 men women and children died. About 850 survived of the 1250 settlers. John Rolfe, the former son-in-law to the deceased Powhatan, was apparently killed in the attack.

The 1622 massacre may be the single most deadly and treacherous attack on whites by any Indian tribe in America's history. It showed the power of deceit, betrayal and treachery in the DNA of this area, started by the Indians and fanned into flame by our British ancestors.

The English Respond

English reprisals against the Indians were equally violent. A year after the 1622 massacre, Captain William Tucker and Dr. John Pott worked out a spurious truce with the Powhatan Indians and proposed a toast, using wine laced with poison. In May 1623, the colonists arranged a meeting to discuss a truce with Opechancanough through friendly Indian intermediaries.

On May 22, Captain Tucker and a force of musketeers met with Opechancanough and other prominent Powhatans on neutral ground along the Potomac River, allegedly to negotiate the release of English women taken from Martin's Hundred Plantation by the Indians in the 1622 attack on English plantations and settlements along the James River.

But Tucker's objective was the slaughter of Powhatan leaders. After the captain and the Indians had exchanged "manye fayned speeches,"[34] approximately 200 of the Powhatans who had accompanied their leaders unwittingly drank poisoned wine that Jamestown's resident physician and later governor, Dr. John Pott, had prepared for the occasion. Many of the Indians fell sick or immediately dropped dead, and Tucker's men shot and killed about fifty more.[35]

There was no further fighting between the English colonists and the Indians on a large scale until 1644 when Opechancanough led the last uprising, in which he was captured and murdered at Jamestown in 1646.[36]

He had waited 22 years to strike again! This ended the Powhatan Empire and fulfilled the Indian prophecy of 1607 that people "from the Chesapeake bay should arise, which would dissolve and give end to His Empire," speaking of Powhatan's empire.[37] That Indian seer, using demonic prophetic gifts, had correctly discerned the coming of the English to destroy the Powhatan confederacy.[38] Historian T.J Stiles writes:

> It was as if Jamestown was under a curse that bound Opechancanough to strike, despite prosperity, despite friendship, despite alliance. It was as if the soil of Virginia must be watered with blood. Indeed, the

colony's cycle of treachery and murder would not end until Jamestown itself was destroyed, more than fifty years later.[39]

God says in Habakkuk 2:12, "Woe to him who builds a city with bloodshed, And founds a town with violence!"

Could there be legitimate Native American curses and a God-given curse on Tidewater and America for its sins against the Indians? Jamestown's history has all the earmarks of curses working against it. The next chapter has a lot more to say about God-give curses for sin.

Discussion Questions

1. Why do you think Paqiquino's war party killed the Spanish priests and brothers who brought him back to his tribe?

2. How honest were the Spanish and English with the native people when they arrived in the Jamestown region?

3. How well did the settlers get along in the early years of the colony?

4. Whys did some men desert the colony to live with the Powhatans?

5. What did the two Dutch deserters teach the natives? Why?

6. What does it tell you about John Smith that his favorite author was Machiavelli?

7. How did the owners of the Virginia Company lie?

8. Describe what happened in 1622? What motivated the Powhatans to do this? How did the English respond?

---

1. Thomas C. Parramore et al, Norfolk: The First Four Hundred Years (Charlottesville: University Press of Virginia, 1994), 2.
2. http://www.virginiaplaces.org/settleland/ajacan.html (17 March 2020)
3. See Chapter 9
4. Ibid, also with the eight Jesuit adults was a young Spanish boy, **Alonso Olmos**, called Aloncito, who came to serve Mass with the priests. Paquiquino spared his life and he was later rescued by the Spanish. He is the source of information about this massacre

5. Ibid., 8.
6. Plans are under way to officially **canonize Father Segura as a Catholic saint**. There is also the possibility of putting up a statue to the martyrs near the York River where they died. **Protestants and Catholics could both celebrate the zeal and faith of those six Jesuit martyrs who came here to seek and save the lost in Jesus' Name**!
7. Ibid., 3.
8. John Smith, "The Settlement of Jamestown" http://www.nationalcenter.org/ SettlementofJamestown.html (17 March 2020)
9. http://blogs.britannica.com/2008/09/the-real-john-smith-remembering-our-first-president/ (17 March 2020).
10. http://www.virtualjamestown.org/timeline2.html (17 March 2020)
11. Marshal, 88.
12. http://www.apva.org/tour/jsstat.html (18 May 2006)
13. Peter Marshall and David Manuel, 88.
14. Edward Wright Haile, Jamestown Narratives: Eyewitness Accounts of the Virginia Colony, (Champlain: Roundhouse, 1998), 502.
15. Stiles, 55.
16. Marshall, 92.
17. Ibid
18. George F. Willison, Behold Virginia: The Fifth Crown (New York: Harcourt and Brace & Co., 1952), 147.
19. Stiles, 32.
20. Stiles, 68.
21. Willison, 147.
22. http://www.virtualjamestown.org/exist/cocoon/jamestown/fha/J1003 (26 Dec. 2022)
23. Fischer, 210.
24. https://www.pbs.org/wnet/secrets/death-jamestown-interview-william-kelso/1438/ (19 March 2021)
25. Ibid
26. Marshall, 90.
27. Ibid., 99.
28. Ibid.
29. Ibid.
30. Willison, 107.
31. Marshall, 99.
32. http://www.virginiaplaces.org/nativeamerican/secondanglopowhatan.html (26 Dec. 2022)
33. **Friday is an important day the healing of this area.** The first Christian martyrs were slaughtered by great treachery by a professed Indian believer and his warriors near Yorktown while celebrating the **death of Jesus in the Catholic Mass on *Friday*, Feb. 9, 1571**. The Mass celebrates the crucifixion of Jesus. The 1622 Massacre also occurred on the day Christian's commemorate the death of Jesus, this time on **Good Friday,** March 22, 1622. For three years, some of us **planted small crosses** and stakes with scriptures on them around the perimeters of Tidewater—first the entire area and then the boundaries of each city. We did it to claim the land for Jesus. We did it on Good Friday each year!
34. https://www.historynet.com/powhatan-uprising-of-1622.htm

(17 March 2020)

35. http://en.wikipedia.org/wiki/Jamestown,_Virginia (17 March 2020)
36. https://www.historyisfun.org/sites/jamestown-chronicles/timeline.html (17 March 2020)
37. Parramore, 24.
38. Acts 16: 16-18 in the Bible tells about the girl with a demonic spirit of divination who also spoke revelatory truth, but from an evil source.
39. Stiles,157.

CHAPTER 19

THE SPIRITUAL WAR

AGAINST THE COLONY

"For our struggle is not against flesh and blood, but against the rulers,
against the powers, against the world forces of this darkness, against
the spiritual *forces* of wickedness in the heavenly *places"(Eph.6:12)*.

THE DEMONIC SPIRITUAL WARFARE AGAINST THE SETTLERS IN THIS
region was massive, powerful, and not well understood by our founding
fathers. Fighting pagan spiritual power was not common knowledge
among many Christians back then—*or today!*

To make matters worse, the settlers acted like they were unsaved,
poorly-discipled, and/or very carnal in their behavior. "Reading the
story of Jamestown is similar to reading the list of curses in
Deuteronomy 28."[1]

This created the "Perfect Storm" for skilled, native witch doctors
to use demonic oppression against them with hideous results that defy
logic. Despite the extensive education and technology available to
English leaders, the suffering of Jamestown is hard to believe. PBS.org
describes it this way:

> The death rate in the colony was nothing short of astounding! Disease
> killed nine out of ten who had come in the first three ships by the

second year of arrival.[2] This frequency of death went on for years. "Of the 1,200 people who went out to Virginia in 1619, only 200 were alive by 1620."[3]

The disease-filled Jamestown Island of 1607

The Mayflower Society claims tens of millions of Americans descended from the original Plymouth Colony;[4] *Jamestown has no society to compare to Plymouth.* Most of the first settlers at Jamestown quickly died or fled back to England to escape the horrors of Jamestown. [5]

Three Questions

1, Why would it take four painful endeavors for a rich, technically advanced, and powerful nation like England to plant a permanent colony on the shores of another country with many natural resources and relatively uninhabited by natives armed only with stone-age technology?

2. Why was Jamestown infamous for insurrection, meanness, foolish decisions, and homicidal relationships in the first few years?

3. Why were the Indians so persistently opposed to them for decades, unlike other colonies later on?

Underneath the physical, historical answers to those questions, *a great spiritual battle has raged*—more real than the one seen by human eyes—as God discloses in the Bible:

> For our struggle is not against flesh and blood, but against the rulers, against the powers, against the world forces of this darkness, against the spiritual forces of wickedness in the heavenly places. [6]

A Turf War

At Normandy, on D-Day, June 6, 1945, the greatest fury of the German army was unleashed on the first waves of Allied soldiers to attempt landings on their heavily fortified French beaches.

The Germans knew that if the Allies succeeded in getting a beachhead established on the first beach, more enemy soldiers would follow. If they could prevent the first American soldiers from getting a beachhead, the invasion might be defeated. The movie, *Saving Private Ryan*, shows some of the unbelievable horrors those first waves of Allied troops faced as they splashed ashore that day of bloodshed.

According to the Bible, demons are territorial.[7] A high-level demon called the prince of Persia resisted even the angel Gabriel when he was sent by God to Daniel in Persia (Daniel 10:13).[8] That demonic prince of darkness had authority in Persia to resist even an angel from God!

In places like 1 Corinthians 10:20, the Bible says that the idols pagans worship *are demons.* The demons of hell surely claimed Virginia as their own through the centuries of spoken covenants made with the Indians there who worshipped a demon they called *Okeus.* It makes perfect sense that those demons would lead their native followers to violently resist the Jamestown Christian "invaders".

These same demons had already used the Powhatans to defeat Spanish Catholic Christians who attempted to settle there in 1571. Now it was time to defend their territory against these English Anglicans bearing the hated Name of Jesus.

The Spiritual World of the Powhatans

The prince of darkness had deceived, infiltrated, and taken over the tribes of Powhatan centuries before. Native religious men[9] became power brokers with the spirit world for the needs of their tribes, In exchange for covenants of safety and prosperity, the Powhatans were deceived into worshiping Okeus, the vicious god of the Algonquians, who demanded sacrifices of everything valuable, including human life —even children, at times. In return, Okeus and his platoons of demons assigned here claimed to give the tribes spiritual power to conquer their enemies, see into the future, hunt game, produce healthy crops, and father many offspring.[10]

Amazingly, the Powhatan Indians also believed in a good Creator God named *Ahone* who was the source of all good things. A Powhatan Indian told Robert Beverley shortly before 1705:

That, tis true, God is the giver of all good things, but they flow naturally and promiscuously from him; that they are showered down upon all Men indifferently...god do not trouble himself with the impertinent affairs of Men...therefore it was to no purpose either to fear, or Worship him: but on the contrary if they do not pacify the Evil Spirit, and could make him propitious, he'd wou'd take away, or spoil all the good things that God had given them; and ruine the Health, their Peace and their Plenty. [11]

If only the English had helped the Native Americans connect their loving Creator God with the God of the Bible! This is surely what famed author Don Richardson would call a "redemptive analogy" that could have opened the hearts of the Indians to the true God through this striking parallel in their native belief system. [12]

Native American Divination

As we saw earlier, an Algonquin priest accurately predicted that a people from the Chesapeake Bay would come and take over Powhatan's kingdom. In 1585, Thomas Harriot described the Native American conjurers he met near Roanoke Island, NC, just south of Powhatan's confederacy in Tidewater, Virginia.

They have comonlye conjurers or juglers which use strange gestures, and often contrarie to nature in their enchantments: For they be verye familiar with devils, of whome they enquier what their enemys doe, or other suche thinges. They shave all their heads...and fasten a small black birde above one of their ears as a badge of their office...The Inhabitants give great credit unto their speeche, which oftentymes they finde to bee true."[13]

Algonquin "Prophet" who practiced divination

Harriot goes on to write that some Indians in Roanoke prophesied that the English would annihilate them and take their place: "Some woulde likewise seeme to prophesie that **there were more of our generation yet to come, to kill theirs and take their places**, as some thought the purpose was by that which was already done"[14] *This was* *twenty-two years before the similar prophecy in Jamestown by a Powhatan prophet.*

In short, the spiritual world of the Indians was extremely intense and central to their way of life. Virtually all male Indians sought to have a demonic "spirit guide," as many other American tribes also practiced. A demon, masquerading as a spirit guide, would then have strong access to that man. Progression in their society was based more on their religious standing than on their ability in war or hunting ability![15] *You might say that the degree of progression was dependent on the degree of possession*—by a spirit. Indian priests were held in extremely high regard. "They could foretell the future...determine secret things...identify criminals...intuit the motives of foreigners..."[16]

The Spiritual Rules of the Physical

According to the Bible, battles and lives are won or lost more because of what is happening in the spiritual world than the physical world.

Spiritual warfare is real warfare! People can die because of it. The biblical evidence for the priority of the spiritual over the physical in *any battle in the Bible* is overwhelming.[17]

Native & Biblical Examples

Percy, one of the original settlers, wrote that one night the Indians were agitated because they tried to attack the English, but found their arrows couldn't pierce the new coats of mail armor Governor Dale just brought from England. Puzzled, the Indians fell into their "exorcisms, conjuracyons, and charms...making dyabolicall gestures and many ... spells and incantaciones."

[18]These religious acts had "very remarkable effects," according to Percy. While some settlers were sitting in an Indian house nearby, " a fantasy possessed them that they imagined the Salvages were sett upon them, each man taking one another for an Indyan, and so did fall pell-mell one upon another, **beating one another down and breaking one anther's heades**...[19]

Notice the striking similarity here to Judges 7:22 where Gideon and his 300 men blow the trumpets and "the LORD set the sword of one against another even throughout the whole army" of Gideon's enemies.

Another example is in 2 Chronicles 20:1-29: the large army of three nations coming against the Jews begins to fight and destroy each other *as the Israelites begin to worship God!* God's spiritual power confused the enemies and caused them to attack one another. Such power can come from God or from demons to fight battles and wars. This was a biblical concept that Jamestown did not grasp, as is true of most Western societies today.

Child Sacrifices Can Release Great Power

Just as God was honored by the Jewish temple sacrifices of animals in the Old Testament, demons are also honored by animal and human sacrifices to them. Demons sometimes give their followers *great supernatural power* in return for such sacrifices, as the story from II Kings 3 below shows. Demonic wrath came against God's people because the king made an extremely costly *sacrifice of his heir* to win the favor of his god, who is the "face" of a demon masquerading as that god.[20]

> Then he took his oldest son who was to reign in his place, and offered him as a burnt offering on the wall. And there **came great wrath against Israel**, and they departed from him and returned to their own land. [21]

This same kind of wrath probably came against the English colony for the same reasons: child sacrifices to the demon god they called Okeus.

While John Rolfe, husband of Pocahontas, denies that child sacrifice occurred among the Powhatans, [22] other Jamestown witnesses, William White, William Strachey and Henry Spelman all report child sacrifice by the Indians. The testimony of Henry Spelman affirming such practices should not be taken lightly. Spelman lived with the Indians for two years at the request of Captain Smith to learn the Powhatan language. He later spoke it fluently. He was an insider, not just an observer. [23]

If Powhatan, desperate to defeat the people his priest had prophesied would destroy his empire, did sacrifice children or adults to Okeus, then the incredible struggles with famine, disease, mutinies, treachery, stupidity, and homicide the Jamestown colony suffered are more easily explained from a spiritual perspective: great wrath had gone out against them from demonic powers worshipped by the Powhatans as they sacrificed children and adults to Okeus to defeat the English.

God's People Have Done the Same

Before we judge Native Americans too harshly for sacrificing children or adults to their gods for extreme needs, it should be noted that even God's people, the Jews committed this great sin, too, at times the Jews burned their own children alive to worship Molech, a false god in Israel (Jer.32:35). "They even sacrificed their sons and their daughters to the demons." Solomon built an altar to Molech (1 Kings 11:17) and King Ahaz of Judah seems to have sacrificed his son in the fire (1 Kings 16:3).

A Powhatan Curse Fulfilled?

William Strachey, a colonial leader, wrote in 1609 that the Powhatans had an angry song they sang against the British which may have been chanted around a campfire "which concludeth with a kind of petition unto their Okeus and to all the host of their idols, **to plague the tassantasses, for so they call us, and posterities...**"[24]

Most people would call that a curse. According to Strachey, the priests prayed that those curses **would fall on the descendants of those British settlers—that's Americans!**

Eventually, it seems that the curses of Powhatan and his priests against the British invaders finally came true as the *British were driven from Powhatan's land* by American soldiers, French sailors, and German troops in 1781 not far from Jamestown.

Chanting around a fire

Curses Against America?

Are there just curses against America today due to our abuse of the Native Americans in Virginia and elsewhere? I believe there are. However, repentance by Christians can break those curses.

Curses Are Real!

Besides the curses coming from demonic sources, the Bible teaches that people in authority, like parents, can bless and curse. For instance, Noah cursed his son Canaan for his voyeurism and blessed his other son Shem.

> Cursed be Canaan; A servant of servants He shall be to his Brothers... Blessed be the LORD, The God of Shem; and let Canaan be his servant.

Later, the descendants of Shem—the Israelites—would conquer and subjugate the descendants of Canaan, who were always idol worshippers. As noted earlier, Jacob pronounced *a curse on Reuben,* his firstborn. He was not honored, as the firstborn normally would be, because of his sexual sin.[25]

Joshua's Curses

Even more amazing is the story of how Joshua, the main leader of Israel, put a curse on anyone who would rebuild Jericho.[26] Joshua's curse said that they would lose their firstborn son for rebuilding the foundation and lose their youngest son for restoring the gates. That godly curse was precisely fulfilled generations later:

> In his days Hicl, the Bethelite built Jericho; he laid its foundations with the loss of Abiram his firstborn, and set up its gates with the loss of his youngest son Segub, according to the word of the LORD, which He spoke by Joshua the son of Nun.[27]

While this is a very unusual example, it shows the reality of a curse proclaimed against a place that had been dedicated to evil by someone with high authority from God.

God's Curses

The Bible describes God using curses at times to enforce his commands, as in Genesis 12:3: "I'll bless those who bless you, but I'll curse the one who curses you."

Even in the New Testament, we see Peter telling Ananias and Sapphire they are going to immediately die due to their sins. Paul makes a man blind for a while when the man interferes with Paul's ministry (Acts 13:11). Paul later warns us against preaching a Gospel different from the one he preaches in Galatians 1:8: "But even if we or an angel from heaven should preach a gospel other than the one we preached to you, let them be under God's curse!"

Breaking Generational Curses Due to Sin

We have already seen in Chapter Eight how God sent a famine on Israel during David's reign because the previous king had broken an ancient covenant with a pagan people by trying to annihilate them. [28]

This is one of the clearest biblical examples of a previous generation's sin negatively affecting the present generation through a God-given curse! But King David broke that curse through repentance and God blessed Israel again even more.

Jesus Can Break Curses

We cannot conclude this chapter on the power of evil without remembering the good news of the New Testament. Whether the curse is from God or a demonic source, Jesus came to earth to take them away from people. As He proclaimed this truth in His "job description" that he read in His hometown synagogue from Isaiah 61:1.

The Spirit of the Lord GOD is upon me, because the LORD has anointed me to bring good news to the afflicted; He has sent me to bind up the brokenhearted, to proclaim liberty to captives and freedom to prisoners...

Jesus came to break curses off of us:

Christ redeemed us from the curse of the Law, having become a curse for us—for it is written, "CURSED IS EVERYONE WHO HANGS ON A TREE"—in order that in Christ Jesus the blessing of Abraham might come to the Gentiles so that we would receive the promise of the Spirit through faith. [29]

As Christians, if we follow the guidelines of scripture in trying to love God, love others, forgive others, and confess and repent of our sins and the sins of our ancestors, we can experience freedom from almost any curse. Jesus came to take our curses off us and to heal our land and fill it with blessings and new life!

For a better understanding of curses and how to deal with them, I suggest three books:

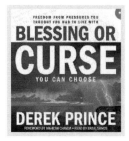

BLESSING OR CURSE: You Can Choose by Derek Prince. "Derek draws on real-life experiences of people who dealt with curses, some of which originated in a previous generation. He shows you how to recognize a curse at work and to find release in God's blessings!"[30]

THE BONDAGE BREAKER by Dr. Neil T. Anderson. [31] We don't have to be trapped in frustration, bitterness, and discouragement. *The Bondage Breaker*, with more than 1.3 million copies sold, helps readers discover how to break negative thought patterns, control irrational feelings, and break out of sinful behavior.

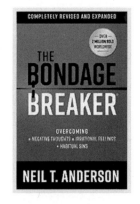

Power Healing by John Wimber.[32] This is my all-time favorite book on healing. Besides very helpful biblical teaching, John tells *real-life stories* about how to deal with the many causes of physical, emotional, spiritual, or relational sickness, including curses.

As a pastor for over thirty-five five years, I have seen what he taught in action! Many Christian leaders consider John Wimber to be one of the most important Christian leaders of the 20th century.[33]

If Only

If only the English had come in the power of the Spirit and in obedience to the Word of God, the battle against these demonic strongholds could have been won with much less bloodshed.

God loves the Indians. Jesus died for them. He longed to set them free from demonic idolatry so they could know Him and receive all His blessings for this life and the next.

If only the British had loved their enemies, returned good for evil, blessings for curses, and wept for their conversion to Jesus, the history of America would have been different...and so much better right up to today.

But it is not too late. Our generation can still obey those commands and win our enemies to Jesus as we confess, repent and work together to heal our land.

Let's do that!

☙❦❧

Discussion Questions

1. Describe the spiritual world of the Powhatans.

2. What did the two predictions by two different Algonquins say about the British? Were they true?

3. What was the purpose of the song that William Strachey describes? Could those words be affecting us today?

4. Describe what happened in II Kings 3: 26-27. Could this have happened against Jamestown by a similar sacrifice?

5. Describe the effects of Joshua's curses in I Kings 16:34.

6.. Do curses from God have any power in New Testament times? What about curses from demons?

---

1. John Dawson, Healing America's Wounds (Ventura: Regal, 1994), 43.
2. Marshall, 93.
3. Marshall, 93.
4. https://www.themayflowersociety.org/ (17 March 2020).
5. Fischer 226.
6. Ephesians 6:10-13
7. Dr. **Gary Grieg** notes: **"Demonic principalities were called "gods" in the biblical world** and were associated with specific peoples and specific territories or lands in the ancient Near East: See Deut. 32:8 "When the Most High gave the nations their inheritance, when he divided all mankind, he **set up boundaries for the peoples according to the number of the sons of God** [i.e., **"according the number of the angels"** following, as most Old Testament scholars do, the Septuagint and Qumran versions of the text of Deut. 32:8]" on which see Gregory Boyd, *God at War: The Bible and Spiritual Conflict* (Downers Grove, IL: InterVarsity Press, 1997), p. 135, 339 note 72; Deut. 31:16 "the gods of the land they are entering"; Judges 10:6 "the gods of Sidon, the gods of Moab,

the gods of the Ammonites, the gods of the Philistines"; Ruth 1:15 "her people and her gods"; 2 Kings 18:34-35 "the gods of Hamath and Arpad . . . the gods of these lands"; Jer. 2:11 "Has a nation ever changed its gods?"; Micah 4:5 "All nations may walk in the name of their gods. . . ."; See also Gregory Boyd, *God at War: The Bible and Spiritual Conflict* (Downers Grove, IL: InterVarsity Press, 1997), pp. 9-10, 135-37; E. T. Mullen, *The Assembly of the Gods: The Divine Council in Canaanite and Early Hebrew Literature* (Harvard Semitic Monographs 24, 1980); H. Bietenhard, *Die himmlische Welt im Urchristentum und Spätjudentum* (Tübingen, 1951); J. L. Cunchillos, *Cuando Los Angeles Eran Dioses* (Salamanca Universidad Pontificia, 1976)."

8. Boyd, God at War, 9-10 and notes 1-2: Boyd shows in notes 1-2 that a majority of Old Testament scholars and commentaries support this interpretation of Daniel 10:13.

9. https://docsouth.unc.edu/nc/hariot/ill7.html (17 March 2020)

10. Edward Wright Haile, editor, Jamestown Narratives: Eyewitness Accounts of the Virginia Colony (Champlain: Roundhouse, 1998), 140 quoting colonist William White.

11. O'Rourke, 14 quoting Robert Beverley, The History and Present State of Virginia [1705], ed. Louis B. Wright, University of North Carolina: Chapel Hill, NC, 1947, 200.

12. Dr. Richardson's classic book, *Eternity in Their Hearts*, describes many thrilling accounts of tribes and peoples whose own folklore seems to have striking parallels with parts of the Bible. Many groups have come to Jesus through use of these "redemptive analogies" in their culture. *Peace Child*, the first of Don's books describes how he discovered this principle in the jungles of New Guinea. It is the only missions book ever printed in Readers Digest!

13. Thomas Harriot, . A Briefe and True Report of the New Found land of Virginia (New York: Dover Publications, Inc.,1972), notation under illustration XI. The Conjuerer. Picture is also from this book.

14. Ibid, 29.

15. O'Rourke, 13: quoting Roy Dudley, President of The Order of Cape Henry 1607, in a taped interview.

16. Ibid., 15: quoting Helen Roundtree, *Pocahontas's People: the Powhatan Indians of Virginia through Four Centuries*, University of Oklahoma Press, Norman, OK, 1990, 11.

17. II Chronicles 20:1-29, II Kings 3:27, Exodus 17:11-12, Judges 1-16, Habbakuk 1:5-11, etc

18. Willison, 383.

19. Ibid.

20. Deuteronomy 32:17, Psalm 106:37, I Corinthians 10:20

21. II Kings 3: 26-27

22. Author Edward Wright Haile notes that colonists **William White, William Strackey and Henry Spelman all report child sacrifice by the Indians** while, John Rolphe, husband of Pocahontas denies it. It is easy to see why Rolfe would want to protect his father-in-law, Powhatan and Pocahontas from such a scandalous report. Spelman's testimony is especially powerful **because he actually lived with the Indians for two years and spoke their language fluently.** He was an insider, not just an observer.

23. Haile, 481.
24. Haile, 642.
25. Genesis 49:4
26. Joshua 6:26
27. I Kings 16:34
28. II Samuel 21
29. Galatians 3:13-14
30. https://www.dpmuk.org/product/blessing-or-curse-you-can-choose (17 March 2020). Good videos on curses by Derek can be seen on Youtube, such as https://www.youtube.com/watch?v=uPmrpSWAWeo
31. https://freedominchrist.com/ (17 March 2020).
32. My Book
    (17 March 2020)
33. http://en.wikipedia.org/wiki/John_Wimber (17 March 2020)

CHAPTER 20

LAND & LAWS THAT
SUPPORTED ABUSE

SYSTEMIC CULTURAL ABUSE PATTERNS
BEGAN HERE

"Vindicate the weak and fatherless. Do justice to the afflicted and destitute. Rescue the weak and needy. Deliver them out of the hand of the wicked" (Ps. 82:3-4).

THE LAND

It is ironic that the very things that made Tidewater so attractive and fruitful as a land also contributed to the scope, capacity, and growth of human rights abuses in Tidewater.

In the 1600s and 1700s, Tidewater was a great land of opportunity for those who wanted to own land and make plenty of money growing tobacco. The British government had plenty of former Indian land to give away, and there were 6,000 miles of navigable water in Tidewater next to that land on which one could transport goods to markets anywhere in the world. **Every farm on the water was an international port!**

Trans-Atlantic sailing ships would anchor near the shore in the deep water of the Chesapeake Bay, or in its many tributary rivers, while slaves on small barges would haul hogsheads (large barrels) of tobacco out to the ship. Goods imported from England or France would then come ashore for the farmer in the returning barge in exchange for the tobacco. What the farmer could not buy right off the ship from England near his dock could be made, especially with many slaves to help.

> "The Potomac, Rappahannock, York, and James rivers...bore colonial merchant traffic as far inland as the rocky fall line [where the river met rocky falls]. The flat, rich peninsulas between the tidal rivers were covered with forests broken by large fields of wheat, corn, and, above all, tobacco."[1]

No Need for Cities

This ability to maintain a prosperous lifestyle from the comfort and safety of one's farm meant that there was little need for cities. Virginia farmers were like rulers of little fiefdoms, masters of all they surveyed, isolated from most other people, and able to live independently from others. They were, in effect, **a law unto themselves.**

Farmers owned a large number of their servants and slaves. Whatever evil they did to their servants and slaves would be hardly noticed by other families, or by the law, due to the isolation of the farms from the community at large. The planter, as the farmer was called, "was at the apex of his plantation community, of which the slaves formed the base."[2]

This physical isolation, plus the proud, rough-hewn nature of these frontier planters, created **a culture capable of large-scale abuses** of servants and slaves for the first 300 years in Virginia.

VIRGINIA'S IMMIGRATION LAWS FACILITATED ABUSE

The Statue of Liberty in New York Harbor is inscribed with the famous words of poet Emma Lazarus. It ends with the well-known cry:

> 'Keep ancient lands, your storied pomp!'
> Cries she with silent lips.
> 'Give me your tired, your poor,
> Your huddled masses

yearning to breathe free,
The wretched refuse of your teeming shore.
Send these, the homeless,
tempest-tost to me.
I lift my lamp beside the golden door!'[3]

Jamestown's version might have read:

Give us your tired, your poor,
Your illiterate longing to be free.
I have men of pomp longing to use you,
Abuse you and then free you...for a fee!

As eminent historian David Hackett Fischer is quick to point out, the variety of settlers who came to the Virginia colony did not happen by chance:

"Virginia's great migration was the product of policy and social planning. Its royalist elite succeeded in shaping the social history of an American region partly by regulating the process of immigration."[4]

Virginia: England's First Penal Colony

In addition to the poor, illiterate, rural folks the colony deliberately imported as servants for the tobacco farmers, Parliament passed laws in 1717 sending criminals to Virginia by the droves! England would not found Australia as an English penal colony until 1786!

Eventually, the arrival of many convicts became unpopular with many colonists—although it did initially provide cheap, indentured labor for many farmers. One Virginia pastor wrote in 1747 that the importation of so many criminals had made Virginia

"**a mere Hell upon Earth**, another Siberia...so that few large bodies of people − have been induced willingly to transport themselves to such a Place..."[5]

By 1776, "20,000 convicts and loose women...were shipped to

Virginia. There they were sold as indentures of seven years for minor offenders and of fourteen years for those guilty of serious crimes."[6]

We Americans should thank the British for sending us so many willing men to fight them in 1776 among those 20,000 deportees who were probably not very fond of England! By 1786, England sent her criminals to Australia. Did you know we shared that unusual heritage with our Aussie friends?

Recruitment of the Younger Sons of Nobility

In 1641, the most important leader since perhaps John Smith strode on the scene in the Virginia Colony in the person of **Governor William Berkeley**. He would rule and shape Virginia with an iron fist for the next 35 years.

Besides his illegal covetousness mentioned earlier, he "bullied those beneath him, and fawned on people above."[7] By force or by flattery, he had to be in control at all times. He controlled the legislature and wrote many of the laws himself,[8] and was a gifted politician in many ways.

He was also immensely popular as governor with other Virginia leaders.[9]

Governor Berkeley of Virgina

Berkeley got things done to the liking of those with power and money, even if he had to abuse the common folk in the process. Again, we see **the abuse of power by a privileged few at the expense of the poorer masses**, another Tidewater DNA sin pattern that runs deep in our state and national character.

Governor Berkeley was very good for Virginia in many ways as a lawgiver and governor, but his most profound heritage to Virginia came from his immigration policies. He recruited dozens of the younger sons of the English Royalist elite to Virginia between 1642 and 1676 when he served as governor.

These royalist immigrants were refugees from oppression in England now that the Puritans had won England's Civil War against both King Charles I and Charles II.

"When they arrived, he promoted them to high office, granted them large estates and created **a ruling oligarchy** that ran the colony for generations."[10]

"These 'distressed cavaliers' founded what later would be called the first families in Virginia." Almost all were *disinherited younger sons of nobility* in England. As such, they were very eager to find wealth and fame in Virginia.

Most came in the 1650s. Sixty-eight percent came from the South and West of England, mostly close to London and Bristol.[11] Berkeley was himself a younger son of nobility: "This 'younger son syndrome,' as one historian has called it, became a factor of high importance in the culture of Virginia."[12]

These younger sons had no hope of inheriting their father's estate. In addition, they had little hope of ever living the life of a rich gentleman in England like their fathers and their eldest sons.

"The founders of Virginia's first families came here to reconstruct from American materials a cultural system from which they had been excluded at home."[13]

Birth order and war made them refugees looking for a fresh start where they could rule in style as their ancestors did. With them, younger sons brought the culture of the London gentry denied them in England. They would do almost anything to get and keep it in Tidewater. Selfish ambition and jealousy, fueled by rejection and fear of failure in England made them ripe to abuse anyone who got in their path to success as a Virginian gentleman.

Far from being democratic, Berkeley's social engineering created a society of **Virginia's "first families"** so closely intermarried and intertwined that no one could do anything in Virginia without the consent of these ruling families who formed a massive political and financial force.

To offend one was to incur the wrath of all. The "first families" would not rest until they had ruined the offender. This **ruling Royalist oligarchy was almost like the mafia**—only more benign for the most part—if you were not in their way. John Randolph very freely cautioned against disobliging or offending any person of note in the colony:

For either by blood or by marriage, we are almost all related, and so connected in our interests, that whosoever of a stranger presumes to offend any one of us will infallibly find an enemy of the whole. Nor, right or wrong, do we forsake him, till by one means or other his ruin is accomplished.[14] The elite controlled almost everything in Virginia to maintain their wealthy style of life. This great power corrupted them enough to abuse others around them for personal gain. As Lord Acton so famously wrote in 1887:

"Power tends to corrupt and absolute power corrupts absolutely. Great men are almost always bad men." [15]

The Pride of Virginia's Ruling Families

These elite families—most of them descended from high-standing English families—believed that they had a divine right to rule others and to have more liberties than others did. They loved to rule others, as they saw fit; the elite believed others were born to submit to them based on their fortune in life, just as Indian Brahmins look down on Indian untouchables in India today. The tyrannical Governor Berkeley himself "wrote repeatedly of 'prized liberty' as the birthright of an Englishman."[16]

Virginia's ruling elite families were nothing if not arrogant and proud. They defined themselves by their ability to live independently as gentry and serve no one, except whom they chose to serve.

One observer wrote that "the public and political character of the Virginians corresponds with their private one: they are haughty and jealous of their liberties, impatient of restraint, and can hardly bear the thought of being controlled by a superior power."[17]

Far from seeing freedom as equality for all, British Virginians saw liberty as their freedom to rule others and not be ruled by others! James Thomson (1700-1748) immortalized this belief in a famous poem:

When Britain first, at Heaven's command,

Arose from out of the Azure main,
This was the charter of the land,
And guardian angels sang this strain:
Rule, Britannia, rule the waves;
Britains will never be slaves.[18]

Even the Virginia Flag conveys this message of British Virginia's defiant and proud resistance to any form of domination by others—even by Britain itself. The Code of Virginia, Section 7.1-26, describes the Virginia flag. "Virtus, the genius of the Commonwealth, dressed as an Amazon[19]...her left foot on the form of Tyranny represented by the prostrate body of a man..."[20] The Latin

The State Flag of Virginia

inscription "Sic Semper Tyrannis" translates: "Thus always tyrants." Virtuous Virginia is thus depicted conquering the British tyrant George III.

The Roots of Abuse: Pride

The many cases of abuse of people cited above, the sexual perversions of the gentry, their passion for fortune-telling astrology and the like, may have their roots in the extreme pride of the ruling families of Virginia, who were models for everyone else aspiring to success in the colony.

The elements for such a situation might be:

1. The arrogance of British pride to rule—at any cost to others,
2. combined with the freedom to make laws of their choosing in a frontier environment,
3. the labor needs of large farms filled with poor, illiterate, powerless indentured servants, and

4. involvement in the occult through astrology to gain knowledge and power all coalesced to create a situation where too few have too much power over others.

Selfish pride still seems to be one of the chief sins underlying all the defective DNA of Tidewater...and of America.

❦

Discussion Questions

1. Describe how Tidewater's geography encouraged the abuse of people.

2. How did the immigration laws in the Jamestown Colony contribute to the abuse of slaves and servants?

3. Describe the culture of the ruling elites in Virginia who made the laws and their treatment of the non-elites?

4. What do you think motivated them to act that way?

---

1. George Washington Birthplace brochure (National Park Service: GPO-2004, reprint 2001).
2. Ibid.
3. https://www.poetryfoundation.org/poems/46550/the-new-colossus (17 March 2020)
4. Ibid., 232.
5. George F. Willison, Behold Virginia: The Fifth Crown, Harcourt & Brace & Co., NY, 1952, 387.
6. Ibid., 396.
7. Ibid, 209.
8. Ibid, 212.
9. Willison, 408.
10. Ibid, 212.
11. Ibid, 214.
12. Ibid.
13. Ibid.
14. Ibid, 224.
15. https://oll.libertyfund.org/quote/lord-acton-writes-to-bishop-creighton-that-the-same-moral-standards-should-be-applied-to-all-men-political-and-religious-leaders-included-especially-since-power-tends-to-corrupt-and-absolute-power-corrupts-absolutely-1887 (11 Dec 2022)
16. Ibid, 410.
17. Ibid, 411.

18. Ibid.
19. No one is quite clear why "Virtue" has to have her left breast uncovered. During the Civil War, it was covered. This author, for one, would prefer to see it covered again to show more respect for the dignity of women, especially because they were so abused by men for centuries in Virginia.
20. https://law.lis.virginia.gov/vacode/1-500/ (19 March 2021)

CHAPTER 21

TIDEWATER'S SPIRITUAL GATES

TO HEAVEN & HELL

"He had a dream, and behold, a ladder was set on the earth with its top reaching to heaven, and behold, the angels of God were ascending and descending on it" (Genesis 28:12).

SPIRITUAL GATEWAYS IN TIDEWATER

There is evidence that Tidewater, and Virginia Beach, in particular, is a wide gateway to the spiritual worlds—*of both heaven and hell.* This area seems to be heavily guarded by enemy spiritual forces opposed to the significance of this land dedicated to the Gospel in 1607!

This land comprises the first "gateway," the spiritual and physical "birth canal", for the birth of America. So, Tidewater—much like the city of Jerusalem—is still intensely fought over by those opposed to the God of Israel and His Messiah. Holy ground often draws intense attacks from enemy spiritual forces.

If it is true that the healing of America is somehow tied to the spiritual healing of Tidewater/Hampton Roads, it makes perfect sense why this is such a hotly contested region by the forces of darkness and the Host of heaven.

Gateways

A spiritual gateway is a modern term for an ancient concept among many religions, including Christianity. It's a place where God and/or demonic forces interact with humanity more intensely than in other places.

In Genesis 28:13-17, God speaks to Jacob in a dream where angels are moving between earth and heaven continuously via a gateway.

> Then Jacob awoke from his sleep and said, 'Surely the Lord is in this place, and I did not know it.' He was afraid and said, 'How awesome is this place! This is none other than the house of God, and **this is the gate of heaven'**...He called the name of that place **Bethel** (Gen 28:16-17)."

In these verses, we see Jacob's ladder as a pictorial metaphor for a spiritual gateway between earth and heaven.

Biblical Examples of Spiritual Gates

The biblical truism that God is everywhere (Psalm 139) does not negate the biblical examples of certain spiritual experiences being limited by God to one location, temporarily or permanently.

When God decided to speak to Jacob again (Genesis 35), God sent Jacob back to the same place: Bethel.

The Tent of Meeting in the wilderness is another example. God continually required Moses to meet Him "... **at the doorway of the tent of meeting** before the LORD, where I will meet with you, to speak to you there" (Ex. 29:42).

Later, it was **the Temple in Jerusalem**, which was the only permissible location for sacrifices to the Lord. God's manifest (easily discernible) Presence only dwelt in the Ark inside the Temple (Ex.25:22).

In the New Testament, Jesus designated the Mount of Olives near Jerusalem as the only place in Jerusalem He will return to someday. (Acts 1:12, Zechariah 14:4). *Jerusalem itself is a spiritual gate*—a place of special access to the spiritual realm.

Colonial Clues

As noted in Chapter Nineteen, Native American priests in this region had highly refined divination powers. Colonial Virginia gentlemen also had an obsession with knowing their fortunes through forms of astrology and divination.

Colonial British Divination

Divination: Discovery of what is hidden or obscure by supernatural or magic means. — Oxford English Dictionary

It seems that later generations of settlers in Tidewater were also deceived into practicing divination just as the Powhatans had.

As eminent historian David Hackett Fisher points out: "In most seventeenth-century cultures, religion was closely linked to what the modern world calls magic. Virginians were deeply interested in magic —even obsessed by it."[1]

Gentlemen Virginians were very interested in "the study of stars, planets, spheres, and portents—not as signs of God's purpose, but as clues to their fate. They believed that every man possesses a certain fixed quality called fortune, which could be understood by knowledge of these things. The idea has been widely accepted in Elizabethan England."[2]

Many men kept "fortune books" full of magical and astrological data that they believed helped give them good luck in just about everything: "One such fortune book included an entire chapter on marriage with entries on 'whether a man shall marry, the time of the marriage, how many husbands a woman shall have, who shall be the master of the two, how they shall agree after marriage, and whether the man or the wife shall die first and the time when."[3]

Two observations:

This fascination with spiritual revelation from sources other than God is a form of divination. It is serious sin! This is just as sinful as the Christians who go to church and later seek out the voodoo doctors in Haiti for help. It is religious syncretism: blending scriptural practices with non-biblical spiritual practices —the kind that got ancient Israel in big trouble with God.[4]

This fascination with divination probably brought spiritual defilement into the Anglican churches then since everyone was required to attend church. *What did the colonial Anglican Church have to say about this?* Has this ever been renounced and repented of by Anglicans in America then or now? Acceptance of extra-biblical sources of spirituality in the American Church started in Tidewater.

Could this flaw in America's DNA be part of the reason that several major Christian cults started in America: Mormons, Jehovah's Witnesses[5], Christian Science and Scientology?

Latter-Day Saints (Mormons), in particular, rely heavily on extra-biblical sources of revelation like the Book of Mormon, the Pearl of Great Price, and the Doctrine and Covenants.[6] Smith first obtained the Book of Mormon by putting a "seer stone" into a hat, then putting his face into the hat and dictating the Book of Mormon hour by hour.[7]

Modern Evidence of Gateways

Pat Robertson, one of the most spiritually astute observers of Tidewater since coming here in the late 1950s, writes:

> In 1959, the Tidewater area of Virginia was literally a spiritual wasteland. For years it had been in the grip of demon power. **Virginia Beach was advertised as the psychic capital of the world.** It was the headquarters of Edgar Cayce and the Association of Research and Enlightenment (ARE). Mediums, clairvoyants and necromancers flocked to Virginia Beach saying the "vibrations" in the air made their work much easier.
>
> These Satanic vibrations, which traverse space and time, are the communication channels to which sensitives or mediums must attune themselves, and Virginia Beach was renowned as the prime receiving station of the Universal Transmitter (Satan). Stories abound of **how people discovered their psychic sensitivity** while visiting in the area. Spiritualist centers dotted the Norfolk, Virginia Beach area.[8]

Even a casual review of the web for pagan, Wicca and occult sites in Hampton Roads shows a high concentration of activities and groups dedicated to occult practices and beliefs.[9] Occult activity is strong in Virginia Beach according to the police who had a special division some years ago assigned to investigate the sacrificing of cats and other animals.

The Virginia Beach oceanfront, where psychics and sinners congregate to enjoy the pleasures of sin, is almost a spiritual desert. Evangelical churches do not thrive there, with few exceptions.

One of the first **Freemason's Lodges** in America was probably started in Norfolk in about 1778 (some say Richmond), not far from Virginia Beach.[10] Freemasonry is very strong in the Tidewater region, especially in Norfolk and Chesapeake. In the opinion of many evangelical leaders, modern Freemasonry has some serious theological issues that must be addressed by Christians who are also Masons.[11] Most Masons are not told that Freemasonry honors a pantheon of pagan gods in their upper-level ceremonies. This is a form of idolatry that brings a curse from God on their descendants as the firsts of the Ten Commandments as discussed in Chapter Eight. This website has more information on that.[12]

CBN

Pat Robertson's CBN complex of ministries in Virginia Beach, just a few miles inland from the First Landing Cross, is one of the most spiritually fruitful Christian ministries in the world.

CBN is a major testimony to the existence of a "spiritual gate" from heaven to earth in this region.

CBN has taken the Gospel all over the world to hundreds of millions of people! They now broadcast Christian programs in 79 nations in 70 languages! By satellite, over 200 nations can see their programs. As of 2006, over 410 million around the world have become Christians because of those broadcasts!

Over 70 million have called CBN for prayer in the last 40+ years! CBN is, unquestioningly, one of the major harvesting ministries of Christendom—a ministry started just a few miles from where Rev. Hunt prayed in 1607.

CBN's massive global ministry may be related to the prayer that Rev. Hunt is said to have uttered as he dedicated this new land to the spread of the Gospel worldwide on April 29, 1607. Research seems to show that Pat Robertson is a descendant of Rev. Hunt!

Edgar Cayce's A.R.E. Center

Edgar Cayce, the world-renowned spiritualist, claims that Virginia Beach is one of the earth's spiritual "power centers."[13] Cayce built his international center for psychic readings on the beachfront in Virginia Beach where the "spiritual vibrations" allegedly occur—not far from where the first landing of English colonists occurred.

His center is called the Association for Research and Enlightenment (A.R.E.). It offers spiritual healings from New Age spiritualist sources.

It is probably the oldest and best-known such center in America. Cayce (1877–1945) was an "American folk

Cayce's Association for Research and Enlightenment

healer" who staunchly believed in the non-Christian idea of reincarnation. In his book about Jesus, Cayce claims **Jesus had been reincarnated** many times before becoming the Christ of the New Testament.

He was active as a **"psychic diagnostician"** between 1901 and 1944, performing thousands of "life readings." He is the most documented psychic of the 20th century. He wandered across the United States, spreading his ideas, before settling in Virginia Beach, Va. in 1925, where he established the Cayce Hospital (1928) and the Association for Research and Enlightenment (1931). People apparently do get healed through his spiritual assistance, but **he does not give Jesus any credit for those healings.** His works have enjoyed a renewal among adherents of New Age spirituality." [14] In fact, the A.R.E. bookstore is full of New Age and spiritualist books.

Despite the serious spiritual dangers to anyone using A.R.E.'s services, no church or ministry in Tidewater has yet produced even a pamphlet to warn people about this massive spiritualist center. Someone needs to write one.

In Conclusion

All these facts point to the conclusion that Tidewater is a portal for both the demonic world and for God that must be brought under

God's control so Tidewater and America can be free to receive all that God will do in the Great Awakening to come! Confession and repentance pave the way to that freedom!

Only a repentant, holy, loving, united, praying Church can "bind the strong man"[15] over this region and give control of the land back to the Lord. Every city in America needs this also to see the full blessing of God in their city!

The 1607 landing is near the Cayce Spiritualist Center

Discussion Questions

1. Give examples of spiritual gateways in the Bible. Which one surprises you the most?

2. What evidence could you cite to show that Tidewater may be a spiritual gateway for God? For the devil?

3. Why would the devil want to resist the Gospel in Tidewater more than in other places?

4. What can the Christians in Tidewater do to resist the devil so he will surrender control of this land to the Kingdom of God?

---

1. Fisher, 340.
2. Ibid., 341.
3. Ibid.
4.
5. https://www.factmonster.com/world/religion/us-religious-sects-originating-19th-century (19 March 2021)
6. http://scriptures.lds.org/ (17 March 2020)
7. https://mit.irr.org/translation-or-divination (28 Dec. 2022) as recorded by Smith's wife.
8. Pat Robertson, Shout It From the Housetops (Plainfield: Logos International 1972), 104 quoted by Jerry Graham in *Toward a Spiritual Mapping of South Hampton Roads, Virginia*, 16.
9. https://witchvox.com/ used to describe pagan activity in our region in 2006. The site is shut down now. Thank God. (19 March 2021)

10. http://www.norfolkmasonictemple.com/history-of-freemasonry-in-virginia.html (177 March 2020)
11. This website shows how Freemasonry could be theologically reformed to a great extent. It can be found at http://www.dear-mr-mason.com/Main.html and it is in eight languages. (1 Dec 2022)
12. http://www.dear-mr-mason.com/Main.html (27 Dec. 2022)
13. Graham, 19.
14. The Columbia Electronic Encyclopedia, Sixth Edition Copyright © 2003, Columbia University Press.
15. Mark 3:27

CHAPTER 22

WHY THE COLONY SURVIVED

"And He has made from one blood every nation of men to dwell on all the face of the earth and has determined their preappointed times and the boundaries of their dwellings" (Acts 17:26).

HUMANLY SPEAKING, THIS COLONY SHOULD NOT HAVE SURVIVED. But God had other plans. America was God's idea...and nothing the devil could do, nothing weak human flesh could do, would deter Him from creating a nation founded on His scriptures, His Son and His Great Commission. America is that nation—not only because of us—but also, despite us.

As discussed in Chapter 10, **God uses imperfect people to do great things.** God used stiff-necked, rebellious Israelites to start the nation of Israel under Moses. God used Rahab the prostitute, the immoral Tamar and Judah and the adulterous and murderous King David and Bathsheba in the family genealogy of His Messiah, Jesus! God even used a donkey to speak to a money-hungry prophet.[1]

Obviously, it was not because of the colonists' righteousness or wisdom that Jamestown survived: *God sovereignly preserved the colony!* The ninth chapter of Romans is good to review as it reveals God's ultimate control over the destiny of people based on *His* choices, not theirs "so that God's purpose according to His choice would stand, not because of works [of people] but because of Him who calls..."[2]

God wanted to raise up a nation that would send out more missionaries and more missions and finances around the world than any other nation has ever done. God wanted to fulfill Rev. Hunt's prayer that "from these shores, the Gospel would go forth to the ends of the earth." He did!

God Built Jamestown

God is completely sovereign. He raises up nations and brings them down at His good pleasure. He creates and controls the boundaries of nations and people as Acts 17:26 declares in the first quote above.

Jamestown and America would not be here unless God had ordained them. And because America was His idea, the colony survived!

Unless the Lord builds the house the laborers build in vain; unless the Lord guards the city, the watchman stays awake in vain.[3]

A CITY SET ON A HILL

I conclude this chapter with the words that Puritan Governor John Winthrop wrote of his Massachusetts colony in 1630. These words were quoted at the magnificent memorial service for former President Ronald Reagan on June 11, 2004.

As a strong believer and former president of our nation, President Reagan requested that these words be read at his memorial service as an encouragement—and warning—to America today. They are, I believe, as prophetic for our day as they were in 1630 AD when Governor Winthrop wrote them...or in 725 BC when the prophet Micah wrote his famous words quoted within Governor Winthrop's following text:

Now the only way to avoid this shipwreck, and to provide for our posterity, is to follow the counsel of Micah, to do justly, to love mercy, to walk humbly with our God. For this end, we must be knit together, in this work, as one man. We must entertain each other in brotherly affection. We must be willing to abridge ourselves of our superfluities, for the supply of others' necessities. We must uphold a familiar commerce together in all meekness, gentleness, patience and liberality. We must delight in each other; make others' conditions our own; rejoice together, mourn together, labor and suffer together, always having before our eyes our commission and community in the work, as members of the same body.

So shall we keep the unity of the spirit in the bond of peace. The Lord will be our God, and delight to dwell among us, as His own people, and will command a blessing upon us in all our ways, so that we shall see much more of His wisdom, power, goodness and truth, than formerly we have been acquainted with. We shall find that the God of Israel is among us, when ten of us shall be able to resist a thousand of our enemies; when He shall make us a praise and glory that men shall say of succeeding plantations, "may the Lord make it like that of New England.

For we must consider that we shall be as a city upon a hill. The eyes of all people are upon us. So that if we shall deal falsely with our God in this work we have undertaken, and so cause Him to withdraw His present help from us, we shall be made a story and a by-word through the world. We shall open the mouths of enemies to speak evil of the ways of God, and all professors for God's sake. We shall shame the faces of many of God's worthy servants, and cause their prayers to be turned into curses upon us till we be consumed out of the good land whither we are going. Therefore, let us choose life that we, and our seed, may live by obeying his voice, and cleaving to Him, for He is our life and our prosperity. [4]

May God help the American Church to be that city on a hill in the gathering darkness of our nation. America's future rests in the hands of the American Church.

Discussion Questions

1. Why do you think the Jamestown Colony might have failed to survive?

2. How do you see the hand of God in preserving the colony?

3. What gives you hope for America now in this morally dark time of our history?

4. How can you and your church be a "city on a hill" to the community?

---

1. Numbers 22:28
2. Romans 9: 11
3. Psalm 127:1
4. https://billofrightsinstitute.org/activities/a-city-upon-a-hill-winthrops-modell-of-christian-charity-1630 (3 Dec. 2022)

CHAPTER 23

A BIBLICAL SCHOLAR'S INSIGHTS

INTO IDENTIFICATIONAL REPENTANCE

THIS BOOK HAS SPOKEN A LOT ABOUT IDENTIFICATIONAL repentance as a biblical practice that helps break spiritual penalties for past sins. However, it seems that most Christians and many pastors are not familiar with it.

So, I have asked a friend, **Dr. Gary S. Greig,** Ph.D. to write this chapter from a biblical scholar's perspective. Dr. Greig is a former Associate Professor of Old Testament at Regent University in Virginia Beach as well as the former Vice-President for Bible and Content at Gospel Light Publications.

Much of the material cited here has been taken from Dr. Greig's teaching notes at Regent University.[1] While this section is for the more theologically trained, if you read and look up the references in the first few pages (up through his answers to Objection #3), you'll have the essence of it.

✦

WHAT Is Identificational Repentance

Identificational Repentance is a term that was coined by John Dawson in his book[2] called *Healing America's Wounds.*

As International Director of Urban Missions for Youth With A Mission (YWAM), John has personal experience with this biblical concept.

He defines Identificational Repentance as a type of prayer that identifies with and confesses before God the sins of one's city, nation, people, church, or family. It may also involve formally apologizing to and asking the forgiveness of representatives of the victims of the corporate sins (such as white Christians repenting of racism and asking a representative group of black people for forgiveness in a public ceremony).

Cindy Jacobs, President, and co-founder with her husband, Mike Jacobs, of Generals International, has also taught for over a decade about healing the nations and reaching them for Christ through corporate prayer and repentance for corporate sins, **present, and past.**[3]

MODERN EXAMPLES

Identificational repentance is not a new kind of prayer never before seen in the Church, as some suggest.

Episcopal

For example, corporate confession of sin is a well-established category, distinct from the individual confession of sin, going back almost 500 years in the worship tradition of the Anglican Church. In the **Book of Common Prayer 1559** (the Elizabethan Prayer Book), for example, we find the following prayer:

> Remember not Lord our iniquities, **nor the iniquities of our fore-fathers.** Spare us, good Lord, spare thy people, whom thou hast redeemed with thy most precious blood, and be not angry with us forever. Lord have mercy upon us. Christ have mercy upon us. Lord have mercy upon us.[4]

The 1789 ratified Book of Common Prayer of the Episcopal Church in the U.S.A. includes the Psalter to be used for congregational prayers. The introduction to the collection of Psalms for daily prayers explains that "the Psalter is a body of liturgical poetry. It is designed for vocal, congregational use, whether by singing or reading."[5]

The Psalms designated for morning and evening prayers, for example, specify on the twenty-first day of evening prayer the reading of Psalm 106. This chapter of the Bible includes a corporate prayer confessing generational sin: "**We have sinned as our forebears did; we have done wrong and dealt wickedly.** (Psalm 106:6)"[6]

In addition, the Book of Occasional Services of the Episcopal Church, U.S.A., contains a prayer of corporate confession of generational sin:

Teach your Church, O Lord, to mourn the sins of which it is guilty, and to repent and forsake them; that, by your pardoning grace, the results of **our iniquities may not be visited upon our children** and our children's children; through Jesus Christ our Lord; Amen.[7]

Colin Dunlop, former Dean of Lincoln Cathedral, articulates the nature of corporate identity and confession in Anglican worship with these words:

We make our confession as members of the Church, 'members one of another.' We confess not only our own private sins, but . . . our share in that **whole aggregate of sin** which all but crushed our Master in the Garden of Gethsemane.[8]

Lutheran

At the end of World War II, in October 1945, the newly formed United Evangelical Lutheran Church, under the influence of one of its leaders, the prominent anti-Nazi theologian, and pastor, Rev. Dr. Martin Niemöller, who resisted the Nazis alongside the famous Christian martyr Rev. Dr. Dietrich Bonhoeffer, issued the "Stuttgart Confession of Guilt" (Stuttgarter Schulderklärung). In the Stuttgart Confession, the German Lutheran church identified with and confessed the corporate guilt of the German people for the widespread suffering perpetrated by the former Nazi government with words like:

With great pain we say: Through us, unending suffering has been brought upon many nations and countries...Now a new beginning should be made in our churches.[9]

As you can see, Lutheran denominational leadership felt that identificational repentance should be kept with their theological understanding of Christian confession. This corporate confession of national guilt has been articulated and discussed over the past decades by German theologians like Dr. Martin Honecker and Dr. Gerhard Besier,[10] as well as by German New Testament scholars including Dr. Bertold Klappert of the University of Göttingen.[11]

RECENT EVANGELICAL TEACHING

Many Evangelical Christian leaders have written about the practice of prayer with corporate confession of corporate and generational sin at the family level, as well as at the level of cities, people groups, and nations—**Cindy Jacobs** (Possessing the Gates of the Enemy, 192ff., 236ff.; The Voice of God, 237ff.), **John Dawson** (Taking Our Cities for God, 19ff.; Healing America's Wounds, 15ff), **Bob Beckett** (in C. P. Wagner's, Breaking Strongholds in Your City, 160-162), **Dr. C. Peter Wagner** (Confronting the Powers, 260), **Dr. Ed Murphy** (Handbook for Spiritual Warfare, 437-438), **Dr. Neil T. Anderson** (Bondage Breaker, 201), **Dr. Charles H. Kraft** (Defeating Dark Angels, 74-75), **Francis Frangipane** (The Divine Antidote, 68-69), and **Tom White** (Believer's Guide to Spiritual Warfare, 150).

All these leaders, to one degree or another, have taught or advocated the Old Testament model of corporate confession. On a personal level, this means confessing and repenting in whatever way possible of the sins of one's parents and ancestors.

On a national level this means the Church identifying with the nation as a "royal priesthood" (I Pet. 2:9), confessing the sins of the nation, repenting of those sins in whatever way possible, and asking God to heal our nation (II Chronicles 7:14) and turn it to Christ.

Objections and Answers from the Bible[12]

Is identificational repentance biblical? Does the New Testament teach us to follow the Old Testament model of confessing corporate sin, generational sin, and national sin in addition to personal sin?

The question is really the following: Is the confession of corporate sin—which includes generational sin and national sin—still a legitimate category of confession in New Testament faith, as it was in the Old Testament?

First, it should be clear from the start that we are saved not by keeping Old Testament covenantal law but by faith in Christ and the atonement of His blood for our sins (Rom. 6:14; Gal. 2:16; 5:6; Eph. 2:8). However, this does not mean that the deeper principles of God's character mentioned in Exodus. 34:5-7 or the deeper principles of the Ten Commandments mentioned in Exodus. 20:3-17 and Deut. 5:7-2 are nullified by faith in Christ. Paul emphatically teaches this: "Do we, then, nullify the law by this faith? Not at all! Rather, we uphold the law." (Rom. 3:31) New Testament faith fulfills or establishes the deeper principles of Old Testament law according to Romans 8:4; 13:8.

The OT Was the Bible of the Early Church

Second, *the Old Testament was the only Canon of authoritative Scripture the New Testament Church* had before the New Testament documents began to be collected in the late first century A.D. When Paul wrote in II Timothy 3:16 "All Scripture is God-breathed and is useful for teaching . . . and training in righteousness" he meant "All the Old Testament is God-breathed and is useful for teaching . . . and training in righteousness."

Since the Old Testament was the Bible of the early church pictured in Acts, this means that the Old Testament's view of sin and *the Old Testament's model of confession was the only scriptural view of sin and model of confession the New Testament church had.* New Testament passages which explicitly teach about confessing sin, including James 5:16 and I John 1:9, are written against the background of the Old Testament's concept of sin and confession.

We also need to understand that **the New Testament offers no new framework of sin and confession apart from that found in the Old Testament.** The only fundamental modification in the New Testament is that Christ is now the eternal sacrifice for all sin in place of all Old Testament sacrifices for sin (Matt. 26:28; Mark. 14:24; Luke. 22:20; John. 1:9; Heb. 9-10; I John. 2:2).

Many Old Testament and New Testament scholars have pointed out that the New Testament concept of sin and the New Testament framework of public confession of personal and corporate sin pictured in such passages as I John. 1:9 and James. 5:16 is entirely shaped by the Old Testament concept of sin and confession.

Not surprisingly, references from **intertestamental Jewish religious literature**[13] indicate that the Jewish community of Jesus' day, out of which the Early Church was born, **continued to follow the Old Testament model of confessing personal as well as generational and national sins,** as the fifth century B.C. Jewish community of Jerusalem had done before them in Neh. 9:2.

Exodus 34:5-7 and Exodus 20:5-6 and their parallel Old Testament passages [14]show that the heart of the Lord's character is that He shows compassion and love toward thousands of generations of those who love Him, but His holiness causes Him **to visit the iniquity of parents upon their descendants** to the third and fourth generation of those who hate him.

Some translations are inaccurately periphrastic in rendering Exo. 20:5 and 34:7 "punishing the children for the sin of the fathers," since the Hebrew simply says "visiting the **iniquity** of the fathers on the children"—parental sin patterns and sin guilt (Hebrew for "awon" primarily denotes "iniquity, [state of] guilt," and the meaning "punishment" is a less certain secondary sense of the word) will be visited upon, repaid to (Heb., Isa. 65:6; Jer. 32:18), or measured out (Heb. Isa. 65:7) upon the children.

The children will not be punished for their parent's sins but challenged and influenced by the sin-weaknesses and sin-tendencies of their parents *along with any accompanying spiritual bondage.* (Spiritual bondage is explicitly referred to in Hos. 4:12-13: see below.) The implicit challenge to the children in these passages (made explicit in Ezek. 18:20 and Jer. 31:29-30 which will be discussed later) is to repent and make a break with parental and generational sin rather than continue in it.

The Old Testament model of receiving forgiveness of sins is by confessing and repenting of our sins according to Prov. 28:13 ("whoever confesses and forsakes [sins] finds mercy"). In the Old Testament's view, one should confess not only personal sin but also parental and national sin according to Lev. 26:38-40.

Nehemiah's prayer in Neh. 1:6-9 shows that he understood that both confession and repentance are taught in the Covenantal Law codes of the Pentateuch and that both are necessarily inseparable aspects of turning away from sin and returning to the Lord.

We see the kind of confession of personal and corporate, generational sin which is prescribed in Lev. 26:40 practiced throughout Israel's history by Jeremiah (Jer. 3:25; 14:7, 20), the author who composed Ps. 106:6, and the congregation for whom it was written, by Daniel (Dan. 9:8, 20), by Ezra (Ezra 9:6-15), Nehemiah (Neh. 1:6-7), and by the restoration Jewish community of fifth century Jerusalem in Neh. 9:2.

This form of prayer is part of the covenantal background of the oft-quoted promises of II Chronicles 7:14: "If my people, who are called by my name, will humble themselves and pray and seek my face and turn from their wicked ways, then will I hear from heaven and will forgive their sin and will heal their land."

Furthermore, **Jesus, Peter, and Paul all assumed and made passing mention of the Old Testament concept of generational sin as an ongoing reality** in Mat. 23:32-35 ("Fill up then the measure [of the sin] of your forefathers," alluding to Gen. 15:16 and Lev. 18:25; "upon you will come all the righteous blood," alluding to the theme of blood-guilt in such passages as Isa. 59:3; Ezek. 9:9; and Lev. 20:9), in I Thess. 2:16 ("so as always to fill up [the measure of] their sin," alluding to Gen. 15:16 and Lev. 18:25), and I Pet. 1:18-19 ("the empty way of life handed down to us from our forefathers" which many scholars believe is a reference to pagan idolatry as in Exo. 20:5; Deut. 5:9).

Jesus states in **John 9:3** that the blindness of the man who was born blind was not caused by the man's sin or by his parent's sin. Many claim that this pronouncement of Jesus signals an end to the Old Testament principle of generational sin being visited upon later generations.

But this is simply not true. *Jesus simply asserts that in this case genera-*

tional sin and personal sin are not the cause of the man's blindness. Jesus could hardly be denying the general principle of generational sin in John 9:2-3 since he clearly assumes it in **Matt. 23:32-35** and two of his most devoted followers, Paul and Peter are likewise seen to be assuming it in I Thessalonians 2:16 and I Pet. 1:18.

I Peter 1:18-19 states that the precious blood of Christ saves us from the empty pattern of ancestral sin handed down to us by our forefathers. It is important to remember in connection with I Pet. 1:18-19 that the blood of Christ redeeming us at conversion does not dispense with our need to continue to confess sin and be cleansed by Christ's blood after putting our faith in Christ. I John 1:7-9 was written to believers:

> If we walk in the light...the blood of Jesus, his Son, purifies us from all sin. If we claim to be without sin, we deceive ourselves...If we confess our sins, he...will forgive us our sins." Interestingly, the word "purifies" is the Greek katharízei—a present indicative denoting an imperfective aspect or ongoing action that "keeps on purifying.

The fact that the Old Testament concept of generational sin is assumed in the New Testament suggests that the Old Testament corollary concept of confessing corporate, generational, and national sin is still a legitimate category of confession in New Testament faith.

And this conclusion is borne out by examples of corporate confession in later Christian confessional traditions, such as the Anglican corporate confessional prayer tradition and the post-World War II example in the German Lutheran Stuttgart Confession of Guilt.

But why...should we take responsibility for past sins in our family lines or the sins of our nation which we have not committed?

We Are A Royal Priesthood

First, I Peter 2:9 says that we are a "royal priesthood," and there is a priestly aspect to biblical examples of identificational repentance prayer. Even in cases where we have not personally committed corporate sins, we are confessing before God, John Dawson points out that "we can all identify with the roots of any given sin."[15] We may not have had an abortion, but we can identify with the lust, the love of comfort, the love of money, the rejection, and the unbelief which are the sinful root attitudes leading to abortion.

Jeremiah did not commit the sins he confessed in Jer. 3:25; 14:7, 20. Rather, he prophesied against the sins of Judah and Jerusalem and was persecuted for it (Jer. 2:1—5:31; 11:18-23; 12:6; 18:18-20; 20:2; 37:15-16; 38:6). Still, Jeremiah confessed Judah and Jerusalem's sins nonetheless according to the instruction of Lev. 26:40 (Jer. 14:20 "we acknowledge our wickedness and the iniquity of our fathers; we have . . . sinned against you"). When Ezra (Ezra 9:6-15), Nehemiah (Neh. 1:6f.), and Daniel (Dan. 9:8, 20) confessed the sin of their people, no evidence in any of the texts suggests they had personally committed all those sins. But in obedience to Lev. 26:40, they confessed their people's sins anyway, as Jeremiah before them had done.

Such Prayer Breaks Demonic Opposition

There is a second benefit to prayer involving identificational repentance for our families, churches, and nation. Daniel's example of identificational repentance in Daniel 9 and 10 shows that identificational repentance **breaks through the spiritual opposition of satanic principalities and powers.** Repentance from sin smashes the work of the devil because the devil and his forces work through sin in the world and in our lives (I John. 3:7-9; Eph. 4:26-27 and context).

> We have sinned, committed iniquity, acted wickedly, and rebelled, even turning aside from Your commandments and ordinances. Moreover, we have not listened to Your servants the prophets, who spoke in Your name to our kings, our princes, our fathers and all the people of the land. (Daniel 9:5-6)

Daniel's identificational repentance led to **a spiritual breakthrough in Dan. 9:20-22** when the angel Gabriel appeared to him. Dan. 9:3 mentions that Daniel was praying and fasting when he confessed his people's sins on that occasion. Dan 10:2-3, 12 shows that Daniel was praying and fasting on a second occasion. Prayer and fasting were often associated with confessing sin in the Old Testament (I Sam. 7:2-6; II Sam. 12:13, 16; Neh. 1:4-7; 9:1-2; Ps. 51:1ff.). This fact and the thematic similarity of Dan 9 and 10 suggest that in Dan. 10 Daniel would have been praying a prayer similar to the one he prayed in Dan. 9 including confessing his sins and the sins of his nation.

CAN WE SEEK FORGIVENESS FOR THE SINS OF OTHERS?

Doesn't the Bible show that we can only seek and receive forgiveness for our own sins and that we cannot remit the sins of others—we cannot receive God's forgiveness or apply God's forgiveness to the sins of others, whether families, corporate bodies, or nations from which we come or to which we belong?

If it were true that the Bible teaches one cannot seek or receive God's forgiveness on a corporate level for the sins of others, one would have a hard time explaining **why Moses did just that for Israel after their sin with the golden calf** (Exo. 32:9-14; 34:8-9; Deut. 9:18-29; 10:10-11; Ps. 106:23).

In Exo. 34:8-9 **he identifies himself with sins he did not commit,** "Forgive our wickedness and our sin." In Num. 14:13-20, he asked for the Lord's mercy and forgiveness for Israel's rebellious refusal to enter Canaan after the spies' bad report. And Moses received forgiveness for Israel: "The Lord replied, 'I have forgiven them as you asked" (Num. 14:20). **The Lord's intention to destroy Israel was abated because of Moses' intercession**. Moses did remit the sins of Israel; he sought and received God's forgiveness for them.

This kind of prophetic intercession was so basic to prophetic ministry from Moses onward that Samuel the prophet said it would be a sin for him not to pray for Israel regularly (I Sam. 12:23). This is precisely the kind of intercession the Lord looked for to avert His wrath and to extend forgiveness to His people according to Ezek. 22:29-30: "I looked for a man among them who would build up the wall and **stand in the breach** before me on behalf of the land so I would not have to destroy it."

In John 20:23, Jesus gives the disciples **the authority to forgive the sins of others**—to apply God's forgiveness to others. Paul also seems to expect the Corinthians to exercise such forgiveness toward a repentant member of the church in II Cor. 2:7-10. Again, this seems to suggest **a priestly function** which reflects the fact that we are a "royal priesthood" (I Pet. 2:9) who can receive and apply and proclaim God's forgiveness to others we pray for and pray with.

Similarly, **Ezra's** identificational repentance in Ezra 9:6-15 on behalf of the fifth century B.C. Jewish community of Jerusalem in Ezra 10:1-4, resulted in the people, for whom he was praying, being moved more freely to repent of their sins. **Nehemiah's** confessing his people's sins before God and asking God to forgive them on a corporate level in Neh. 1:6 along with Ezra's identificational repentance in Ezra 9:6-15 also seems to have released God's grace on a corporate level to move the community to weep openly and repent of their sins in Neh. 8:9-11 and 9:1-2, when Ezra read the Law.

Thus, the cases of Moses, Ezra and Nehemiah show that on *a corporate level,* God's mercy and forgiveness can be sought and received for those one identifies with through prayer. Individuals are still responsible to repent personally of their own sins (cf. Exo. 32:33-34; Num. 14:21-35, 37), but identificational repentance releases a measure of God's grace and forgiveness on the corporate level that helps move individuals to repentance and faith.

෩෨

Discussion Questions

1. What did you learn from this chapter?

2. What questions do you still have about identificational repentance?

3. Can Christians today do for America what Moses did for Israel when they sinned? If not, why not?

4. Is it possible God has withdrawn his promise to "remember the land" when we confess our sins and the sins of our forefathers as Lev. 26:39-42 states?

5. If what Dr. Greig writes is true, what will you do in response?

---

1. Gary Greig, "Healing the Land: What Does the Bible Say about Identificational Repentance, Prayer and Advancing God's Kingdom?" (Regent University Class Notes: August 22, 1996)

2. John Dawson, Healing America's Wounds (Ventura: Regal, 1994), 15.
3. Cindy Jacobs, Possessing the Gates of the Enemy (Tarrytown, Revell, 1991), 192ff., 236ff.; id., The Voice of God (Ventura,: Regal, 1995), 237ff.
4. J. E. Booty, ed., The Book of Common Prayer 1559: the Elizabethan Prayer Book (Washington: Folger Shakespeare Library, 1976), 300 (part of "The Order for the Visitation of the Sick").
5. Ibid., 582.
6. C. M. Guilbert, ed., The Book of Common Prayer (1789 Ratified Version of the Protestant Episcopal Church in the U.S.A.; New York: Church Hymnal Corp., 1979), 742.
7. The Standing Liturgical Commission of the Episcopal Church in the U.S.A., The Book of Occasional Services (New York: Church Hymnal Corp., 1979), 64 (Eighth Station of the Cross in the Service of the Way of the Cross).
8. C. Dunlop, Anglican Public Worship (London: SCM Press, 1953), p. 95.
9. "Mit grossem Schmerz sagen wir: Durch uns ist unendliches Leid über viele Völker und Länder gebracht worden. . . . Nun soll in unseren Kirchen ein neuer Anfang gemacht werden." Cited by M. Honecker, "Individuelle Schuld und Kollektive Verantwortung: Können Kollektive Sündigen? (Individual Guilt and Corporate Responsibility: Can Corporate Entities Sin?)," Zeitschrift für Theologie und Kirche 90 (1993): 217; id., "Geschichtliche Schuld und Kirchliches Bekenntnis (Historical Guilt and Ecclesiastical Confession)," Theologische Zeitschrift 42 (1986): 132-158; G. Besier and G. Sauter, Wie Christen Ihre Schuld Bekennen. Die Stuttgarter Erklärung (How Christians Confess Their Guilt. The Stuttgart Confession), Göttingen: Vandenhoek Ruprecht, 1985.
10. Ibid.
11. B. Klappert, Bekennende Kirche in Ökumenischer Verantwortung (The Confessing Church in Ecumenical Responsibility), (Munich: Chr. Kaiser, 1988).
12. This section is quoted only in part from Dr. Greig.
13. Baruch 1:15-3:8; Tobit 3:1-17; I Esdras 8:74-90; Qumran Manual of Discipline 1.23-26; etc.
14. Lev. 18:25; Num. 14:18, 33; Deut. 5:9; 7:10; Isa. 65:6-7; Jer. 32:18; cf. Job 21:19; Ps. 79:8; 109:14-16
15. Dawson, 95.

CHAPTER 24

A SAMPLE REPENTANCE SERVICE

FOR HAMPTON ROADS VIRGINIA

"If I shut up the heavens... and My people who are called by My name
humble themselves and pray and seek My face and turn from their
wicked ways, then I will hear from heaven, will forgive their sin and
will heal their land" (II Chron. 7:13-14).

THIS REPENTANCE SERVICE OUTLINE BELOW CAN BE MODIFIED FOR
use anywhere in the world to repent for past and current sins of any
group, city, region or nation so that God's Kingdom may come there in
greater power and blessing.

After all, Christians are a "royal priesthood"[1] who has direct access
to God to continue the work of Jesus in reconciling mankind to God.
We can "stand in the gap" on behalf of others so that God will nullify
His earthly penalties for sin by confessing our sins and the sins of our
forefathers. When we do that, God promises to heal our land.

Here in the Tidewater/Hampton Roads region, Christians, because
of their location, probably have special authority to confess and repent
for the deepest root sins of our Christian forefathers that began in the
Jamestown Colony!

"If the first piece of dough is holy, the lump is also; and if the root
is holy, the branches are too" (Rom 11:16).

How to Repent

In many ways, repenting as a group for corporate sins is not much different from repenting as an individual. When I wrong someone, I need to admit to myself exactly what was wrong, confess the specific sins to God, if possible, apologize to those wronged for specific offenses and make a commitment to God and to those offended not to commit that offense again. God puts a high value on such reconciliation between people.

> First, be reconciled to your brother, and then come and present your offering (Matt. 5:23-24).

Former FBI Special Agent, James Spence, has a website and book called Operation Heal America with detailed guidelines for churches to use to fast, confess and repent for sins in order to heal America.

Another friend, Pastor Jeffrey Daly, has several small books out on this subject. He even leads successful repentance movements in other nations.[2]

To repent, **I also may need to forgive** if I feel wronged. If we do not choose to forgive offenses, it opens us up to attack by the devil as Eph. 4:26-27 declares: "In your anger do not sin": Do not let the sun go down while you are still angry, and do not give the devil a foothold."

Also, if I can reverse the effects of my offense or make restitution for my mistakes, I would do that, too. This is the way that Christians normally should repent.

An Unforgettable Example

I'll never forget the day I got a knock on my door just before Christmas in Foley, Minnesota where I first pastored a church. I opened the door to see the Police Chief, a big, burly man, standing there with a little boy of about 10.

The officer said, "Go ahead, son. Tell him." Then, with a grimace born of much emotional pain (and perhaps some rear-end reinforcement), the little boy haltingly recounted how he had stolen some of the small, colored bulbs from our outdoor Christmas decorations and later smashed them for fun. He had done it to several homes.

"He's willing to pay for them, sir... Son, give them the money." The little boy sheepishly held out his hand with two crumbled dollars. I took them only because I knew what the father was doing was good for his son.

I was dumbfounded. Here was a father who knew how to lead his son in repentance. I so admired the humility of that Police Chief and the meek obedience of his reluctant son! It was a living parable of how we all should act when we as an individual... as a city...or as a nation have wronged others.

TWO SCRIPTURAL MODELS FOR HEALING AMERICA'S SOUL

Besides the clear promises and conditions of II Chronicles 7:14, in chapters eight to ten of Nehemiah[3], we see *God healing Israel's soul* as the Jews humbly repented for their sins and the sins of their ancestors.

As you may know, in 587 BC God banished His beloved Jews in Jerusalem to 70 years of cruel captivity in Babylon because they had turned their back on God for generations despite the many warnings of the prophets He sent calling them to repent.

Let's weave the principles from II Chronicles and Nehemiah above to construct a worship service outline for the Christians in Hampton Roads as they do their part to heal America's soul. Read Nehemiah 8-10 first to make this outline more understandable.

LEADERSHIP FOR THIS REVIVAL REPENTANCE SERVICE

Who organizes and leads this service is crucial. God looks:

1. at their hearts for holiness, purity and deep humility,
2. for people on both sides of the offenses with His authority to repent and forgive for full restoration to happen,
3. for people who closely represent the offending and offended parties (II Sam 21),

4. for people gifted in reconciling others to one another.

The **highest level of religious leaders** should participate in the leading of the service. Ezra, Nehemiah, the priests, and the Levites helped run the service (Neh.8:7, 9; 9:4-5).

The highest levels of government and business leaders attended and publicly committed themselves by signing a document to obey the scriptures that they and their ancestors had disobeyed repeatedly (Neh.9:38-10:39).

Leaders from Four Groups That Must Be Represented

Native Americans, Blacks, Women and Non-Anglican Christian Denominations who suffered discrimination by early Anglicans.

Leadership representatives should include:

1. **British people**, especially:
2. British businesspeople: God used businesspeople to establish Jamestown and to run the slave trade that started here in America.
3. Anglicans: Practically every offense was committed by those representing the Anglican faith in the earliest years of the colony. Later Anglicans purged the area of any non-Anglican Christians.
4. British Government people: Jamestown was founded by a royal charter from King James and it became a royal colony in 1624.
5. British Military: they enforced the laws that often sinned against others.
6. **Americans,** especially:
7. Businesspeople, in particular, city and regional business leaders: As members of the business community in Tidewater, they can repent with the British businesspeople who sent the colony here.
8. Anglican and Episcopal Leaders: As members of the Anglican Communion, only Episcopal priests representing congregations who have not endorsed homosexuality as a godly lifestyle would have the proper

spiritual authority to repent for the sins of their Anglican forbears here.

9. Denominational leaders: including Baptists, Quakers and others specifically discriminated against in early Tidewater.
10. Native Americans: Especially Virginia tribal chiefs.
11. Blacks: Especially those descended from Virginian slaves.
12. Whites: Especially those descended from Virginian indentured servants.
13. Women: Especially those with Virginia ancestors who were not landowners.
14. Tidewater government leaders: Mayors, city councils and police leaders.
15. Tidewater military leaders: especially the Navy and Marines have cultural ties to the British military.
16. A Jesuit leader to represent the first Christian martyrs in Virginia. Native American leaders could ask forgiveness for the treacherous slaughtering of the Spanish priests and brothers at Mass in 1571.
17. A Spanish government leader who can both confess their sins against the Native Americans here and forgive the Native Americans for the murder of their clergy. *In 2007, a Spanish Embassy staff person, Jose Marco, actually did this at Christopher Newport University in Tidewater on June 3, 2007.*

CALL FOR A SACRED ASSEMBLY

"And all the people gathered as one man at the square which was in front of the Water Gate." New. 8:1

It must be a large, public, lengthy and very official service. The more people, the better. All the exiles attended the service in Nehemiah 8:1. Today, a large stadium would work well.

While they stood in their place, they read from the book of the law of the LORD their God for a fourth of the day; and for another fourth, they confessed and worshiped the LORD their God.[4]

HUMBLE OURSELVES

Humble Themselves, Pray and Seek My Face (II Chronicles 7:14).

Confessing sins to heal a region or nation—past and present—demands real humility. God will know if we are sincere or not. In prayer, long before the service, we must ask God to search our hearts and show us **our personal sins and the sins of our corporate identities**—present and past—the groups we are part of and connected to:

Search me, O God, and know my heart; Try me and know my anxious thoughts; and see if there be any hurtful way in me, and lead me in the everlasting way.[5]

We humble ourselves with fasting, prayer and seeking God's face for days before the service with extended times of private and corporate communion with God and meditation on the scriptures.

"Now on the twenty-fourth day of this month, the sons of Israel assembled with fasting, in sackcloth and with dirt upon them."[6]

As we fast, we are seeking to know what we and our ancestors have done to offend God and to offend others that would bring God's wrath on our land.[7]

We also should humbly ask representatives of those we or our ancestors have sinned against to suggest **what we can do to bring reconciliation** between us so that they can bless us as a people.

When God brought a three-year famine on Israel due to the sins of the former King Saul, David asked God for direction and then went to those offended—and that led to the healing of the land.[8]

Pastors, especially, and other Christian leaders in Hampton Roads should attend while fasting and walking in humility before God and each other.

WORSHIP HIM!

"If My People" (II Chronicles 7:14)

Worship the Father and thank Him for our precious, saving relationship with Him through Jesus, for all he has done for us and our group, city or nation.

Thank and praise Him for specific blessings He has given your group now and, in the past. (Nehemiah 9:5-33)

You must have God's Presence with you in power whenever you come to Him with regional or national sins. The stakes are high and God's Spirit must be in control of the whole process or it will fall short of what you need and what God wants.[9]

If the ones offended will come, invite them to join you in this celebration of who God is and who we are in Him.

SCRIPTURE MUST BE READ

"Then Ezra the priest brought the law before the assembly of men, women...He read from it before the square which was in front of the Water Gate from early morning until midday."[10]

Generous amounts of God's commands must be read to specifically remind us of where we and our ancestors have failed to obey God's commands.[11]

CONFESS SINS

"Turn from Their Wicked Ways" (II Chronicles 7:14)

"The descendants of Israel separated themselves from all foreigners, and stood and confessed their sins and the iniquities of their fathers..."
[12]

Specific personal and corporate sins—current and past— must be thoroughly confessed by the leaders present before the entire gathering. The list of sins in Chapter Two is a good place to start.

COMMIT TO REPENT

Reaffirm that we are committed to fully obey God out of love for Him and holy fear of His discipline as Our Heavenly Father (Hebrews 12:5-11). According to Jesus, that is how we show God our love (John 14:15, 21; 15:10; I John 2-3 2, John 1:6).

Here we can also publicly renounce living for the world, the flesh or the devil and recommit ourselves to following Jesus in obedience to all His commands to honor the Father by the power of the Spirit!

We can also publicly and formally commit ourselves **in writing** to obey the specific scriptures we and our ancestors have disobeyed:

> Now because of all this, **we are making an agreement in writing**; and on the sealed document are the names of our leaders, our Levites and our priests...[13]are joining with their kinsmen, their nobles, and are taking on themselves a curse and an oath to walk in God's law, which was given through Moses, God's servant, and to keep and to observe all the commandments of GOD our Lord, and His ordinances and His statutes...[14]

The leaders of our region could sign this public statement promising that they and their followers will, by God's grace, never again commit the specific sins that we and our ancestors have committed.

In that written statement, our leaders can also call all believers to **walk in the opposite spirit** to the sins we have just confessed, as in the following examples.

1. Instead of the love of money ruling our lives, we could commit to always following the example and commands of Jesus no matter what the financial consequences.

2. Instead of abusing others—our workers, native people, women,

other denominational believers or immigrants—for personal gain, we can commit to loving our neighbor as ourselves, even when they are our enemy—as Jesus commands in the Sermon on the Mount (Matt. 5-7).

3. Instead of discriminating against women and abusing them sexually, we can commit to treating them with all fairness and purity. (Gal. 3:28; 1 Tim. 5:2)

4. Instead of using lies, deceit and treachery to cover our mistakes and our real motives, we can promise to love each other without hypocrisy (Rom. 12:9; 1 Peter 2:1, 3:10)

See Nehemiah 10: 30-39 for a complete list of the specific scriptures they swore an oath to now follow. They later broke some of these promises (Nehemiah 13). Sadly, this may be part of the reason God gave His beloved Israel over to the Romans to be conquered again in 70 AD. May God protect our nation from that kind of judgment!

HOLD THIS SERVICE ON A FRIDAY

Fifty-one years apart, Native Americans attacked and killed Christians who came to invade their land on a Friday.

On Friday,[15] February 9, 1571, six Spanish Jesuits and four Spanish helpers were betrayed and murdered while the priests said Mass not far from Yorktown.

On Friday,[16] March 22, 1622 (in the British Julian Calendar), thousands of Powhatan Indians murdered 350 settlers.

Those Fridays represent so much of what went wrong among everyone involved in the colony. *Let's reverse the meaning of that day* by coming before God to seek reconciliation with God and with all the groups represented at Jamestown.

BUILD BRIDGES OF LOVE

Before, during, and after this service, believers can build bridges of love with every group represented, regardless of what god they follow. These words of confession and repentance must be authenticated by acts of kindness, friendship, trust and affection for one another if the fruit of this service is to last. Where restitution by individuals can be made, it should be made in whatever way seems appropriate. Let's see each other through the eyes of our loving Father who has shown such deep and consistent mercy to us in Jesus. Love and respect have to be more than words. John Dawson's book and video series, Healing America's Wounds, does a great job of describing how to build bridges of love between groups.

ARE CHRISTIANS IN AMERICA READY FOR THIS?

Every city in America could do such a similar service to bring healing and reconciliation to their region for the sins that have been committed there, present and past. *But will they?*

Probably not yet. Prosperity has lulled many Christians to sleep on issues like this. Most of the American Church may *not be desperate enough* yet to repent deeply for their current sins, not to mention our ancestral sins that started in Jamestown. Sin and repentance are not popular topics in sermons in many churches. *That has to change if America is to be healed.*

But thankfully, *God is more committed to our holiness than to our happiness!* Out of His passionate love for us, He is currently allowing America to grow sicker and sicker with sin to make His Church desperate enough to get right with Him so He can heal America—just as He did with His beloved Jewish nation many times, as seen in the Book of Judges seven times mentioned in Chapter Six.

But here is what I see happening. This is why I have great hope in the midst of America's deepening moral and mental darkness:

As America's soul gets painfully sicker with sin, and society becomes increasingly painful, the pain will eventually awaken **the sleeping giant of the American Church** to prayer, confession, repentance and collaborative action to love and serve our communities with the Gospel in word and deed.
God is going to use it to drive us back into His arms and into another Great Awakening, which alone can save America.

I believe that with all my heart. God is allowing all this current spiritual, political and cultural craziness to prove how badly we need Him. Once we come back to Him, God will release another Great Awakening which alone can save America—the nation He founded and loves. He longs to be gracious to us (Is.30:18), but He is waiting.

"If My people"…God is waiting on us.

Discussion Questions

    1. What would you change in this service?

    2. What parts do you like?

    3. Do you think this could happen one day?

    4. What would you be willing to do to help make it happen?

---

1. I Peter 2:9
2. https://bobfox.org/malawi-kneels-in-repentance/ (29 Dec. 2022)
3. https://www.biblegateway.com/passage/?search=Neh.+8%3A1-10%3A39&version=NASB1995 (22 Dec. 2022)
4. Nehemiah 9:3
5. Psalm 139:23-24
6. Nehemiah 9:1
7. II Chronicles 7:13
8. II Sam. 21
9. See II Kings 13:18-19 when partial obedience led to partial results.
10. Neh. 8:2-3
11. Nehemiah 8:3; 9:3
12. Nehemiah 9:2
13. Nehemiah 9:38
14. Nehemiah 10:29
15. http://www.timeanddate.com/calendar/index.html?year=1571&country=1 (17 March 2020)
16. https://www.dayoftheweek.org/?m=March&d=22&y=1622&go=Go says it was a Friday.
    https://www.genuki.org.uk/big/easter/C?year=1622 agrees
    As does http://5ko.free.fr/en/jul.php?y=1622
    You have to use the Julian calendar, not the Gregorian one we use today that was introduced in October 1582 by Pope Gregory XIII

ABOUT THE AUTHOR

For over 35 years, my wife and I have lived in the Tidewater/Hampton Roads area of Virginia—about 45 minutes from Jamestown, Virginia. In the 50-plus years that Beth and I have been married, God has blessed us with four godly children and thirteen wonderful grandchildren.

I've been a Catholic seminarian, Marine F-4 recon pilot during the Vietnam War, a Naval Reserve Chaplain, database administrator, painting contractor— and for over 35 years, a Protestant church pastor in several denominations. Along the way, I've earned a BA in History and a Master of Divinity— but my love relationship with God has taught me the most important things in life.

Interestingly enough, parts of my life connect with Jamestown. I was born in my grandmother's home in Great Britain (Scotland) and came to America by ship—just like the Jamestown colonists in 1607! After moving here, I always had a sense that the history of this region was part of the reason God brought me here.

My greatest passion has always been to help people around the world make it to heaven through a real relationship with God through Jesus Christ. I pray that this book and *Angel 24* will help send the Gospel around the world through a repentant and revived American Church.

Angel 24

PS. When I wrote this book in 2002, I had no idea that in 2005 God would lead me to write a novel based on it. Sixteen years later, **Angel 24** is that novel. I think you and your children will enjoy it. It is the familiar story of Pocahontas, Captain John Smith and the

Jamestown Colony as you have never heard it! More details are on the next page.

Contact me at:

https://healing-americas-soul.com

More details about me and my books at https://hisherospress.com

Email: bob@healing-americas-soul.com **for a free digital gift from the author.**

Go to our Facebook page below for quick answers to common questions.

If you are reading the digital version, please leave a review on **Amazon here.**

facebook.com/bobfoxbook

instagram.com/bobfox_author

ANGEL 24

A NOVEL BASED ON THIS BOOK

A historical thriller about the intense spiritual warfare between angels, demons and rebel angels that almost destroyed the Jamestown Colony.

Angel 24 tells the dramatic story of an emotionally damaged angel named Scion who survived the Great Rebellion in heaven and now is assigned to protect the 1607 Jamestown Colony from the wicked schemes of his former best friend.

It's the story of John Smith, Pocahontas and her Powhatan tribes as few have ever imagined. Sample chapters at the back of this book!

Book details at https://angel24book.com or use this QR code:

A Historical Fantasy Thriller

Angel 24 is the story of Scion, a powerful angel who was emotionally damaged in the Great Rebellion in Heaven. Now, he has been assigned to protect the 1607 Jamestown Colony from the wicked schemes of his former best friend!

... wildly creative characters will captivate readers of all ages who enjoy an epic thriller
—*Dr. Randy Clark - Network of Global Awakening*

... uniquely and creatively brings light to the realities of the wars in the unseen realms...
—*Doug Stringer - Somebody Cares International*

ANGEL 24

BOB FOX

SPIRITUAL WARFARE AUTHOR
BOB FOX

ANGEL 24

FIGHTS TO DEFEND THE 1607 JAMESTOWN COLONY FROM THE WICKED SCHEMES OF HIS FORMER BEST FRIEND!

APPENDIX A

This apology is in response to the many tragic human rights abuses and broken treaties that our federal government oversaw for hundreds of years against Native Americans. **But it never passed.**

HISTORIC RESOLUTION OF APOLOGY TO NATIVE PEOPLES INTRODUCED IN U.S. CONGRESS

A historic Resolution of Apology to the Native American peoples was introduced in the U.S. Congress by Senators Sam Brownback (R-KS), Ben Nighthorse Campbell (R-CO) and Daniel K. Inouye (D-HI) on the evening of May 6, 2004, National Day of Prayer.

It was reintroduced as RESOLUTION S.J RES. 15 on April 19, 2005. It has been forgotten by Congress.

In his remarks on the Senate floor, Sen. Brownback stated, "This is a resolution of apology and a resolution of reconciliation. It is a first step toward healing the wounds that have divided us for so long-a a potential foundation for a new era of positive relations between Tribal Governments and the Federal Government. Before reconciliation, there must be recognition and repentance. Before there is a durable relationship, there must be understanding."

REMARKS ON SENATE FLOOR AND TEXT OF RESOLUTION S.J. RES. 37
From the Congressional Record, May 6, 2004

MR. BROWNBACK. Mr. President, I rise today to introduce before this body a joint resolution that seeks to address an issue that has long lain unresolved. That issue is our Nation's relationship with the Native peoples of this land.

Long before 1776 and the establishment of the United States of America, this land was inhabited by numerous nations. Like our Nation, many of these peoples held a strong belief in the Creator and maintained a powerful spiritual connection to this land. Since the formation of the American Republic, there have most certainly been numerous conflicts between our Government and many of these Tribes —conflicts in which warriors on all sides fought courageously and in which all sides suffered. However, even from the earliest days of the Republic, there existed a sentiment that honorable dealings and peaceful coexistence were preferable to bloodshed. Indeed, our predecessors in Congress in 1787 stated in the Northwest Ordinance:

"The utmost good faith shall always be observed toward the Indians."

Many treaties were made between this Republic and the American Indian Tribes. Treaties, as my colleagues in this Chamber know, are far more than words on a page. Treaties are our word, our bond. Treaties with other governments are not to be treated lightly. *Unfortunately, too often the United States of America did not uphold its responsibilities as stated in its covenants with the Native American Tribes.* **Too often, our Government broke its oaths to the Native peoples**.

I want my fellow Senators to know that this resolution does not dismiss the valiance of our American soldiers who bravely fought for their families in wars between the United States and different Indian Tribes. Nor does this resolution cast all the blame for the various battles on one side or another. What this resolution does is recognize and honor the importance of Native Americans to this land and our Nation—in the past and today—and **offers an official apology to the Native peoples for the poor and painful choices our Government sometimes made to disregard its solemn word.**

This is a resolution of apology and a resolution of reconciliation. It is a first step toward healing the wounds that have divided us for so long—a potential foundation for a new era of positive relations between Tribal governments and the Federal Government. It is time—it is past time—for us to heal our land of division, all divisions, and bring us together as one people.

Before reconciliation, there must be recognition and repentance. Before there is a durable relationship, there must be understanding. This resolution will not authorize or serve as a settlement of any claim against the United States, nor will it resolve the many
challenges still facing the Native peoples. But it does recognize the negative impact of numerous deleterious Federal acts and policies on Native Americans and their cultures. Moreover, it begins the effort of reconciliation by recognizing the past wrongs and repenting for them.

Martin Luther King, a true reconciler, once said, "The end is reconciliation, the end is redemption, the end is the creation of the beloved community." This resolution is not the end. But perhaps it signals the beginning of the end of division and the faint first light and first fruits of the creation of beloved community.

S. J. RES. 15

[Report No. 109-113]

To acknowledge a long history of official depredations and ill-conceived policies by the United States Government regarding Indian tribes and offer an apology to all Native Peoples on behalf of the United States. ß

IN THE SENATE OF THE UNITED STATES

1. April 19, 2005

Mr. BROWNBACK (for himself, Mr. DORGAN, Mr. DODD, Mr. INOUYE, Mr. COCHRAN, Mr. AKAKA, Mrs. BOXER, Mr. CRAPO, Mr. JOHNSON, Ms. LANDRIEU, Mr. LAUTENBERG, Ms. CANTWELL, and Mr. INOUYE) introduced the following joint resolution; which was read twice and referred to the Committee on Indian Affairs

1. July 28, 2005

Reported by Mr. MCCAIN, without amendment
JOINT RESOLUTION
To acknowledge a long history of official depredations and ill-conceived policies by the United States Government regarding Indian tribes and offer an apology to all Native Peoples on behalf of the United States.

Whereas the ancestors of today's Native Peoples inhabited the land of the present-day United States since time immemorial and for thousands of years before the arrival of peoples of European descent;

Whereas the Native Peoples have for millennia honored, protected, and stewarded this land we cherish;

Whereas the Native Peoples are spiritual peoples with a deep and abiding belief in the Creator, and for millennia their peoples have maintained a powerful spiritual connection to this land, as is evidenced by their customs and legends;

Whereas the arrival of Europeans in North America opened a new chapter in the histories of the Native Peoples;

Whereas, while the establishment of permanent European settlements in North America did stir conflict with nearby Indian tribes, peaceful and mutually beneficial interactions also took place;

Whereas the foundational English settlements in Jamestown, Virginia, and Plymouth, Massachusetts, *owed their survival in large measure to the compassion and aid of the Native Peoples in their vicinities*;

Whereas in the infancy of the United States, the founders of the Republic expressed their desire for a just relationship with the Indian tribes, as evidenced by the Northwest Ordinance enacted by Congress in 1787, which begins with the phrase, `The utmost good faith shall always be observed toward the Indians';

Whereas Indian tribes provided great assistance to the fledgling Republic as it strengthened and grew, including invaluable help to Meriwether Lewis and William Clark on their epic journey from St. Louis, Missouri, to the Pacific Coast;

Whereas Native Peoples and non-Native settlers engaged in numerous armed conflicts;

Whereas the **United States Government violated many of the treaties ratified by Congress and other diplomatic agreements with Indian tribes;**

Whereas this Nation should address the broken treaties and many of the more ill-conceived Federal policies that followed, such as **extermination, termination, forced removal and relocation, the outlawing of traditional religions, and the destruction of sacred places;**

Whereas the United States forced Indian tribes and their citizens to move away from their traditional homelands and onto federally established and controlled reservations, in accordance with such Acts as the Indian Removal Act of 1830;

Whereas many Native Peoples suffered and perished—

(1) during the execution of the official United States Government policy of forced removal, including the **infamous Trail of Tears and Long Walk;**

(2) during bloody armed confrontations and massacres, such as the Sand Creek Massacre in 1864 and the Wounded Knee Massacre in 1890; and

(3) on numerous Indian reservations;

Whereas the United States Government condemned the traditions, beliefs, and customs of the Native Peoples and endeavored to assimilate them by such policies as the redistribution of land under the General Allotment Act of 1887 and the **forcible removal of Native children from their families to faraway boarding schools**

where their Native practices and languages were degraded and forbidden;

Whereas officials of the United States Government and private United States citizens harmed Native Peoples by the **unlawful acquisition of recognized tribal land and the theft of tribal resources and assets from recognized tribal land;**

Whereas the policies of the United States Government toward Indian tribes and the **breaking of covenants with Indian tribes** have contributed to the severe social ills and economic troubles in many Native communities today;

Whereas, despite the wrongs committed against Native Peoples by the United States, the Native Peoples have remained committed to the protection of this great land, as evidenced by the fact that, on a per capita basis, more Native people have served in the United States Armed Forces and placed themselves in harm's way in defense of the United States in every major military conflict than any other ethnic group;

Whereas Indian tribes have actively influenced the public life of the United States by continued cooperation with Congress and the Department of the Interior, through the involvement of Native individuals in official United States Government positions, and by the leadership of their own sovereign Indian tribes;

Whereas Indian tribes are resilient and determined to preserve, develop, and transmit to future generations their unique cultural identities;

Whereas the National Museum of the American Indian was established within the Smithsonian Institution as a living memorial to the Native Peoples and their traditions; and

Whereas Native Peoples are endowed by their Creator with certain unalienable rights, and that among those are life, liberty, and the pursuit of happiness: Now, therefore, be it

Resolved by the Senate and House of Representatives of the United States of America in Congress assembled,

I. **SECTION 1. ACKNOWLEDGMENT AND APOLOGY.**

The United States, acting through Congress—

(1) recognizes the special legal and political relationship the Indian tribes have with the United States and the solemn covenant with the land we share;

(2) commends and honors the Native Peoples for the thousands of years that they have stewarded and protected this land;

(3) recognizes that there have been years of official depredations, ill-conceived policies, and the breaking of covenants by the United States Government regarding Indian tribes;

(4) apologizes on behalf of the people of the United States to all Native Peoples for the many instances of violence, maltreatment, and neglect inflicted on Native Peoples by citizens of the United States;

(5) expresses its regret for the ramifications of former wrongs and its commitment to build on the positive relationships of the past and present to move toward a brighter future where all the people of this land live reconciled as brothers and sisters, and harmoniously steward and protect this land together;

(6) urges the President to acknowledge the wrongs of the United States against Indian tribes in the history of the United States in order to bring healing to this land by providing a proper foundation for reconciliation between the United States and Indian tribes; and

(7) commends the State governments that have begun reconciliation efforts with recognized Indian tribes located within their boundaries and encourages all State governments similarly to work toward reconciling relationships with Indian tribes within their boundaries.

1. **SEC. 2. DISCLAIMER.**

Nothing in this Joint Resolution—

(1) authorizes or supports any claim against the United States; or

(2) serves as a settlement of any claim against the United States.

ANNOTATED BIBLIOGRAPHY

Please use this link or the QR to buy some of these books.

 Dawson, John. *Healing America's Wounds* (Regal Books, CA, 1994) Without a doubt, **the first and finest treatment of identificational confession and repentance** that I know of. I just rediscovered this book as I was doing this 2023 Study Edition. The book and the video series by the same name are much better than this book for understanding how *relationships between people groups are healed through identificational confession and repentance*. John has been preaching and teaching on this since the 1990s. I highly recommend it. The video series brings the book to life with powerful interviews with Christian leaders in the white, Native American and black communities, along with great historical footage.

Dawson, John. Taking Our Cities for God (Creation House, Lake Mary, FL, 1989) is Similar to *Healing America's Wounds* which came later (1994), but with detailed chapters on spiritual warfare and spiritual mapping.

Fischer, David Hackett. *Albion's Seed: Four British Folkways in*

America (Oxford University Press, New York, 1989). This book was recommended to me by Dr. Charles Wolfe, President of The Plymouth Rock Foundation there (https://plymrock.org/). He *considers Fisher's book a masterpiece.* T.J. Stiles calls this book a "provocative, staggeringly detailed study...truly a seminal work and the source of many of my numbers and names" (ibid, p.xɪv). Albion's Seed is so crucial to what I have written in this book that I quote below what the publisher, Oxford University Press, says of it:

"This book is...a history of American folkways as they have changed through time, and it argues a thesis about the importance for the United States of having been British in its cultural origins.

From 1629 to 1775, North America was settled by four great waves of English-speaking immigrants. The first was an exodus of Puritans from the east of England to Massachusetts (1629-1640). The second was the movement of a Royalist elite and indentured servants from the south of England to Virginia (ca. 1649-75). The third was the "Friends' migration,"—the Quakers—from the North Midlands and Wales to the Delaware Valley (ca. 1675-1725). The fourth was a great flight from the borderlands of North Britain and Northern Ireland to the American backcountry (ca. 1717-75).

These four groups differed in many ways—in religion, rank, generation and place of origin. They brought to America different folkways which became the basis of regional cultures in the United States. They spoke distinctive English dialects and built their houses in diverse ways. They had different ideas of family, marriage and gender; different practices of child-naming and child-raising; different attitudes toward sex, age and death; different rituals of worship and magic; different forms of work and play; different customs of food and dress; different traditions of education and literacy; different modes of settlement and association. They also had profoundly different ideas of comity, order, power and freedom which derived from British folk traditions. *Albion's Seed* describes those differences in detail and discusses the continuing importance of their transference to America.

Today most people in the United States (more than 80 percent) have no British ancestors at all. These many other groups, even while preserving their own ethnic cultures, have also assimilated regional folkways, which were transplanted from Britain to America. In that sense, nearly all Americans today are "Albion's Seed," no matter what their ethnic origins may be; but they are so in their different regional ways. The concluding section of *Albion's Seed* explores the ways that regional cultures have continued to dominate national politics from 1789 to 1988, and still control attitudes toward education, government, gender, and violence, on which differences between American regions are greater than between European nations. (Emphases mine) *What Professor Fischer calls "folkways" roughly defines what I call the "spiritual DNA" of a people or region.*

Graham, Jerry L. *Toward the Spiritual Mapping of south Hampton Roads, Virginia*. (Unpublished paper submitted to Regent University Virginia Beach, VA, 1996.) Dr. Graham is a former engineer, pastor, church consultant and now personal coach. I not only appreciate his scholarship but his encouragement to me as a new writer.

Greig, Gary "Healing the Land: What Does the Bible Say about Identificational Repentance, Prayer and Advancing God's Kingdom?" (Regent University Class Notes: August 22, 1996) Dr. Greig's friendship, expertise and passion for this subject helped me to believe that I could write about it with greater biblical precision and confidence.

Haile, Edward Wright. *Jamestown Narratives: Eyewitness Accounts of the Virginia Colony*, (Roundhouse, Champlain, Virginia, 1998). The finest one-volume collection of first-person, primary source documents on the first 10 years of the Virginia colony's history: fascinating details and fairly easy reading.

Harriot, Thomas. *A Briefe and True Report of the New Found Land of Virginia* (Dover Publications, Inc., New York, 1972). The 1590 edition by Theodore de Bry with illustrations by John White.

Tremendous, first-hand accounts of life in the Outer Banks area of what is now North Carolina and what was then first called Virginia. Harriot and White both helped found this ill-fated colony in 1585-1590. *Harriot's concern for the salvation of the native people and their keen interest in the Gospel is especially revealing (pp.27,71).* One of America's earliest and most accurate descriptions of life in the New World.

Horn, James. *A Land As God Made It: Jamestown and the Birth of America (Basic Books, New York, 2005).* A very readable story of the first

168 years of our nation as British colonists (1607-1775) written by a local Tidewater historian who is the Director of the John D. Rockefeller, Jr. Library at The Colonial Williamsburg Foundation. A fair, well-documented and enjoyable book!

Johnson, Paul. *A History of America* (New York: HarperCollins, 1998). This British historian has written a much-acclaimed, very readable history of the United States with a strong conservative perspective and a high regard for the role of religion in American history.

O'Rourke, Marty. *Community Transformation*, (Unpublished Paper for Regent University, Virginia Beach, VA., 2001). The Rev. Dr. O'Rourke is one of my best friends and my favorite "repenters"s for the sins of colonial Anglicans. He and others have lovingly walked with me through the many years that birthed this book. He is a pastor's pastor.

Otis, George Jr. *Informed Intercession* (Ventura, CA: Renew Books, 1999). His books, videos and the class I took at Regent University have been tremendous catalysts for my understanding and passion for this kind of research and revival preparation.

Parramore, Thomas C. with Peter C. Stewart and Tommy L. Bogger. *Norfolk, The First Four Centuries* (University of Virginia, Charlottesville, 1994). This is standard work on this region and was written by three history professors, two from the Norfolk area.

Raeburn, M.J. *America's Dedication to God Series: Booklet One: Richard Hakluyt's Contribution (His* Story Seminars, Virginia Beach, VA., 1994). George and Jan know more about Rev. Hakluyt than anyone I know. They are keen defenders of America's Christian roots.

Spelman, Henry. *Relation of Virginia, 1609*, quoted by Edward Wright Haile, editor, *Jamestown Narratives: Eyewitness Accounts of the Virginia Colony*, (Roundhouse, Champlain, VA. 1998). The most complete, single-volume collection of first-hand accounts from Jamestown I've found. A goldmine of references.

Stiles, T.J., ed *In their Own Words: The Colonizers* (The Berkley Publishing Group, New York, 1998). A wonderfully arranged collection of first-hand accounts from the first European colonists of America with good sections on Jamestown. *T.J., the author, was a teenager in the First Presbyterian Church of Foley, MN while I was the pastor!* Small world!

The Columbia Electronic Encyclopedia, Sixth Edition (Columbia University Press, 2003) Licensed from Columbia University Press. www.cc.columbia.edu/cu/cup/ and very easy to use.

Upton, Rachel. *History of the Suppression/ Oppression of Women: Tidewater Virginia* (Unpublished paper for Regent University Master's level class, 1998). Rachel was an intern with me in city-church work when she wrote this. Her conclusions greatly influenced a women's conference led by Dr. Cindy Jacobs here soon after as they grappled with the generational sins of this area. Rachel's husband is Jason Upton—one of the most gifted revival, prophetic singer/musicians in the world today. Check out the music reviews about him on the web. He has a message and a song for reconciliation, renewal and unity that is an awesome instrument for revival in God's hand. His webpage: www.jasonupton.com

Wagner, C. Peter. *Breaking Strongholds In Your City: How to Use Spiritual Mapping to Make Your Prayers More Strategic.* (Ventura, CA. Regal Books, 1993). Dr. Wagner was a former professor of mine at Fuller Seminary and has been a model for me over the last 30 years. He is a global missionary statesman with apostolic gifts to build networks of Christian leaders around emerging God-given ministry frontiers on several fronts.

Willison, George F. *Behold Virginia: The Fifth Crown,* (Harcourt and Brace & Co., NY, 1952). One of the best-researched and least sanitized books on the founding of Virginia. He calls a spade a spade.

Wink, Walter, *When the Powers Fall: Reconciliation in the Healing of Nations,* (Fortress Press, 1998). Dr. Wink is a well-known theologian with special insight into important topics many writers miss. This is one of them. His book about how Jesus dealt with demons is excellent.

ANGEL 24: SAMPLE

PROLOGUE

ANGELS WERE EVERYWHERE.

Thousands of six-foot choir angels swirled above the fiery Throne of God in an ever-expanding cone of concentric circles, moving in opposing, alternating directions as high as the eye could see. Faces of brown, black, yellow, and white spun together in a blur of light and motion. Their childlike shouts of joy and their ringing peals of laughter formed a contagious counterpoint to the massive choruses of praise echoing across the vast expanse of heaven.

Just below that whirlwind of worship, a rippling, iridescent rainbow arched regally over the Throne. Lightning and thunderous, staccato voices shot up into the angelic cone from the throats of dozens of eight-foot, golden-headed Cherubim and Seraphim who sang as they soared up and down its center, adding a complex vocal drumbeat to the rhythm of the rotating choir.

All around them, watchful and majestic, a hundred thousand fierce, ten-foot Warrior Angels with faces like burning bronze lined the walls of heaven—wings furled, arms akimbo, massive swords at the ready. Multitudes of the six-foot angels sped past them, racing out of Heaven's Gates, headed for Earth with assignments to serve the saints.

☙❦❧

IT HAD NOT ALWAYS BEEN that way.

Once, there were no huge Warrior Angels or swords in heaven— just one hundred eighty thousand, unarmed, six-foot angels to serve the Court of Heaven. They all lived in great contentment, enjoying one another and the incredible pleasures of heaven. Although the angels were males, their love for one another was stronger, deeper, and purer than any human could ever know.

But, just as God decided to make Adam and Eve, eighty thousand beautiful angels disappeared in a way no angel could have ever foreseen.

Lucifer rebelled against God! He and sixty thousand of his rebel angels were cast out of heaven in what God called the Great Rebellion. Twenty thousand loyal angels died in the fierce battle to protect heaven. The sixty thousand became Lucifer's Dark Angels. The remaining one hundred thousand in heaven lost their best friends, closest companions and comrades-in-arms . . . forever!

Because of this, the Great Rebellion was immediately followed by the Great Grief. God himself grieved deeply for centuries at the loss of eighty thousand beloved sons.

For hundreds of years, the Great Grief muffled the joy of heaven. Angel poets later wrote that God and the angels released their tears of sadness on the Earth during Noah's time, flooding the Earth with water.

Shortly after the Great Rebellion, the Lord of Hosts restructured heaven for war. God immediately gave many of his remaining angels ten-foot-tall, massive physiques and long, sharp swords. They became the Warrior Angels in the Host of Heaven, the ones who now protect heaven under Archangel Michael's leadership. God also established a War Room where Michael and his angelic staff would coordinate heaven's plans against Lucifer's Dark Angels. At roughly the same time, Lucifer somehow spawned billions of new creatures that would later be called demons.

But after thousands of years of vicious combat between the Host of

Heaven and Lucifer's evil forces, God revealed his ultimate solution to rescue mankind. God planned to send his Son, Jesus, to destroy Satan's wicked works on Earth! The angels were ecstatic!

Next, God began to create billions of new angels to serve the vast throngs of people on Earth who would soon become disciples of Jesus. Their assignments varied. Sometimes, they passed messages to a Christian from the Holy Spirit. At other times, they guide the person away from danger in ways that are usually unnoticeable.

These new angels were called Mod1 Angels. They are six-foot-tall, handsome males with glowing skin in stunning shades of black, brown, beige, yellow and red. Their eyes were mesmerizing, sparkling hues of brown, green, blue and grey framed by shoulder-length hair. Even though they carry no sword, these muscular Mod1s look formidable in flight with their massive, pearly white twelve-foot wingspans, glistening white robe that hung down to the ankles, cinched at the waist with a wide, golden belt.

At the same time, the Lord created six million Mod2 Scout Angels to monitor the movements of Satan's forces. Mod2s are small and harder to detect by the enemy. They range in size from fourteen to eighteen inches. However, they are equipped with the most powerful visual and auditory sensors any angel has ever had.

To the surprise of every angel in heaven, God made all Mod2s *female*—the first ever seen in heaven. Most male angels were in shock when they heard it. They were even more stunned when God allowed the small, female Mod2s to change the color of their hair, clothes and wings as often as they desired.

In order to train all those new angels for service in the Earth war zone, God created Angel Academy. After six months of intense training, each angel would be released to serve the saints on Earth. Every angel could hardly wait for the day when they would fight to protect God's people from demonic temptations and every form of evil.

Finally, God decided to save one continent on Earth from discovery by men for thousands of years. From that continent, the Lord planned to launch His final assault on Lucifer, whom he now called Satan. So, in the 1500s of earth time, God allowed Great Britain to start a colony of Christians on that continent. God planned to use this new settlement to birth a nation unlike any other—a nation that would help vast numbers of people from all over the globe make it to heaven. For this special job, God decided to use a special angel—but one that the other angels would never have chosen.

Angel 24.

ANGEL 24: SAMPLE
CHAPTER ONE

12,000 BC

Deep in the frigid, inky fringes of the universe, a dazzling, golden angel sped past a pale, red planet as he furiously wrote in a notebook. He was measuring the rate of expansion of the universe at its outer limits. He tried to focus on the final complex mathematical measurements he was making, but his mind was elsewhere. He was one of twenty-four prototype angels in Archangel Academy being trained to become heaven's first Earth archangels. Although this flight was just a class exercise, the platinum-haired scout knew he had to do his very best. After all, Lucifer, the Headmaster of Archangel Academy, had personally chosen him for this difficult task. He also wanted to look his very best. As soon as he returned to heaven, he would have to report directly to Lucifer. So, just before he left for deep space, he borrowed a pair of new shoes from another angel at the academy.

Now, after a week of hard work far from heaven, he was anxious to finish the last few measurements and return to heaven. Just before he left on this mission, his best friend at the academy, Kai, had nervously confided to him that Lucifer was planning a big surprise for heaven. Kai was not allowed to say what it was—just that heaven would never forget it. Now, even in the four-hundred-and-fifty-four-degrees-below-zero vacuum of space, the lone angel felt warm all over just imagining the excitement and fun that surprise would be. Lucifer was famous for being bold and creative. *No angel had ever planned to surprise all of heaven,* Scion mused. *This is going to be spectacular!*

But there was something about how Kai acted that still puzzled Scion. He has never seen Kai so passionate. When he told him about Lucifer's surprise plans, Scion noticed that Kai's hands trembled a little and his eyes filled with tears. Stranger still, just before Kai left him, he hugged Scion so tightly and for so long that Scion almost felt embarrassed. Then, Kai suddenly flew off, looking back with that smile of love Scion always treasured. All Scion could think now was *Wow! That was different. Kai was so emotional! Whatever it is, I can't miss it. I gotta get this done and get back to heaven* the golden scout vowed silently just as he completed the last steps of a mission no other student had wanted.

Who could blame them? The assignment required that an angel go to the very edge of the universe for an entire week *alone* and be out of contact with other angels the entire time. Like every other student at Archangel Academy, Scion didn't want to be alone in deep space that long. But when Lucifer personally asked him to do it, his love for the Headmaster made him say yes. "And now, I can go home to that fantastic surprise Lucifer is planning," he sighed into the darkness. A wide smile filled his face as he took one more look at the pulsating edge of creation just yards away from his brilliant, golden wings.

Just as he was about to turn around and head back to heaven, he saw three Sentinel angels speeding toward him. Normally, Sentinels were the more introverted angels who silently stood guard over remote sectors of the universe. But as the trio drew closer, Scion saw that something was terribly wrong. Terror covered the faces of each angel.

"Treason! Treason!" the three shouted to Scion. "Lucifer has gone mad. He is leading a rebellion against the Lord, and many angels are following him. Come at once. General Michael has ordered everyone to return to heaven and fight off the rebels."

As the terrified Sentinels sped off to alert others across the cosmos, Scion froze with a fear that no angel had ever felt. He had recently shared a Throne Room secret with Lucifer that had enraged Lucifer.

What Scion had feared was now happening. His hands shook so violently that he dropped his notebook and pen. His heart raced. His entire body felt limp. With a scream of sheer agony, the huge angel dove toward the surface of the dark planet faster than he had ever flown. But after a few thousand feet of descent, he suddenly passed out and tumbled head over heels, slicing through the hot, volcanic surface with such force that his body did not stop until he finally splashed into the fiery, molten core, ten thousand miles underground.

۞

LIGHT YEARS AWAY, all hell was breaking out in heaven. The once glorious choirmaster of heaven was enraged with wounded pride as he savagely sliced through a dozen angels with one swipe of his eight-foot sword. His once brilliant blue eyes were now fiery black with hate. Thousands of rebel angels swarmed around him, fighting for him with a fury never seen before in heaven. Angel wings, arms, and heads flew everywhere as twenty thousand unarmed, loyal angels were beheaded and dismembered by their fellow angels who now had swords—something no angel had ever possessed. Agony filled the air as angels were butchered by old friends. Hideous, rhythmic sounds of death filled heaven: a cry for mercy—then *thwack*—a scream of terror—*thwack*—a surprised shout of the attacker's name—*thwack*. The swords of death hacked down the unarmed angelic ranks with monstrous precision.

When the attack began, the emotions and bodies of the loyal angels were frozen with shock. Slowly, their eyes grew big and their bodies began to tremble. They had neither weapons nor desire to fight their friends. Then, as if on some invisible cue, tears of grief burst forth on all the faces of the innocent angels. In the flick of a moment, heaven was filled with the ear-piercing wails of totally distraught angels. Their eyes were filled with tears that they could hardly make out the faces of their attackers. Like lambs led to the slaughter, most of them died without any resistance.

But all was not lost. The Four Living Creatures who guarded God's Throne Room shot into heaven's blue canopy, high above the battle. Each Creature had six wings and a huge body completely covered with eyes. They moved like lightning above the battlefield, seeing everything and giving rapid orders to General Michael and his army of Cherubim and Seraphim warrior angels. But none of them had swords. *They had something better.*

As Lucifer and his sixty thousand rebels pushed forward toward the Throne of God, the Four Living Creatures guided Michael to array the remaining hundred thousand angels around God's Throne in sixty-four rows—six-winged Seraphim at the front and Cherubim in the rear ranks. Michael's voice rang out like a deafening trumpet call to battle, "Worship!"

Instantly, one hundred thousand loyal angels fought back their tears of shock, grief and anger and began to worship, "Holy, holy, holy is the Lord God, the Almighty, Who was and Who is and Who is to come. Worthy are You, our Lord and our God, to receive glory and honor and power; for You created all things, and because of Your will they existed and were created." The piercing staccato blasts of many golden trumpets released a powerful anointing that looked like a glistening, golden blanket floating down on the thundering worship of the weeping angels.

Then, the air suddenly became electrified with the unseen Presence of Almighty God. Lucifer and his rebels halted for a second as they felt the atmosphere shift. An instant later, Lucifer roared defiantly and charged the Throne even more ferociously.

As the rebels came within three hundred feet of God's Throne, they raised their swords for the final slaughter of the unarmed angels surrounding the Throne. The Seraphim on the front ranks were now so close to the rebels that they could recognize the faces of former friends, former teammates in games, and former choir members. As the Seraphim beheld those beautiful angels' faces now darkened with evil, many began to weep for their deranged and murderous fellow angels they had loved since heaven began.

It was over in an instant. Michael shouted, "Fire!" and six thousand Seraphim angels—whose name means "burning ones"—shot a wall of white-hot flames one thousand feet high out of their eyes and mouths. Lucifer and his rebels slammed into each other as they fell to the golden streets of heaven just before hitting the wall of fire. Within moments, Lucifer realized he would never reach God's Throne that day. With a hideous howl, Lucifer commanded his army to retreat to Earth. Michael's army pursued them until they reached the upper atmosphere of the new, blue planet.

The Great Rebellion had begun.

ANGEL 24: SAMPLE

CHAPTER SIX

The storm-battered Spanish galleon lurched into the mouth of the dark river just as Angel 442 swooped in from heaven. Scion had sent her there to record what the Spanish were doing and to get as much data as she could on Okeus if he showed up. The petite angel checked her sensors' data display embedded in her left arm to confirm her location. As usual, she was right on target.

Angel 442

Standing at fourteen inches tall, with bright rainbow-colored hair, sparkling purple eyes, and a deep beige, velvety face, Angel 442 was stunning to behold. When in flight, the multicolored tips of her trailing wing feathers twinkled to the beat of whatever song she was singing—and she sang a lot. Like most angels, she wore a tunic that covered her arms to the wrists and her legs to her ankles. But the tight golden belt around her slim waist left no doubt that beneath that garb was a very athletic, female body. Today, her tunic color was hot pink. She never wore white like all the Mod1 male angels do.

Some had said that she was sassy. But she has only ever admitted to quirkiness, which she claims, simply goes with being a risk-taker. Some others have said that she thinks "out of the box." She would probably prefer to say that she *lived* "out of the box." What is clear is that she is one of the most intelligent, innovative, and emotionally sensitive angels in heaven. She was top of her Mod2 class. Although she is a sensory detection marvel, as are all Mod2s, she loves human history. Her final thesis was on the romantic lives of humans. She has always said that if she were human, she would have been a romance novel writer.

"I DON'T CARE a damn about the storm!" the ship's captain shouted. "I don't care if you all die! Get that boy, you idiots! Don't you understand that we need him to convince his tribe not to resist our conquistadors when they arrive? That boy is going to make us all rich!"

The man who was responsible for guarding the entire fleet of Spanish treasure ships against pirates had come to collect a treasure. But tonight, Admiral Pedro Menéndez de Avilés, Captain-General of the Fleet of the Indies,* had come for something far more valuable than a boatload of gold. He had come for a boy.*

"But, Admiral, the waves . . . they are too big—"

"You idiot! If Spain is ever to rule here, we have to have the boy!" Menéndez ranted above the howling wind.

Like thousands of angry hands, frothy black waves slapped the heaving hull as it tacked north out of the great bay known as Bahia De Santa Maria* and into Powhatan River.* Smelling the earthy scent of land nearby, Captain Menéndez's sharp brown eyes scanned the eastern bank for their rendezvous point near the Powhatan village of Kiski-ack,* in the land the Spanish called Ajacán.*

FIFTEEN HUNDRED PAIRS of fiery yellow eyes squinted back at him. But no one on the ship saw the mocking demon eyes or the colored lights that flickered from their bodies. Looking on from his perch high above the storm, a large, huge, dinosaur-like spirit watched with amusement. Okeus was the ruling spirit of Ajacán—and he looked every inch the part.

His sixteen-foot-tall body was covered with seaweed-green armored hide. Atop his muscular torso, a huge reptilian head with frog-like lips rose to display a wide mouth full of six-inch, razor-sharp orange teeth. Beneath his formidable eating apparatus, two short but powerful arms ended in six-fingered claws that could wield a mighty sword or flick a foolish demon across the room with one claw finger. His wide, short legs descended into a thick, fearsome, spiked tail. He normally sat upright with his thick tail curled beneath him, somewhat like a monkey. He was strong as a dozen oxen, and yet he could glide effort-lessly for miles on thirty-six-foot, semi-transparent green wings like those of a flying fish. And speaking of fish, Okeus loved to eat raw fish. His breath usually reeked of rotting fish, and was almost overwhelm-ing, even to the strongest demons who served him.

But his most impressive feature was his eyes—large, yellow eyes, set in bright red sockets full of cunning and cruelty that was only surpassed by Lucifer himself. Every demon under his command feared him immensely—or at least that is what his bright yellow, very obese, demon assistant Snookus always told him to curry favor.

Snookus stood next to Okeus and pretended to enjoy watching the Spanish intruders. He always mimicked his master's moods—the better to avoid a beating. His octopus-shaped body had already lost three of his eight tentacles to the wrath of Okeus years ago. Unlike the octopi of Earth, the three severed arms of Snookus would never grow back. Okeus used his dark powers to make sure they wouldn't. But despite his cruelty towards Snookus, Okeus enjoyed having the only gas-powered demon in North America. Because Snookus did not have wings, he propelled himself by shooting inky gases from a tube under his head. Landings were awkward and thumpy, but no winged demon moved faster in the air than Snookus—a fact that always brought a smile to his light-green eyes as he shot past every other demon in flight.

⚜

SUDDENLY, a sailor sighted the small torch on the riverbank about one hundred yards off the port bow. "There's the village chief, the werowance, Capitan! And I see the boy with his mother!" the sailor shouted out in a husky voice, barely audible above the rumble of the storm.

"Make for shore and send in the landing boat with my cabin boy, Raqīb," Menéndez barked. He wiped the cold rain from his dark, well-trimmed beard. "We'll get that little Powhatan and set sail as quickly as we can before this accursed storm tears us to shreds. And if the tribe spots us taking the boy, they will attack us."

Raqib looked at the tall captain and asked, "But what if the parents refuse to give us the boy as they promised last week when we came ashore?"

"Foolish question, son. The father of the boy is as greedy for gain as we are. He'll comply."

⚜

AS SOON AS the landing party approached the shore, hundreds of large, dark red, horned guard demons circled overhead. They glided in the night sky with monstrous bat-like wings, swords drawn, and bright orange fangs exposed as they scanned for signs of the Heavenly Host among the Spanish invaders. Soon these aerial guards would report on these invaders to their master.

⚜

FINALLY, the six sailors landed their boat and hid it under an overhanging tree. Raqīb—a swarthy young man with a strange glow in his eyes—was their leader. "Let's go," he whispered to the Algonquian family huddled nearby. Then they quickly disappeared into the bushes to avoid being seen by other members of the tribe.

As the sailors handed over a small chest of beads, trinkets, knives, and copper to the native husband, Raqīb ran into the forest and buried a small, black rock next to a towering oak tree. He was careful not to let the other sailors see him so they would not report it to the captain. He was on a secret mission for his god. Once the rock was hidden, he hurried back, then grabbed the weeping boy and tore him away from his distraught mother. "*Vámonos, vámonos! El Capitan esta esperando*! We have to leave now. The captain is waiting," he ordered.

The boy screamed, and his mother collapsed into the arms of her husband who hardly noticed her fall. As he gently slid her to the forest floor, the crewmen threw the boy into the small boat.

"Papa, Papa, I don't want to leave!" the boy cried. "Please let me stay. I'll be good. I promise!"

Mercifully, beyond their eyesight, their boy was being hauled up the side of the ship. He still cried out to his parents but they could not hear him in the heavy winds. The small boat was cranked aboard, the anchors were winched in, and the sails slowly extended. The great ship spun around so fast in the whistling winds that the forward mast cracked a little.

❧

OKEUS WATCHED the Spanish plot play out from his usual roost in the clouds high above the churning bay. "Let them take the boy, the fools. They want that young man to help them conquer this land. Little do they know that that boy will one day conquer them! I know what to do when that boy comes back. What the stupid Spanish mean for their good, I mean for evil. It's so juicy, I can almost taste it!" Okeus roared above the thunder, "How I love to deceive and kill! It makes me feel so alive. I was made for this!" Okeus bellowed at his bloated assistant, who bobbed beside him trying to smile but choking on the blast of pungent breath from his master. Then, without another word, Okeus bolted into the night sky toward his throne in the great swamp just miles away. Tonight, he would celebrate with his royal court of demons. Once more, Okeus was to have the pleasure of killing Christians when the boy returned.

🙖🙥

FINAL THOUGHTS

I hope you enjoyed these samples from Angel 24.
Book details at https://angel24book.com

MANY BLESSINGS on you and your loved ones as you all pursue God's highest and best for yourselves and America!

AMERICA'S SOUL *will* be healed. The Church in America *will* become the holy people of God who will repent and open up the floodgates of God's mercy on America!

GOD *WILL* BRING A GREAT, national and global revival that will shake the world—one more time—before Jesus returns.

I BELIEVE Jesus is coming back in *my* lifetime— *and I am already old!*

LET'S be and do all we can— to be ready.

GRATEFUL FOR HIM and for you,

BOB FOX